Repentance

Repentance

Thomas Goodwin

Sovereign Grace Publishers, Inc.
P.O. Box 4998
Lafayette, IN 47903
2001

Printed In the United States of America
By Lightning Source, Inc.

CONTENTS

THE NECESSITY OF REPENTANCE
Thomas Boston

REPENTANCE
Thomas Goodwin

THE NECESSITY OF REPENTANCE.

LUKE xiii. 5.

I tell you, Nay: but except ye repent, ye shall all likewise perish.

WHEN we consider the abounding sin and hardness of heart prevailing under a preached gospel, it must needs let us see, that the doctrine of repentance is both necessary and seasonable, to pluck the brands out of the burning ; or if that will not do, to leave men without excuse. Sinners stave off repentance, as if they were resolved to persist in sin come what will, or at least as halting betwixt two opinions : But here is a peremptory decision of the case in this text, " I tell you, Nay : but except ye repent, ye shall all likewise perish."

In these words we have two things.

1. An abuse of a dispensation of providence corrected : " I tell you, Nay." Some had told our Lord the news of Pilate the Roman governor's falling on some Galileans, with his soldiers, and killing them, while they were sacrificing. It seems the tellers of this news, or others in the company, were apt to think, that these were sinners beyond others, because an unordinary judgment had fallen on them. Our Lord tells them, that it would not bear such a conclusion. He puts them in mind of another remarkable providence, viz. the tower of Siloam in Jerusalem its falling on and killing eighteen persons : but here he shews that this did not befal them, because they were greater sinners than all the rest in Jerusalem ; nay there were as great sinners as those, which missed that stroke, and others like it too.

2. The right use of the dispensation instructed : " But except ye repent, ye shall all likewise perish." The right use is to learn repentance from the ruin of others ; if others give us an example at their own cost, that we take heed to it and improve it to our repentance and reformation. This is the import of the particle *but*. These words are a peremptory certification given to sinners by our Lord. And the proposition in its own nature includes a twofold certification.

1*st*, A certification of ruin upon impenitence. Sinners go on in their course, yet hope that all may be well. No, says our

Lord, deceive not yourselves; for if ye do not repent, there is no hope of saving you. There is here,

(1.) The matter on which the certification is given, " Except ye repent ;" i. e. If ye do not repent, if ye be not duly humbled for your sins, and sincerely turn from them. If ye harden your hearts under your guilt, keep still your sinful courses, and refuse to let them go, they will ruin you.

(2.) The thing certified, which is perishing likewise; not perishing in that very manner, but ye shall perish as surely as they did. The judgments of God shall pursue you, and ye shall perish for ever.

(3.) The extent of the certification, " All—perish." This clears the perishing to be meant of everlasting death. Q. d. Though signal temporal judgments do pursue all that are impenitent, yet eternal punishment will ; no impenitent sinner shall escape that, however they may escape temporal strokes of signal vengeance.

(4.) The peremptoriness of it. This appears in two things. 1. That solemn assertion, " I tell you," supposed to be repeated in the last clause. Take it out of the mouth of the Lord himself, that ye shall perish except ye repent. Q. d. This has been told you by many, but ye would not believe : but now I tell it you out of my own mouth. And to hear this out of the mouth of the Saviour, may strike a sinner with concern, and let him see, that Christ's blood will never be laid out on a person continuing impenitent, to save him from death. 2. In the relation intimate to be between the punishment of those so signally smitten by the hand of God, and the future punishment of all impenitent sinners; the former is a pledge of the latter. This is intimated by the particle *likewise*.

2dly, A certification of life and repentance. This is implied here as Gen. ii. 17. God has made as sure connection betwixt repentance and life, as betwixt impenitence and death. Be your sins never so great, if you repent of them, and turn from them, they shall never be your ruin.

Before I come to the main point I design, I shall lay before you some observations from the words.

Obs. 1. That those who meet with more signal strokes than others, are not therefore, nor are to be accounted greater sinners than others. The Lord spares some as great sinners, as he signally punisheth, I tell you, nay.

Reasons of this dispensation of Providence.

1. Because of God's sovereign power and absolute dominion, which he will have the world to understand : Matth. xx. 15. " Is it not lawful for me to do what I will with mine own ?" Thus our Lord

accounts for the dispensation of the man's being born blind, John ix. 3. All men have that in them and about them, which may make them liable to the heaviest strokes that any of the children of men meet with; And therefore whatever any suffer, the Lord does them no wrong, since he punishes them less than their iniquity deserves : but amongst many whom justice may strike, sovereignty picks out some, and causes them to smart. And who may say, "what dost thou ?"

2. Because we are now under the mixed dispensation of providence; not the unmixed, reserved to another world, when all men shall be put into their unalterable state. Now, hereunto this is very agreeable that God signally punish some of a society, while others as guilty do escape, that the whole may, with David, Psal. ci. 1, "sing of mercy and judgment too." And thus the dispensation of divers colours is held up in the world, as a display of the manifold wisdom of God.

3. Because the mercy of God to some is magnified by his severity on others. As black set by white makes the white appear the better; so God's severity against some, may be a looking-glass to others, wherein they may see how much they stand obliged to free grace and mercy, Rom. xi. xxii. Men are never fairer to prize health in themselves, than when they see others tossed on sick beds; nor to prize the exercise of sense and reason, and other mercies, than when they see what miserable and pitiful sights they are that are deprived of these. And this should make folk patient and thankful under the strokes of the Lord's hand, because if he take away a mercy, health for instance, or perhaps a member or limb of their body, being taken away, it may be more serviceable for him, than when they had it, in so far as it shall serve to magnify the mercy of God to others, that see and notice the hand of the Lord. See Matth. xxi. 3.

4. Because in very signal strokes very signal mercies may be wrapped up. So it was in Joseph's case ; there was a very singular blessing on the head of him that was separated from his brethren. Job's troubles were but a dark hour before a very glorious day. The halt Jacob got in his thigh, was more excellent, as a badge of his wrestling with the angel, than Esau's retinue of four hundred men.

5. *Lastly*, Because this dispensation is in some sort necessary to confirm us in the belief of the judgment of the great day. God punishes some remarkably, that the world may see that there is a God that judgeth on the earth ; he does not so punish all, that men may be assured that there is a judgment to come. If none were

punished here, the world would improve that for Atheism; if all were punished, it would be improved to Sadducism.

Use 1. Then learn that unordinary strokes may befall those that are not unordinary sinners; and therefore be not rash in your judgment concerning the strokes that others meet with. It is true, whatever we or others meet with, it is deserved at the Lord's hand; and when God follows an unordinary seen sin with an unordinary judgment, as in the case of Korah, Dathan, and Abiram, it is no breach of charity to judge that that stroke comes for that sin. But when people, in whose conversation ye see no signal sin, meet with signal strokes, beware of harsh judging. For in the way of the Lord's dispensation, some will meet with a signal stroke for some sin, such as the world would think little or nothing of, if they knew it.

2. Then adore the mercy of God to you, and wonder at his sparing you, when ye see others smart under the hand of God, which ye do not feel. Acknowledge, that whatever others meet with, the same might have been your lot, if the Lord had dealt with you as ye deserve; as the church did, Lam. iii. 22, "It is of the Lord's mercies that we are not consumed, because his compassions fail not."

Obs. 2. That the strokes which any meet with, are pledges of ruin to impenitent sinners. But "Except ye repent, ye shall all likewise perish."

Reasons of this are,

1. Because they show how hateful to God sin is, in whomsoever it is: Is. xlii. 24, "Who gave Jacob for a spoil, and Israel to the robbers? did not the Lord, he against whom we have sinned? for they would not walk in his ways, neither were they obedient unto his law." God has no delight in the misery of his own creatures, Ezek. xviii. 23. He must therefore have a mighty hatred against sin, in that he is so heavy oftentimes on the work of his own hands for it. Not only his enemies smart for sin, but his dear friends; yea, his dear Son smarted for it, when it lay on him but by imputation. And therefore how can impenitent sinners think to escape? Luke xxiii. 31, "For if they do these things in a green tree, what shall be done in the dry?"

2. Because they shew how just God is. He is the Judge of all the earth, and cannot but do right, Gen. xviii. 25. Now, though justice may delay the punishment of one longer than another, yet it will not allow to punish some, and for ever to spare others, in the same state. For that would be manifest partiality, which God hateth, Ezek. xviii. 20. And therefore the apostle tells us, 2 Thess.

i. 6. that "it is a righteous thing with God to recompense tribulation to them that trouble" the saints.

3. Because whatever any meet with in the way of sin, is really designed for warning to others, as is clear from the text. See 1 Cor. x. 11, 12. And they that will not be taught by the example of others, may expect to be made examples to teach others, as Lot's wife was. But the wise will have their eyes in their head, while impenitent sinners pass on and perish, as those that will not take warning. Hence it comes to pass, that the stroke afar off not prevailing, is oftentimes brought nearer home.

4. *Lastly,* Because all those strokes which sinners meet with in this life, are the spittings of the shower of wrath that abides the impenitent world, after which the full shower may certainly be looked for. As the joys in believing are the pledges of eternal joy, flowing from one fountain with it; the first-fruits of Canaan's land, which will be followed with the full harvest; so all the outlettings of God's wrath on sinners here, are the pledges of eternal wrath, and first-fruits of hell, which will be followed with the harvest of misery, being the same in kind, Rev. xx. 14.

Use 1. Be not unconcerned spectators of all the effects of God's anger for sin going abroad in the world; for your part and mine is deep in them. There is none of them but says to us, as in the same condemnation, " Except ye repent, ye shall all likewise perish." O how unconcernedly do many look on the miseries of others, how far are they from taking a lesson to themselves therefrom! But a hard heart and seared conscience, which cannot be awakened by the dispensations of providence far off from them, do but invite the heavy stroke to fall on themselves.

2. Consider, O impenitent sinners, how can ye escape, when your ruin is insured by so many pledges thereof from the Lord's hand, while ye go on in sin? When a sinner goes out of God's way, he leaves his soul in pawn for his return by repentance; but the impenitent sinner never returns to loose his pawn, and so loses it. When God lets out any of his wrath in any measure on the children of men, that is God's pawn for his bringing eternal wrath on the impenitent; and we may be sure, that however careless we be of our pawns, God will not lose his. Therefore consider your ways, and repent.

Obs. 3. The strokes that others meet with, are loud calls to to us to repent. That is the language of all the afflicting providences which we see going on in the world. To confirm this, consider,

1. God does not strike one for sin with a visible stroke, but with an eye to all. The reason which God gives in his law for punishing

some transgresssors severely, is, that "all Israel might hear, and fear, and do no such thing." In the infancy of the Jewish church, he consumed Nadab and Abihu with fire, Lev. x. 2. compared with ver. 9. In the infancy of the Christian church, Ananias and Sapphira were struck dead for a lie. Why all this, but to be a warning to all that should come after?

2. Thereby we may see how dangerous a thing sin is to be harboured; and if we will look inward, we may ever see, that there is sin in us also against the God of Israel. If we saw one stung by a serpent which he had taken up, would not we quickly throw away one which we had taken up too, lest we should fare no better? How can we think to prosper in that way, where we see it goes so very ill with others?

USE 1. We may see that none go on impenitently in a sinful course, but over the belly of thousands of calls from Providence to repent, besides all those they have from the word. Look abroad into the world, O sinner, and consider how many have fallen into ruin, and are still falling by their iniquity. As many as there are of these, so many mouths are there calling thee to repent, and turn from thy sin. " Who did ever harden himself against God, and prosper ?" And dost thou think, that thy case shall be an exception to the general rule? No; so many witnesses give their testimony to thee, that " except thou repent, thou shalt likewise perish."

2. Impenitency under the gospel cannot have the least shadow of excuse. The calls of Providence common to the whole world, are sufficient to leave the very heathens without excuse, Rom. i. 20: how much more shall the calls of the word and Providence too make us inexcusable, if we do not repent? Sinners make many shifts for themselves, to preserve the life of their lusts, and to keep themselves from this unpleasant exercise : but they will be but figleaf covers before the Lord.

3. How much more do strokes from the hand of the Lord on ourselves call us to repent? Hos. ii. 6, 7, " Therefore behold, I will hedge up thy way with thorns, and make a wall, that she shall not find her paths. And she shall follow after her lovers, but she shall not overtake them; and she shall seek them, but shall not find them : then shall she say, I will go and return to my first husband, for then was it better with me than now." What Absalom's design was in burning Joab's corn-field, is the design of afflicting providences. And therefore impenitency and hardness of heart under the strokes of the Lord's hand, is highly aggravated, Jer. v. 3. Every cross that we meet with, is a charge from heaven to

turn from our sinful course, and from the particular ills of our way. I come now to the principal doctrine of the text.

DOCTRINE. Sinners, except they repent, shall perish. This is an except without any exception. Be who they will, if they be sinners, they must repent or perish. All are sinners, and by sin depart from God ; and they must come back again to him by repentance, else they are for ever ruined. Be they sinners of a greater or lesser size, they must be penitent sinners, or it had been better for them they had never been born.

In discoursing this doctrine, I shall,
I. Explain the nature of repentance.
II. Apply.
I. I shall explain the nature of repentance. And here we may consider,
1. What it is in its general nature.
2. How it is wrought in the soul.
3. The subject of true repentance.
4. The parts of repentance.
FIRST, We may consider what repentance is in its general nature. It is a saving grace: 2 Tim. ii. 25, "In meekness instructing those that oppose themselves; if God peradventure will give them repentance to the acknowledging of the truth." It is a grace given us of God freely, enabling and disposing a soul to all the acts of turning from sin unto God ; and it is saving, as in its own nature distinguishing a man from a hypocrite, and having a sure connection with eternal salvation. To unfold this more particularly, consider,

1. It is not a transient action, as Papists and some ignorant creatures imagine, as if a sigh for sin, an act of sorrow for it, a confession of it with a " God be merciful to me a sinner," were repentance. No, no; these may be acts of repentance while they proceed from a truly penitent heart. But repentance itself is not a passing act, but an abiding grace, Zech. xii. 10; a continuing frame and disposition of the soul; a principle lying deep in the heart, disposing a man to mourn for and turn from sin on all occasions.

2. It is not a passing work of the first days of one's religion, as some professors take it to be ; but a grace in the heart, setting one to an answerable working all the days of his life. It is a spring of waters of sorrow in the heart for sin, which will spring up there while sin is there, though sometimes through hardness of heart it may be stopped for a while. They that look on repentance as the

first stage in the way to heaven, and looking back to the sorrowful hours which they had when the Lord first began to deal with them, reckon that they have passed the first stage, are in a dangerous condition. And whoso endeavours not to carry on their repentance, I doubt if they ever at all repented yet. As when Moses had smote the rock in the wilderness, and the waters began to gush out, those waters ran (it is thought, 1 Cor. x. 4.) and followed them while in the wilderness: so the heart first smitten with repentance for sin at the soul's first conversion to God, the wound still bleeds, and is never bound up to bleed no more, till the band of glory be put about it in heaven, Rev. xxi. 4.

Hence initial and progressive repentance, though the former be the repentance of a sinner, the latter of a saint, are no more different kinds of repentance, than the soul's virgin love to Christ, and their love to him through the course of their spiritual marriage with him; or than faith in its first, and after actings. But as the mid-day and evening sun are the same with the morning sun, so are these; though the rising morning sun may be most noticed by the traveller, who having travelled in the night, was thereby brought from darkness to light.

3. It is not a common grace, but a special saving one. Men may have a repentance for their sin, gnawing their consciences, and tormenting their hearts, which they will carry on in hell through eternity: being only the first movings of the worm in the soul that never dieth: as Judas's repentance seems to have been Simon Magus's and Pharaoh's. They may bitterly rue their sin, as Esau, Gen. xxvii. 34. who never truly repent of it, Heb. xii. 17; and the stony heart may be broken in a thousand pieces, while yet every piece remains a stone. They may have a superficial sorrow for sin, and a light joy succeeding it, whose hearts were never pierced to the quick; and therefore the joy goes, as the effects of a scud of rain on the parched ground, Matth. xiii. 20, 21. But true repentance is a repentance never repented of, kindly working in the soul.

SECONDLY, We may consider how repentance is wrought in the soul. And here two questions must be answered, and two points cleared, namely,

1. Who works repentance, or is the author of it? And that is the sanctifying Spirit of Jesus Christ: Zech. xii. 13. "And I will pour upon the house of David, and upon the inhabitants of Jerusalem, the spirit of grace and of supplications, and they shall look upon me whom they have pierced, and they shall mourn for him, as one mourneth for his only son, and shall be in bitterness for him, as one that is in bitterness for his first-born." Sometimes notorious

prodigals become true penitents; as a persecuting Saul turned to be a preaching Paul: so that the world is amazed with the change, and are ready to say as in Saul's case, 1 Sam. x. 11. "What is this that is come unto the son of Kish? Is Saul also among the prophets? But that query, ver. 12. "But who is their father?" gives a rational account of the matter. All sort of timber to divine grace is alike easy to hew. And forasmuch as the house of God is ordinarily built of the knottiest wood, publicans and harlots entering into the kingdom of God before Scribes and Pharisees, it may plainly appear, that repentance is not the work of nature, but of grace; not of men's own spirit, but Christ's Spirit.

This is evident from the word, Jer. xiii. 21, " Can the Ethiopian change his skin, or the leopard his spots? then may ye also do good, that are accustomed to do evil." It is the Lord's own work to "take away the stony heart, and give an heart of flesh," Ezek. xxxvi. 26. It is the office of the exalted Mediator to give repentance, in whose hand it is to send the Spirit, Acts v. 31. Ministers may preach repentance, but cannot work in it themselves, and far less in others. They may sow the seed, but cannot make it grow, 1 Cor. iii. 6, 7. It is but a peradventure if God give repentance, when they have done their utmost, 2 Tim. ii. 25. But if at all their weapons be mighty, it is through God, 2 Cor. x. 4.

2. By what means does the Spirit work repentance? That is by the word, whether read or preached. The word is the channel wherein the influences of the Spirit flow; and from these it has its piercing, melting, and heart-softening virtue, as the pool of Bethesda had its healing virtue from the angel's troubling the water: Acts xi. 20, 21. "And some of them were men of Cyprus, and Cyrene, which when they were come to Antioch, spake unto the Grecians, preaching the Lord Jesus. And the hand of the Lord was with them: and a great number believed, and turned unto the Lord." Junius, who was deeply plunged in Athiesm, was brought to repentance by reading John i. in a New Testament which his father had purposely laid down in his chamber, if perhaps he might take it up and read it. Augustine was converted by reading Rom. xiii. 13, 14. " Let us walk honestly as in the day; not in rioting and drunkenness, not in chambering and wantonness, not in strife and envying. But put ye on the Lord Jesus Christ, and make no provision for the flesh, to fulfil the lusts thereof." Three thousand we find were wrought on by one sermon, Acts ii.

Many and various are the occasions of repentance, which the Lord blesseth for bringing home the word to the soul, and the soul by it unto God. Personal afflictions have been so in the case of many, Hos. ii. 7. The sight of strokes on others has been blessed to some. The first occasion of Luther's turning serious was a fright by the violent death of a dear companion of his. Nay, God has made falls into gross sins occasions of repentance unto many, whereof there are several instances, as Achan, the thief on the cross, &c. Flavel gives an account of one, in the case of an attempt of self-murder. Augustine heard a voice, saying, "Take up, and read." Nay, God can make a dream in the night such an occasion, Job xxxiii. 15, 16. But these are not properly the means, but the occasions which bring men to consider of the word, which is the true and proper means. And here the Spirit of the Lord makes use of both parts of the word.

1st, The law, to break the hard heart: Jer. xxiii. 29, " Is not my word—like a hammer that breaketh the rock in pieces ? saith the Lord." It goes before like John Baptist to prepare the way of the Lord into the heart. And the Spirit of the Lord making use of it in a soul, is called " the Spirit of bondage," Rom. viii. 15. And here each part of the law has its proper use.

(1.) The commands of it, to convince the soul of sin : Rom. vii. 7, I had not known sin," says the apostle, " but by the law : for I had not known lust, except the law had said, Thou shalt not covet." The commands of the law, held forth to the soul in their spirituality and vast extent, are the looking-glass wherein the sinner is made to see his black face, the sins and sinfulness of his nature, heart, and life, which he must repent of.

(2.) The threatenings of it, to convince the soul of judgment : Gal. iii. 10, " As many as are of the works of the law, are under the curse: for it is written, Cursed is every one that continueth not in all things which are written in the book of the law to do them." These carried home on the soul, disturb its rest in sin, and let the man see that he has been sleeping within the sea-mark of divine vengeance, and so give him a frightful wakening. These discover the danger of sin for time and eternity, and tell him that he must turn over a new leaf, else he is ruined.

2dly, The gospel, to melt the hard heart like a fire, Jer. xxiii. 29, " Is not my word like as a fire ? saith the Lord ; and so to bow and bend it from sin towards God," Zech. xii. 10, " And I will pour upon the house of David, and upon the inhabitants of Jerusalem, the spirit of grace and of supplications, and they shall look upon me whom they have pierced, and they shall mourn for him, as one mourneth for his only son, and shall be in bitterness for him, as one that is in bitterness for his first-born." Thus the soul that was driven by the law, is kindly led and drawn by the gospel to repentance. The law serves to make a terrible reel in the conscience and affections: but the gospel is Christ's key to open the heart, and to turn about the will that he may come in, Gal. iii. 2. The stormy wind, and earthquake, may go before in the law; but the still small voice of the gospel is that which the Lord is in. This is evident, if ye consider,

(1.) That repentance is the doctrine of the gospel. I do indeed think, that it cannot be denied but that the law requires repentance as a duty, in so far as it binds the apostate sinner to return to God: but in the meantime it gives no hope of mercy to the penitent, seeing its constant voice is, " Cursed is every one that continueth not in all things which are written in the book of the law to do them." But the gospel gives the glad tidings of place for repentance, and shews how the apostate creature returning will be accepted. And there can be no true returning to God, where there is no hope of acceptance.

(2.) Repentance is a promise of the covenant of grace: Ezek. xxxvi. 31, " Then shall ye remember your own evil ways, and your doings that were not good, and shall loath yourselves in your own sight, for your iniquities, and for your abominations." It is not only the duty of God's elect, but their privilege, made over to them in Jesus Christ, purchased by his death, and bestowed on them by virtue of his exaltation, Acts v. 31. And hence, as one of the benefits of that covenant, it is sealed in baptism, Mark i. 4.

The sum of what is said on this second head, is, that repentance is an evangelical softness of heart, and bent of spirit to turn away from sin, and to turn to God, wrought in a soul by the Spirit of Christ. The Spirit of holiness being given to Christ without measure, he puts the same Spirit in his elect in the day of his power; who by his grace melts the heart for sin, and bends it away from sin to holiness.

USE 1. Repentance is not a man's taking up himself, in the point of his outward conversation. It is one thing to reform the life, another to reform the heart, by changing the will. The former is within the reach of mere nature, the other is not to be effected but by a supernatural hand, Jer. xxxi. 18. The former may make one a painted sepulchre, the latter makes him a new creature.

2. Legal repentance is no true repentance: and therefore though one have it, he may perish; as Pharaoh, Judas, &c. It makes a fretful restless conscience under the terror of God's wrath but mean while it leaves a hard heart, glued to sin. The law and its terrors coming into a sinful soul, may raise the dust ready to choke the sinner, as in a house when a sweeping; but it will never be made

clean, unless the gospel have its efficacy on the heart, as the water which lays that dust. Hence it comes to pass, that sinners sometimes have sharp convictions, but mean while their lusts grow as rampant as ever after.

3. See the folly of delaying repentance, and not striking in with the motions of the Spirit, when one has them. How do people put off repentance from time to time, as if it were wholly in their power to do it at any time! But they that cannot command wind and tide, have need to fall in with them while they serve, least if they go, they be left hopeless. O delay not, lest the Spirit of the Lord be provoked to depart.

4. *Lastly*, Learn whom ye are to look to for repentance. It is the work of the Lord's Spirit; and unto him ye are to look for his grace to loose the bands of wickedness, to soften the hard heart, and to turn you to himself, Jer. xxxi. 18.

Thirdly, We may consider the subject of true repentance, what it is. It is a convinced believing soul. An unconvinced sinner cannot be a true penitent; for what the eye sees not, the heart rues not. Neither can an unbelieving sinner be so; for without faith the heart may be rent for sin, but not from it.

First, The soul wherein true repentance is wrought, is a convinced soul: Job xxxvi. 9, 10, "He showeth them their work, and their transgressions that they have exceeded. He openeth also their ear to discipline, and commandeth that they return from iniquity." Acts ii. 87. 38, "Now when they heard this, they were pricked in their heart, and said unto Peter, and to the rest of the Apostles, Men and brethren, what shall we do? Then Peter said unto them, Repent, and be baptized every one of you in the name of Jesus Christ, for the remission of sins, and ye shall receive the gift of the Holy Ghost." The first particular work in the creation was making light; and the letting in a new light by conviction, is the first work in the new creation. God begins his work, where Satan ends his; who having got the soul asleep in the arms of its lusts, shuts the windows, and draws the curtains, that it may sleep sound, till it awaken in hell. But the Spirit of the Lord by conviction opens them, and awakens the sinner ordinarily, if not always, in a fright. Here consider,

1. How this conviction is wrought. It is done by the erecting of a criminal court within the sinner's own breast, which the man cannot absent himself from, more than he can go out of himself. He must stay and answer, unless he prevail with the judge to let fall the process; as, alas! many do by silencing their consciences one way or other to their own ruin. And in this court,

1*st*, The Spirit of the Lord, awakening the sleepy conscience, sets it upon the bench, so that the man becomes his own judge : John xvi. 8, "And when he [the Comforter] is come, he will reprove the world of sin, and of righteousness, and of judgment." The man searches and tries his own heart and life, which was before neglected as the sluggard's garden. But now every corner thereof is ransacked, and secret things set in the light.

2*dly*, The man is convicted as a sinner by the law. His nature, heart, and life brought to the holy law and compared with it, he is found evidently to be guilty and a transgressor. Hence says the apostle, Rom. vii. 9, " I was alive without the law once : but when the commandment came, sin revived, and I died." The law as a looking-glass is held before his eyes, and he sees his spots. His own conscience is as a thousand witnesses against him, and he cannot deny the charge. So his mouth is stopped, and his sin at length has found him out, Rom. iii. 19.

3*dly*, The man is sentenced and condemned by his own conscience according to the law, adjudging him liable to death, eternal death, for his sins : Gal. iii. 10, " Cursed is every one that continueth not in all things which are written in the book of the law to do them." He is therefore a condemned malefactor in his own eyes, by the sentence of the law pronounced against him. Consider,

2. The effects of this conviction ; which are these.

1*st*, A painful sense of sin, an affecting sight of it, Rom. vii. 9. forecited. For now the sore is lanced ; and they see those sins, and that in sin, which they saw not before ; and their eyes affect their hearts. As when the sun shines into a house, the motes are discovered, which did not before appear : so is it here. And the sin which sat light on them before, becomes a burden too heavy to them to bear ; for now they are roused out of their lethargy, and feel their sores. It is a burden on their spirits, which sinks them ; on their backs, that bows them down ; on their heads, which they are not able to discharge themselves of. Therefore the soul coming to Christ is represented as a man with a burden on him : Psal. lv. 22, " Cast thy burden upon the Lord, and he shall sustain thee." Hos. xiv. 2, " Take with you words, and turn to the Lord, say unto him, Take away all iniquity ;" (Heb.) Lift off iniquity as a burden.

2*dly*, Terror on their hearts : Psal. ix. 20, " Put them in fear, O Lord ; that the nations may know themselves to be but men." The convinced jailor, a man who wore a sword, falls a-trembling, Acts xvi. 29 : for the terror of God is too high for the stoutest heart, that knows not what it is to fear the face of man. The soul that was fearless before, because blind to its own hazard, now that his eyes are opened, is *magor missabib*. For what heart can be strong before an angry God, brandishing the sword of a fiery law over the conscience, which awakened, is the tenderest part of the man?

3dly, Legal sorrow for sin: Acts ii. 37, "Now when they heard this, they were pricked in their heart." There are stounds of grief that go through their hearts like arrows, Psal. xlv. 5; and these are very piercing, Prov. xviii. 14, "The spirit of a man will sustain his infirmity; but a wounded spirit who can bear? The man sees now that he has been murdering his own soul, and he groans out an elegy over his dead self; which is raised the higher, that he thought his soul was alive, when really it was dead. He calls himself fool and beast for doing as he did. But what is very sad, though his heart be rent in pieces for his sin, yet it is not rent from it. What grieves him thus, is purely selfish; his separation from God, without whom he sees he cannot be happy; and his liableness to his wrath and curse, which he sees will ruin him for ever to lie under.

4thly, A racking anxiety how to be delivered out of this state: Acts ii. 37, "Now when they heard this, they said,—What shall we do?" And here many times fear and hope take their several turns in his anxious soul; sometimes hoping, sometimes desponding, like Jonah in the whale's belly, Jon. ii. 4, "Then I said, I am cast out of thy sight; yet I will look again toward thy holy temple." Conviction of sin will make way for care into the most careless head, and will make folk bestow many thoughts on the neglected salvation, that used not to bestow one serious thought upon the business. And this care will swallow up all others, as that of a drowning man to save his life.

USE 1. The unconvinced sinner is an impenitent sinner. Hearken ye young ones, and old, that have lived at ease, and with a hale heart, in respect of your souls' state, all your days. They may sleep sound indeed, whom the devil is rocking in the cradle of a natural impenitent state. But ye will get a wakening yet, either in time to bring you to repentance, or when time is gone, and there is no more place for repentance, Jer. xlviii. 11, 12, "For except ye repent, ye shall perish." Ah poor sinner, thou wast never yet in the next step to repentance. Thy sore has not been lanced yet, therefore surely the filthy matter is never yet cast out by repentance.

2. Convictions and legal qualms of conscience are not repentance: for they do but qualify the subject for it, and that in part only. These are very necessary things I have spoke of under this head; but they are but like the unripe fruit, which must be ripened by

the work of the gospel on the heart, and brought to a perfection by the warm sun of gospel-influences, ere he that has them can be accounted a penitent indeed. Or rather, they are like the blossoms which go before, and differ in kind from the fruit, which often fall off, and no fruit follows at all. Folk may have had these many days and years since, that never repented to this day, Hos. vi. 4. The first-fruits of the second death may be mistaken by many for the pangs of the new birth. And therefore ye that have had them consider well what issue they have had; for it is not enough to have been in them, but to have got right out of them. Wrong curing of some diseases, breeds others, that prove mortal to many.

The right issue out of them lies in three things.

1. It lies in self-denial, or unselfing of the soul, when the soul is shaken out of itself for justification and sanctification too: Jer. xxxi. 18, " I have surely heard Ephraim bemoaning himself thus, Thou hast chastised me, and I was chastised, as a bullock unaccustomed to the yoke: turn thou me, and I shall be turned; for thou art the Lord my God." Compared with ver. 19, " Surely after that I was turned, I repented; and after that I was instructed. I smote upon my thigh: I was ashamed, yea, even confounded, because I did bear the reproach of my youth." They see the heinousness of sin, and the corruption of their nature too, so as they conclude themselves utterly unable to help themselves in either of these points, and so come off from themselves.

2. It lies in faith, or believing; in coming to Jesus Christ for all, in point of justification and sactification too: Is. xlv. 24. " Surely, shall one say, in the Lord have I righteousness and strength." The soul being turned off its own bottom, comes and builds on him for what it wants, and looks to him for his blood and Spirit. Thus " the law is a school-master to bring us unto Christ, that we might be justified by faith," Gal. iii. 24. See Jer. iii. 22, 23.

3. It lies in repentance, or a kindly melting of the heart for sin, Jer. xxxi. 18. Zech. xii. 10. as done against a gracious God, whom the heart is knit to in love. The soul comes from before the throne of justice, where it stood weeping for itself and its own misery, unto the throne of grace, where it stands weeping for having offended such a gracious Father.

They land at this threefold shore, who come rightly out of these depths. But many plunge up and down in them a while, and land again just in the same side they went in at. Some land at the shore.

1. Of formality, or a legal walk, 2 Tim. iii. 5. " Having a form of godliness but denying the power thereof." They change their former ways but retain their old heart. They go indeed to religious

duties, but they never go out of them to Christ. They act not as they did; but still they have the old principle of action, acting from self, and to self; so that though they change their work, they still work to the old master. And thus many continue in a profession of religion, living on their duties, never coming to Christ. Others land at the shore.

2. Of their former security. They are neither better inwardly nor outwardly; but they come out of their qualms of conscience, as one out of a fever, returning just to their old way of living; as was the case with Felix, Acts xxiv. 25. who said to " Paul, go thy way for this time; when I have a convenient season, I will call for thee." Others land at the shore,

3. Of profanity; turning worse than before : Mat. xii. 43, 44, 45, " When the unclean spirit is gone out of a man, he walketh through dry places, seeking rest, and findeth none. Then he saith, I will return into my house from whence I came out; and when he is come, he findeth it empty, swept, and garnished. Then goeth he, and taketh with himself seven other spirits more wicked than himself, and they enter in and dwell there : and the last state of that man is worse than the first." Their lusts dammed up for a while, run with more vigour than ever thereafter.

Secondly, The soul wherein repentence is wrought, is a *believing* soul. Faith is the spring and sourse of repentance so that though the grace of faith and repentance are given together and at once in respect of time, yet, in the order of nature, faith goes before repentance, and the acting of faith goes before the exercise of repentance. And he that would repent, must first believe in Christ that he may repent. I know that some teach otherwise. But this is the doctrine of the Scriptures and our Catechism. To confirm it, consider,

1. That faith is absolutely the leading grace, and the first breathing of a quickened soul : Heb. xi. 6, " Without faith it is impossible to please God ;" therefore it is impossible to repent, for that is very pleasing to him, Jer. xxxi. 20. So John xv. 5, " Without me," *i. e.* separate from me, and there is no union with him but by the Spirit of faith, " ye can do nothing" acceptable to God, therefore ye cannot repent.

2. It is particularly the leading grace to repentance : Zech. xii. 10, " They shall look upon me whom they have pierced, and they shall mourn for him, as one mourneth for his only son." Thus it is represented in fact, Acts xi. 21, " And a great number believed, and turned unto the Lord." If repentance be the emptying of the soul by the dropping of the tears of godly sorrow, it is faith that gene-

rates them in the heart. It is faith that melts the hard heart, which droppeth in repentance. The eye of faith fixes on God in Christ, and then the soul turns to him by repentance, Jer. iii. 22.

3. The scripture usually proposeth the objects of faith, and promises of grace, for motives to repentance; thereby discovering, that it is by a believing application of these, that a soul is brought to repentance: Jer. iii. 14, "Turn, O backsliding children, saith the Lord, for I am married unto you." Ver. 22, "Return, ye backsliding children, and I will heal your backslidings: behold, we come unto thee, for thou art the Lord our God." Joel ii. 12, 13, "Therefore also now, saith the Lord, Turn ye even to me with all your heart, and with fasting, and with weeping, and with mourning. And rend your heart and not your garments, and turn unto the Lord your God: for he is gracious and merciful, slow to anger, and of great kindness, and repenteth him of the evil." Hos. vi. 1, "Come and let us return unto the Lord: for he hath torn, and he will heal us; he hath smitten, and he will bind us up. Chap. xiv. 1, " O Israel, return unto the Lord thy God, for thou hast fallen by thine iniquity." Nay the very law proclaimed on mount Sinai with so much terror, is graciously prefaced with gospel-grace for faith to work on in the first place; " I am the Lord thy God," &c. And thus the doctrine of the New Testament concerning repentance is proposed to sinners, Matth. iii. 2, and iv. 17, " Repent ye : for the kingdom of heaven is at hand."

4. *Lastly*, The nature of repentance plainly teacheth this. It is a cordial turning from sin to God: but is it possible to turn to God, but through Christ? John xiv. 6, " I am the way, and the truth, and the life : no man cometh unto the Father, but by me." And is there any way of coming to Christ, but by faith ? The soul then that would turn and go to God again by repentance, must needs take Christ by faith, by the way. The people indeed wept; but did they put away the strange wives, or set to it, till Shechaniah cried, Ezra x. 2, " We have trespassed against our God, and have taken strange wives, of the people of the land : yet now there is hope in Israel concerning this thing ?" They must not be only prisoners of fear, but of hope that will turn, Zech. ix. 12, " Turn ye to the strong hold, ye prisoners of hope." Repentance is a kindly humiliation and mourning for sin; but the faithless heart may roar under law-horror, will never kindly mourn but under gospel-influences.

OBJECTION. Repentance is placed before faith, Mark i. 15; and sometimes repentance only is mentioned to natural men as the way to salvation, as in our text, and Acts ii. 38, and iii. 19. ANSWER,

(1.) Repentance no doubt is absolutely necessary to salvation; and no man needs pretend to faith, that does not repent, for they are inseparable. But that will no more infer the precedency of repentance to faith, than that, Heb. xii. 14, will infer the precedency of holiness to it. Now, this is all our text aims at. (2.) Repentance being the end, and faith the means to that end, no wonder they be so placed: for the end is first in one's intention, yet the means are first in practice. So Mark i. 15. Christ commands sinners to repent; but then in order to repenting, he commands them to believe. So Acts ii. 38, believing is implied in the command to be baptized. And therefore, speaking of the result of this work, ver. 44, it is said, "And all that believed," &c. So Acts iii. 19, it is implied in being converted; compared with Heb. iii. 12, " Take heed, brethren, lest there be in any of you an evil heart of unbelief, in departing from the living God." And that this is the true reason of this way of speaking, namely, that repentance is the end, and faith the means, is clear from Acts xx. 21, " Testifying—repentance toward God, and faith toward our Lord Jesus Christ :" for that Scripture can bear no other meaning, without destroying that fundamental truth, that Christ is the way to the Father. John preached repentance, Mark i. 4, but how did he direct them to it ? Acts xix. 4, " John verily baptized with the baptism of repentance, saying unto the people, that they should believe on him which should come after him, that is, on Christ Jesus."

Use 1. Then it is not gospel-doctrine, that Christ will receive none but true penitents, or that none but such have a warrant to embrace Christ by faith: Rev. xxi. 17, " And the Spirit and the bride say, Come. And let him that heareth say, Come. And let him that is athirst, come : and whosoever will, let him take the water of life freely." The evil of this doctrine is, that it sets sinners to spin repentance out of their own bowels, and to fetch it with them to Christ, instead of coming to him by faith to get it. And it hinders sensible sinners from coming to Christ, as keeping them back till they be persuaded that they have true repentance. I say, persuaded; for how can a sinner come to Christ till he be persuaded he has a warrant so to do? If Christ will receive none but such as have true repentance, then none other are invited to come; for surely those that are invited, will be welcome upon their coming: if none other be invited, then impenitent sinners are not bound to come to Christ; for none are bound to come, but those that are invited; "for where there is no law, there is no transgression." However, none are here in Christ by faith, but thereupon they become true penitents; and none but true penitents will see heaven.

2. Then for sensible sinners to think that they dare not and ought not to believe, and embrace Christ, till they be more deeply humbled, and do more thoroughly repent of their sins, and in a word, be more fit to receive him, is but a gilded deceit, and a trick of the false heart, to make the soul stay long in the place of the breaking forth of children, and die there at length. The Scripture holdeth forth quite other doctrine: Rev. iii. 20. "Behold, I stand at the door, and knock; if any man hear my voice, and open the door, I will come in to him, and will sup with him, and he with me." Is. lv. 1. "Ho, every one that thirsteth, come ye to the waters, and he that hath no money; come ye, buy and eat, yea, come, buy wine and milk without money, and without price." It is one thing what a sinner will do; another, what he may and ought to do. It is very true, there are many who will never come to Christ, if they be not made more sensible of their need of him than they are. But all that hear the gospel may and ought to come, be their case what it will; and those that come not, will be condemned for their not coming, John iii. 19. Therefore let every sensible sinner under that temptation think, that he is in the case of a drowning man, who if he stand disputing whether he may catch hold of the rope reached to him to hale him to land, a wave may come and sweep him away; and therefore without disputing he must take hold of it.

3. This shews the true way to deal with a hard heart, to soften it, and bring it to hearty repentance. It is to believe. Ye must do like those fowls, that first fly up, and then come down on their prey; first soar aloft in the way of believing, and then come down in true humiliation: Zech. xii. 10.—"They shall look upon me whom they have pierced, and they shall mourn for him." One may otherwise toil long in vain with a hard heart. Unbelief will lock up the heart, as the waters with a hard frost; for hard thoughts of God set the soul at a distance more and more from him, when the believing of the proclaimed pardon touches the rebels' hearts, and makes them come in.

4. *Lastly,* The more faith the more repentance; as the fuller the spring is, the streams run with the more vigorous current. According to your faith be it unto you, is the rule of the dispensation of grace. For faith is the provisor for all other graces, as being the conduit pipe by which grace comes from the fountain of grace to the soul; so that it failing, all fails; and it moving vigorously, the rest do so too.

QUESTION. How are we to act faith in order to repentance?

ANSWER 1. Firmly believe, that whatever your guilt be, God is reconciled to you in Christ Jesus; that there is hope of your case, if ye can attain to the way laid out for bettering it. You have God's word for this: Is. i. 18. "Come now, and let us reason together, saith the Lord: though your sins be as scarlet, they shall be as white as snow; though they be red like crimson, they shall be as wool." Ezek. xviii. 23. "Have I any pleasure at all that the wicked should die? 'saith the Lord God: and not that he should return from his ways and live?" This will quicken your endeavours after the happiness of your souls. Satan strikes at this foundation, to keep the soul from repentance, many ways. He will tell you, it cannot be thought that God can ever love the like of you. But the Lord saith the contrary: Hos. xiv. 4. "I will heal their backsliding, I will love them freely: for mine anger is turned away from him." Again, Satan will tell you, that you were not elected, but made for destruction; though God never set him nor you in the secrets of his decrees: Deut. xxix. 29. "The secret things belong unto the Lord our God: but those things which are revealed belong unto us." But why does he tell you all this, but to make you careless? which being done, he knows you cannot repent.

2. Believe that Jesus Christ is both able and willing to save you from sin and from wrath. You have ground to believe his ability: 1 John i. 7. "The blood of Jesus Christ his Son cleanseth us from all sin." Heb. vii. 25. "He is able to save them to the uttermost, that come unto God by him, seeing he ever liveth to make intercession for them." And you have also ground to believe his willingness: Is. lv. 1. Rev. xxii. 17. both forecited. This will set you a step further on; and truly this being believed by a sensible sinner, the bargain is almost closed. Therefore Satan works against the tossed soul's believing this, to the end he may not come to an anchor or rest, but may plunge up and down in the depths, knowing no landing place. Hence these hellish suggestions, What have you to do with the promises of grace? they will be made out to others, but not to you. But see Acts ii. 39. compared with ver. 36. Hence also the suggestion of having sinned the unpardonable sin. But why is that sin unpardonable? not that the physician cannot or will not cure it, Heb. vii. 25. John vi. 37; but because the sinner will never after desire to come to him, but willfully and maliciously rejects him. Hence also that suggestion, that Christ died not for him. But surely Satan never saw the roll of those whom Christ died for, and knows it no more than we, Deut. xxix. 29. forecited. We ought not to call that in question, but leave that matter to the Lord. It is plain, that we are commanded to believe, 1 John iii. 23. Let us do so, and we shall have evidences that Christ died for us.

3. Christ has given his consent to be yours in his word; believe

it; and do you consent to be his, accepting of the covenant, and of Christ therein to be your head and husband. Take him in all his offices as offered; and solemnly lay the whole weight of your soul, for justification and sanctification, on him. Lay over the burden of your guilt on his blood, of your raging lusts on his blood and Spirit; confidently trusting in him for salvation from sin and wrath. You have good ground to do this: Matt. xxii. 4, "All things are ready: come unto the marriage." Is. xxvi. 3, 4, "Thou wilt keep him in perfect peace, whose mind is staid on thee; because he trusteth in thee. Trust ye in the Lord for ever: for in the Lord Jehovah is everlasting strength." Chap. xliv. 5, "One shall say, I am the Lord's: and another shall call himself by the name of Jacob: and another shall subscribe with his hand unto the Lord, and surname himself by the name of Israel." Chap. xlv. 24, "Surely, shall one say, in the Lord have I righteousness and strength." This being done, the bargain is closed for time and eternity; Christ is yours, and ye are his, and God is your God in him. Satan strives against the soul here; for he knows, that if this be done, the person is no more his. Hence are these suggestions, Christ is a hard master there is no living with; though Christ says the contrary, Matt. xi. 28, 29, 30. Again, it is over soon for that serious work, Psal. xcv. If none of these nor the like will do, then he will tell the person, that it is presumption for him to offer at any such thing. But that is but the devil's doctrine, that it is presumption to do it, since God has commanded it, 1 John iii. 23, "This is his commandment, that we should believe on the name of his Son Jesus Christ." And do what ye will, ye cannot please God unless you do it, John vi. 29, "This is the work of God, that ye believe on him whom he hath sent." Heb. xi. 6, "Without faith it is impossible to please God." Well, if the soul will venture, he is ready to tell him, he had as good let it alone as try it in vain, for Christ will never receive him, nor give his consent to the bargain. But Satan is a liar; for he has given it already: Matt. xxii. 4, "All things are ready: come unto the marriage. Hos. ii. 19, "I will betroth thee unto me for ever, yea, I will betroth thee unto me in righteousness, and in judgment, and in loving-kindness, and in mercies. The soul is like a traveller come to a deep water-side, over which lies a bridge appearing very thin and narrow; it is pouring on rain on this side, it is fair weather on the far side; he would fain be over; and while he is minting to take the bridge, a false friend tells him, that he will never get over, that the bridge will break with him, or that his foot will slip, &c. And thus the poor man stands, sometimes putting on his foot, sometimes drawing it back again, till the flood rising behind him, he sees he must venture or perish. So he ventures with a trembling heart, and gets safe over, and sees that it was an enemy that made him so distrustful of the passage.

4. This being done, believe that Christ is yours, Cant. ii. 16; that God is reconciled to you in him; that your sins are pardoned for Christ's sake, and you are no more under condemnation for them, Rom. viii. 1; that you are now in a state of peace with God, and safe under the covert of blood. This will effectually melt your hearts into sincere repentance. And the stronger your confidence be in this point, the fire will be the more keen to melt the soul. Satan will oppose you in this also, that raising the dust of doubts and fears, your hands may be feeble that should fight against your lusts, the legs weak and trembling wherewith ye should turn from sin unto God. But the more he weakens that, the more he serves his own purpose against you.

5. Stand upon this shore, and look to your sins, and Saviour, Zech xii. 10. When a soul has, by a believing application of the blood of Christ, passed the gulf of condemnation and sees itself safe on the other side, it stands fairest for a hearty melting for sin, and a free and cordial turning from it unto God, Luke vii. 37, 38, compared with ver. 47. It is slavish fear that may be greater before, but it is filial relenting that will be greatest then. The waters of sorrow may make greater noise before, but they will come sweeping down with a more full flood then, as when a hearty thaw comes after a long frost.

6. *Lastly*, Believing the promise of his grace, use the means. There are means of God's appointment to stir up a soul to repentance; namely, serious meditations on the sins of our nature, heart, lip, and life; the evil of it with respect to God, and to ourselves, &c. Rev. ii. 5, "Remember from whence thou art fallen, and repent." Psal. cxix. 50, "I thought on my ways, and turned my feet unto thy testimonies." There are promises of repentance, Ezek. xxxvi. 31, "Then shall ye remember your own evil ways, and your doings that were not good, and shall loathe yourselves in your own sight, for your iniquities, and for your abominations." Acts v. 31, "Him hath God exalted with his right hand to be a Prince and a Saviour, for to give repentance to Israel, and forgiveness of sins." To believe the promise without use of the means is presumption; to use the means without believing the promise, is a selfish unsanctified work. What God has joined, either of these puts asunder, and so must be fruitless. God says to us in this case, as unto Moses, Exod. xvii. 5, 6. "Go on before the people, and take with thee of

the elders of Israel: and thy rod wherewith thou smotest the river, take in thine hand, and go. Behold, I will stand before thee there upon the rock in Horeb; and thou shalt smite the rock, and there shall come water out of it, that the people may drink." The means are as the rock, the faith of the promise the rod of God: the way to get the water was by smiting the rock with the rod.

FOURTHLY, Let us consider the parts of repentance. These are two, namely, humiliation for sin, and turning from sin unto God. These two put together, make up true repentance. Accordingly the Scripture speaks of repenting of sin, 2 Cor. xii. 21. " which have not repented of the uncleanness," &c.; and likewise repenting from sin, Heb. vi. 1, "Not laying aside the foundation of repentance from dead works, &c. So in the Old Testament repentance is expressed by two words; the one denoting remorse and sorrow, Job xlii. 6. " Wherefore I abhor myself, and repent in dust and ashes." Jer. viii. 6, "No man repented him of his wickedness, saying, What have I done?" the other denoting the turning of the soul, viz. from sin unto God, Ezek. xviii. 30. " Repent, and turn yourselves from all your transgressions.

But however these may be distinguished, they cannot be divided in true repentance. The true humiliation issues always in turning; and turning always begins at humiliation. Hence very often the whole of repentance is expressed by returning, and sometimes by humiliation, as Lev. xxvi. 41, " If then their uncircumcised hearts be humbled, and they then accept of the punishment of their iniquity." 2 Chron. xxxiii. 12, " And when he was in affliction, he besought the Lord his God, and humbled himself greatly before the God of his fathers." We have both together, Joel ii. 12, 13, " Therefore also now, saith the Lord, Turn ye even to me with all your heart, and with fasting, and with weeping, and with mourning. And rend your heart and not your garments, and turn unto the Lord your God: for he is gracious and merciful, slow to anger, and of great kindness, and repenteth him of the evil."

1st, To begin with humiliation. This leads the van in the sinner's return to God by repentance. There is never a soul comes back to God, but it comes the low way of humiliation. The sinner gone from God, is set up against him: but grace puts down the sinner from that seat, and lays him down at the Lord's footstool, where the Lord takes him up: 1 Pet. v. 6. " Humble yourselves therefore under the mighty hand of God, that he may exalt you in due time." As it was with Benhadad's servants, 1 Kings xx. 31. 32; so it is with the convinced sinner: faith teaches them, that the King of Israel is a merciful King; repentance girds sackcloth on their loins, and ropes on their heads, and in that posture brings them to him. Now, in this humiliation of the soul there are these five things.

First, A kindly sense of sin, whereby the soul sees and is deeply affected with its sins against a holy, gracious God. I call it so, to distinguish it from the legal convictions spoken of before, which make a terrible reel in the conscience and affections ; whereas this kindly soaks into the heart. The former is at the bottom involuntary, comes in, and is kept on against the sinner's will ; because the natural enmity of the heart against God is not broken ; and makes the man like one under great pain, who would gladly sleep, but still the new stounds awake him, and keep him awake. The latter is voluntary, it is welcome in, and welcome to stay ; because the heart is brought low, and would fain be lower before a holy God. When the light appears at a chink, they would fain draw the curtains, and open the windows, that they may get a better sight of their black face and foul hands, Jer. iii. 18, 19. This sense of sin,

1. For the matter of it, is,

1st, A sense of the plague of the heart, or sin of the nature, 1 Kings viii. 38 ; Rom. vii. 7, 8. The man that is humbled, sees the corruption of his nature, himself to be a mass of corruption and confusion. He discerns the bias of his heart to the wrong side, the aversion to do good, the proneness to evil, that is interwoven with his very nature. The light of the Lord shining into his soul, gives him the affecting sight of the distortion and pravity that is in all the faculties of his soul, the blindness in his mind, rebellion in his will, and carnality in his affections. The want of this is a flaw in the repentance of many, of whom we may say, as Lev. xiii. 44, " He is a leprous man, he is unclean : the priest shall pronounce him utterly unclean, his plague is in his head." They never see the corruption of their nature, and so repent not of it.

2dly, A sense of actual sins : Job xxxvi. 9, " Then he sheweth them their work, and their transgressions that they have exceeded." These are the poisonous streams flowing from the impoisoned fountain : Mark vii. 21, 22, " For from within, out of the heart of men, proceed evil thoughts, adulteries, fornications, murders, thefts, covetousness, wickedness, deceit, lasciviousness, an evil eye, blasphemy, pride, foolishness." Sin now lies at the door ; for those things that were buried out of sight, have a resurrection, and stand before him as an exceeding great army which he has mustered against Heaven. Sins committed many years before, will appear more fresh and green than that day they were committed. What he justified before as no faults, he will be now ashamed of ; and what were reckoned tolerable follies, will be accounted monstrous impieties.

3*dly*, A sense of the particular idol of jealousy, which the man has been most apt to be led away with. The soul is never truly humbled, till deeply sensible of its weak side : Hos. xiv. 3, "Ashur shall not save us, we will not ride upon horses, neither will we say any more to the work of our hands, Ye are our gods." For the penitent will be particularly set against that, as what is particularly offensive to God, Psal. xviii. 22. This right eye smarts and pains him so exceedingly, that now he would gladly have it plucked out. And as it does especially grieve the Lord's Spirit, it specially grieves his, as what has been the great make-bate betwixt God and him.

4*thly*, A sense of the numerousness and multitude of their sins : Job xiii. 23, "How many are mine iniquities and sins ? make me to know my transgression and my sin." A true sense of sin will open men's eyes to see innumerable evils compassing them about, countable only by him who telleth the stars, Psal. xix. 12. Hence the humbled soul is sensible of a cloud of guilt that it has been wrapt up in ; and will see it must plead guilty to every line of the spiritual law : sees itself a mass of iniquity ; "from the crown of the head to the sole of the foot, there is no soundness, but wounds, and bruises, and putrifying sores." Is. lxiv. 6, "We are all as an unclean thing, and all our righteousnesses are as filthy rags," &c.

5*thly*, A sense of the heinousness of their sins, the aggravating circumstances wherewith they have been attended : Luke xv. 18, "I will arise, and go to my father, and will say unto him, Father, I have sinned against heaven, and before thee." Each sin pierces the heart of the penitent. And so it is wonderful to see what a dexterity a repenting sinner has in aggravating his sins, in his prayers and complaints. Time, place, person, and each circumstance, shoots as it were a dart through the liver.

Lastly, A sense of the evil of sin. Men may see sin, that see not the evil of it. Hence professing sin, instead of confessing it ; turning to it, instead of turning from it. But if one saw the serpent's sting, he would not take it into his bosom, Luke xxiii. 34. But the Lord's language to the soul whom he is drawing to repentance, is that, Jer. ii. 19, "Thine own wickedness shall correct thee, and thy backsliding shall reprove thee : know therefore and see, that it is an evil thing and bitter, that thou hast forsaken the Lord thy God, and that my fear is not in thee, saith the Lord God of hosts." And there is a twofold evil in sin, which the soul is now sensible of.

(1.) The evil of it with respect to themselves. They are sensible of the bitter fruits of sin : Rom. vi. 21, "What fruit had ye then in those things, whereof ye are now ashamed? for the end of those things is death." They see now "the vine is the vine of Sodom, the grapes are grapes of gall, the clusters bitter, and their teeth are set on edge." They cry out, as the sons of the prophets in another case, 2 Kings iv. 40, " O thou man of God, there is death in the pot." This is the danger of sin, that they are made sensible of. They see the guilt of it, laying the soul open to temporal, spiritual, and eternal strokes: Jer. xiv. 7, " O Lord, though our iniquities testify against us, do thou it for thy name's sake: for our backslidings are many, we have sinned against thee." Hence " horror takes hold on them, because of God's righteous judgments." They are made to wonder that they are not in hell, drinking the cup of the wrath of God. Their hearts tremble to look back on the ruin that was hanging over their heads in their natural state; that the poisonous cup which they drank has not despatched them. Hence they fear to meddle with sin again, as one would do to take a serpent into his bosom.

(2.) The evil of it with respect to God and Christ; and that in a threefold respect. [1.] As contrary to the holy law of God: 1 John iii. 4, " Whosoever committeth sin transgresseth also the law: for sin is the transgression of the law." By sin one breaks over the hedge, yea, breaks it down, and so steps into the devil's ground; what wonder then a serpent do bite him! Now the sinner sees the equity of God's law, and so plainly perceives the evil of transgression: Rom. vii. 12, " The law is holy; and the commandment holy, and just, and good." And the breaking over this so glorious a hedge, galls the penitent heart, the ingenuous spirit of an evangelical penitent.

[2.] As contrary to the holy nature of God: Hab. i. 13, "Thou art of purer eyes than to behold evil, and canst not look on iniquity." Sin is the worst of evils in itself, and in the eyes of the penitent. There is nothing so contrary to the chief good, and therefore it is the chief evil. Now, the true penitent loves God, his holy nature and perfections; and therefore his sin is heavy to him, because by it he has walked contrary to him: Lam. v. 16, " Woe unto us that we have sinned."

[3.] As the procuring cause of the sufferings of Christ: Zech. xii. 10, " They shall look upon me whom they have pierced, and they shall mourn for him," &c. Mount Calvary is the Bochim to the true penitent; the sufferings of Christ are the commentaries on sin, which the true penitent reads; the groans of a dying Saviour rend their hearts; and by the wounds of a Redeemer they see the ill of sin.

This is the loathsomeness of sin, Is. xxx. 22; whereby it is not only hated for what attends it, but is abhorred for itself, as a thing which on no terms the soul could any longer digest.

2. For the qualities of it. It is,

1st, A particular and distinct sense of sin, not a general and confused one. No man that hears the gospel, having common understanding, but he confesses himself a sinner; but many nevertheless are blind as to particulars. But this puts one in a capacity to lay his hands on his sores, saying, as Psal. li. 4, " Against thee, thee only have I sinned, and done this evil in thy sight." It shews him his particular transgressions wherein he has exceeded, and the particular ills by which he has exceeded and offended in these. As the vermin appear crawling, when the stone is lifted up, which before lay hid; so the ills of the heart and life appear to the penitent: Rom. vii. 9, " I was alive without the law once: but when the commandment came, sin revived, and I died."

2dly, It is real, not imaginary. The Spirit of the Lord realizeth the evil of sin to the soul. And so it goes beyond a merely rational knowledge of sin, as far as the sense of the bitterness of gall got by tasting it, exceeds that got by the bare hearing of it: Jer. ii. 19, " Thine own wickedness shall correct thee, and thy backslidings shall reprove thee: know therefore and see, that it is an evil thing and bitter, that thou hast forsaken the Lord thy God, and that my fear is not in thee, saith the Lord God of hosts." There is a spiritual sensation of spiritual things, arising from the new nature, as well as a natural feeling of what is grievous to us another way: 1 Cor. ii. 14, 15, " The natural man receiveth not the things of the Spirit of God; for they are foolishness unto him: neither can he know them, because they are spiritually discerned. But he that is spiritual judgeth all things."

3dly, It is operative, not dead and idle. The eye of the penitent affects his heart; and the heart being touched, sets all the powers of the soul on work. It is the spiritual physic, that ceaseth not to work till the whole soul be purged; as in the case of Peter's hearers, Acts ii. 37, " who were pricked in their heart, and said unto Peter, and to the rest of the apostles, Men and brethren, what shall we do?" There is a sense of sin which vents itself in nothing but in sighing and going backward, or in dry and fruitless complaints. It is like the disturbance which the sluggard meets with on his bed, which never thoroughly awakens him. But this sense of sin is thorough work.

Lastly, It is an abiding sense of sin, not a transient one in a fit, and so away, Lam. iii. 49, 50, " Mine eye trickleth down, and ceaseth not, without any intermission ; till the Lord look down, and behold from heaven." The humbled soul carries it about with him, as long as he carries the body of sin and death about with him, saying with the apostle, Rom. vii. 24, " O wretched man that I am ! who shall deliver me from the body of this death ?" For it is not a slight touch, which goes as it comes, very easily. The removal of the stroke carries off Pharaoh's sense of sin ; but here the wound is deeper and so more abiding.

USE 1. An insensible sinner is an unhumbled impenitent sinner ; as was the case of the church of Laodicea, who said, " she was rich, and increased with goods, and had need of nothing ; and knew not that she was wretched, and miserable, and poor, and blind, and naked, Rev. iii. 17. They that never digged deep, are not built on the rock. They that have never got a broad sight of themselves in the sinfulness of their hearts and lives, have never yet got a believing sight of Christ. Consider this, ye that have still lived at ease, strangers to any thorough exercise about your soul's case ; though the door is shut, the thief is in the house.

1. This shews how it comes that the pride of people's hearts still remains, though under crying guilt of sin. Though they know their sin, they have no due sense of it. If they had, it would be such a burden on their backs as would soon make them stoop, as Peter's hearers did, Acts ii. 37. Insensible sinners may sit high in the seat of the scornful, while they see not what a God they have to do with : but when the Spirit of the Lord opens their eyes, and touches their hearts, to let them see and feel the evil of sin, they will lie low in the dust. They will, with the afflicted man, " put their mouth in the dust, if so be there may be hope," Lam. iii. 29.

3. See here a difference betwixt the saint's humiliation, and that of the hypocrite's. An Ahab may humble himself from a sense of the danger of sin ; but a true penitent is humbled from the sense of the loathsomness of sin, 1 Kings xxi. 27, 29. Job xlii. 5, 6. A slave may bow himself for fear of the whip ; but the disposition of a son is to be affected with the offence done to a kind father. Many will seem very low under the rod of God, and the apprehen-·sions of his wrath, who are never touched with his love. They will be cast down under the sense of the evil their sin does to themselves, while the dishonour done to God by it lies far from their hearts.

4. *Lastly*, Let me exhort you to get and entertain a deep sense of sin on your Spirits. See your sins, and be duly affected with them, and be humbled for them. O how sad is it, that amongst our many thoughts, sin gets so few of them !

For motives to press this exhortation, consider,

1*st*, That the Lord is anew calling the land by his providence to be sensible of their sins, and to be humbled for them. The Lord took it not long ago as a brand out of the burning; but he is threatening to cast it into the fire again, by a foreign invasion.* For though we were delivered, yet the controversy remains still. We have not been thankful for our deliverance; Atheism, profanity, formality, contempt of the gospel, and a spirit of apostacy and declining from the Lord, and his work and way, wofully abound. How can we miss to fall at length!

2*dly*, Consider the present dispensation of providence towards this congregation, threatening to leave our house desolate.† It fills the mouths of many with what is little worth; would to God it might fill your hearts and mine with a serious inquiry into the causes of it before the Lord. It speaks aloud, O that we were taking up the language of the threatening rod. The melancholy state of this congregation, in the time of the last desolation, needs not be forgot. It would become us all very well on this occasion, to consider what a jealous God we have to do with, and what entertainment has been given to the preached gospel; to lay our hands every one on our own mouths, and consider well what we have contributed to the bringing of the matter to this pass. By taking with our sin, and humbling ourselves befor the Lord, way might be made for the acceptance of prayer through Jesus Christ; and them that humble themselves God will exalt.

3*dly*, Consider, that however lightly your sins may sit on your spirits, they are a burden to the holy Spirit of God: Amos ii. 13. "Behold," says the Lord, "I am pressed under you, as a cart is pressed that is full of sheaves." And we may be sure the Lord will ease himself of that burden sooner or later. And if it be not by our repentance and humiliation, it will be by his accomplishing his wrath on us: Is. i. 24. "Ah, I will ease me of mine adversaries, and avenge me of mine enemies." Therefore consider your ways in order to a returning to the Lord. The lighter that sin sits on us, it is the more grieving to the Spirit of the Lord.

Lastly, Consider, that without sense of sin there is no humiliation; that without humiliation there can be no repentance; and that without repentance there can be no escape from the wrath of God. "For except ye repent, ye shall perish." Insensibleness of sin,

---

* Meaning the unnatural Rebellion that broke out in the year 1715; and an invasion from Sweden, in favour of a Popish pretender, in 1717; in which last year these sermons were preached.

† This probably relates to a design of transporting Mr. Boston to Closeburn, which however did not succeed.

and the evil of it, locks up the heart in obduration and impenitency; and that will shut up the soul under wrath. But God loves
the sensible humbled son: Jer. xxxi. 20. "Is Ephraim my dear son?
is he a pleasant child? for since I spake against him, I do earnestly
remember him still: therefore my bowels are troubled for him; I
will surely have mercy upon him, saith the Lord."

Secondly, In true humiliation there is a kindly sorrow for sin:
Zech. xii. 10, "I will pour upon the house of David, and upon the
inhabitants of Jerusalem, the spirit of grace and of supplications; and
they shall look upon me whom they have pierced, and they shall mourn
for him as one mourneth for his only son, and shall be in bitterness
for him, as one that is in bitterness for his first-born." The soul is
not only filled with remorse, but true grief, for offending a holy, gracious God. He grieved the Spirit in committing sin, his spirit is
grieved in repenting of it. The hard heart is broken, the adamantine
heart dissolved into tears of godly sorrow, the rock is struck by the
rod of the gospel, and the waters gush out. The way to Zion lies
through the valley of Baca: Jer. l. 4, 5, "In those days, and in
that time, saith the Lord, the children of Israel shall come, they
and the children of Judah together, going and weeping: they shall
go, and seek the Lord their God. They shall ask the way to Zion
with their faces thitherward, saying, Come, and let us join ourselves
to the Lord, in a perpetual covenant that shall not be forgotten."
And it is the mourners for sin whom the Lord comforts with the
consolations of his Spirit. This is that brokenness and contrition
of heart, which God calls for, and takes so much pleasure in. This
is the rending of the heart, which God requires, Joel ii. 12, 13.
This is godly sorrow, which hath these properties.

1. It is a sorrow for sin as sin; not only for the guilt of it, but
the loathsomeness of it; not only for the ill it does to ourselves,
but the dishonour and wrong it does to a holy gracious God, Psal.
li. 4; Zech. xii. 10. The penitent in his sorrow, goes farther than
awakened reprobates, who seeing their souls ruined and dead, do
put on their mournings. He grieves at the heart, because of the
offence done to God, the defacing of his image, transgressing a holy
and most just law, furnishing a spear and nails to pierce a Saviour.

2. It is an inward real sorrow. Not the hanging down of the
head like a bulrush, Is. lviii. 5. Not a made sorrow in a disfigured
countenance, which lies all in outward appearance. But it is a
sorrow soaking into the soul, and piercing the very heart, Is. lxi. 3.
And therefore it follows the man in secret, where no eye sees;
making him mourn before the Lord, when the world knows nothing
of it. For it ariseth from an inward principle.

3. It is a lively sorrow. The sorrow of the world worketh death. It stupifies a man, and takes heart and hand for duty from him. But the spiritual pangs of godly sorrow for sin quicken a man to his duty: 2 Cor. vii. 11, "For behold, this self-same thing that ye sorrowed after a godly sort, what carefulness it wrought in you, yea, what clearing of yourselves, yea, what indignation, yea, what fear, yea, what vehement desire, yea, what zeal, yea, what revenge!" It makes the man active in salvation-work. And the reason is, the one springs from slavish fear, which chills the soul, making it cold and stiff, and unfit for action; the other from love, which warms the heart, and disposeth it for action: Luke vii. 47, "Her sins which are many, are forgiven: for she loved much."

4. It is an abiding sorrow. It is not a flash of an affection, which is deceitful, but a "spirit of heaviness," Is. lxi. 3. The sorrows of many are like a summer-shower, that wets the surface of the ground, but is presently dried up, ere it do any good. But godly sorrow is like that, Eccl. vii. 3, "Sorrow is better than laughter: for by the sadness of the countenance the heart is made better." The soul, like Mary, mourns till it find the Lord, Lam. iii. 49, 50. forecited. It may indeed remit of its degrees; but while sin abides, the spring of mourning abides too.

5. It is an universal sorrow. The true penitent heartily grieves for his own sin, Psal. xxxviii. 18, and for the sin of others, Psal. cxix. 136. It is like the letting out of waters: it may begin at one sin, but it does not stop there, but goes through all known sin, Psal. i. 5. and unknown too, Psal. xix. 12, "Who can understand his errors? cleanse thou me from secret faults." They never truly mourn for one sin, that do not mourn for all: for that which moves sorrow in the repenting heart for one sin, is to be found in all sins, namely, its contrariety to the law and nature of God, the loathsomeness as well as danger of it. And hence, when once the floodgate of godly sorrow is opened, it overflows all; and the sweetest morsel becomes bitter.

6. It is deep sorrow. Peter repenting wept bitterly. He that would have a good crop, ploughs well; and he that would build surely, goes deep with the foundation. It was the want of depth of earth that was the ruin of the stony-ground hearers, Matt. xiii. 5. And deep digging was the safety of the house founded on a rock, Luke vi. 48. This sorrow is a rending of the heart, Joel ii. 13; a rending of it as the plough rends the earth, Jer. iv. 3; a pricking and piercing of it as with daggers, swords, and spears, Acts ii. 37, compared with John xix. 34; a cutting it as with a knife, Jer. iv. 4.

It is a question, Whether penitential sorrow exceeds all other sorrows for the comforts of this life, or not? If we measure by the moving of the heart and affections, it is evident, that at least always it doth not exceed other sorrows. But if we measure by the settled disposition of the heart, it is as evident that it does exceed them all. As the deepest waters ordinarily make least noise, so men will be more moved in a lesser joy and grief than in a greater; for they are but the lightest joys that move laughter, and oft-times the greatest sorrows are above tears. It settles more firmly, and continues more than any other sorrow whatsoever in the world.

7. *Lastly*, It is a heart purifying sorrow. It works repentance or forsaking of sin: 2 Cor. vii. 10. "Godly sorrow worketh repentance to salvation, not to be repented of." True mourning and turning are inseparable companions; though there is a mourning for sin, that is not deep enough to turn up the love of sin by the root. True sorrow in the heart is a spring, which as it runneth will work out sin, as to the love, habitual practice, and dominion of it, as a spring works out the mud thrown into it.

USE. 1. There is no repenting with a hale heart, and without repentance no salvation. People must either be broken for their sins in a way of mourning, or God will break them for them in a way of judgment. There are many stout hearts in our day, that will boldly outface challenges from the word and their own consciences, without either breaking or bowing. But let such remember, that there is a day coming when God will make the stoutest heart to tremble, and the heart of adamant to fly in a thousand pieces, Psal. ii. 9. "Thou shalt break them with a rod of iron, thou shalt dash them in pieces like a potter's vessel."

2. How far must they be from humiliation, that sin deliberately, glory in their shame, and rejoice in ungodly courses and practices! I think providences and ordinances are hardening to many in our day; they are not bettered by them, and therefore they are hardened and made worse under them. Our penny weddings and set drinkings, leaving such a stench behind them, and attended with before unheard of profanity, are speaking evidences of this. Are these Christian methods to help poor people? Will God accept the gift, where such a fat sacrifice is offered to the devil? Is that charity for which drinking must open men's hearts and hands to give? If some methods be not fallen on to prevent these things, they will bring wrath on the congregation.* I appeal to the consciences of all

* Penny weddings and drinking bouts were not peculiar to the congregation of Ettrick: they prevailed as much elsewhere, and do so still, to the dishonour of God, and nourishment of profaneness.

sober persons, if it looked not judgment-like, that in that very time when abroad a design was managing to lay the congregation desolate,* at home many were met for a set drinking, carried on to a monstrous height of profanity, in the day and in the night. It becomes us all to mourn for this, lest we involve ourselves in the guilt. And particularly I warn all such as were any way partakers of that scandalous riot, to repent, lest wrath break out upon them. For it is a fearful thing to stand exposed to the lash of these threatenings, Hab. ii. 15, " Woe unto him that giveth his neighbour drink : that puttest thy bottle to him, and makest him drunken also, that thou mayest look on their nakedness." Is. xxii. 12, 13, 14, " And in that day did the Lord of hosts call to weeping, and to mourning, and to baldness, and to girding with sackcloth : and behold, joy and gladness, slaying oxen, and killing sheep, eating flesh, and drinking wine ; let us eat and drink, for to-morrow we shall die. And it was revealed in mine ears by the Lord of hosts, surely this iniquity shall not be purged from you, till ye die, saith the Lord God of hosts."

3. The sorrow of many for their sins, will tend to no good account before the Lord. Few have any remarkable sorrow for their sins at all ; but amongst those whose hearts are really grieved and pained for their sin, how few are there that have any right sorrow ? The danger of it, the disadvantage by it, the shame of it before the world, pains them a little ; but the dishonour done to God by it touches them not effectually. And so their sorrow will be but the beginning of hell, not of repentance.

4. *Lastly*, Be exhorted to mourn for sin. Labour to get your hearts affected with this mournful object, and be not strangers to this exercise. The sins and threatened judgments of this day call for it ; and it is the way to attain particular safety in common calamity : Ezek. ix. 4, " And the Lord said unto him, Go through the midst of the city, through the midst of Jerusalem, and set a mark upon the foreheads of the men that sigh, and that cry for all the abominations that be done in the midst thereof." If we were more in the duty of mourning, we would share more of the gospel-comforts, Matt. v. 4, " Blessed are they that mourn : for they shall be comforted." And the more of the Spirit one has, the more will he be taken up that way.

Thirdly, In true humiliation there is a holy shame upon the account of sin before the Lord : Rom. vi. 21, " What fruit had ye in those things, whereof ye are now ashamed ? for the end of those things is death." The remembrance of sin fills the penitent

---

* Meaning the design of transporting the author to Closeburn.

with shame and blushing : hence says Ezra, chap. ix. 6, "O my God, I am ashamed and blush to lift up my face to thee, my God : for our iniquities are increased over our head, and our trespass is grown up unto the heavens." Shame was never known in the world, till sin entered ; yet sometimes sin comes to such a height with sinners, that it quite banishes shame : but the case of such is very desperate, Jer. iii. 9. "Thou hadst a whore's forehead, thou refusedst to be ashamed." Shame then is the remains of virtue in a sinner, to which whoso are lost, all are lost to all good, Is. iii. 9. "The shew of their countenance doth witness against them, and they declare their sin as Sodom, they hide it not." Now, the grace of God awakens this shame, and sanctifies it in the penitent soul, so that he hangs down his head before the Lord, as ashamed of his way and heart.

There are four things occasion shame, and meet here.

1. Nakedness causeth shame. Hence said Adam to the Lord, Gen. iii. 10, "I heard thy voice in the garden : and I was afraid, because I was naked; and I hid myself." Sin strips the sinners of their beautiful garments, takes away the glory of the rational creature, and leaves them without a covering before the eyes of a holy God. The penitent sees this, and is ashamed ; and so the publican, cannot lift up his eyes to heaven, but smites on his breast, as if he would wound the breast that sin bred in, which has brought him to this shamful case.

2. Pollution and defilement, for that makes one loathsome to others, Job ix. 31, "Thou shalt plunge me in the ditch, and mine own clothes shall abhor me." Sin defiles the soul, takes away and mars all its beauty, and deforms it in the sight of God. And the penitent sees this, and is ashamed, Is. lxiv. 6, "We are all as an unclean thing, and all our righteousnesses are as filthy rags, and we all do fade as a leaf, and our iniquities, like the wind, have taken us away." Never was a man that had been plunged over head and ears in a mire, more ashamed to come before others in that case, than the penitent is ashamed to shew his face before God.

3. Disappointment of raised expectations, Jer. ii. 36, 37. The sinner in his impenitent state, looked for his happiness and satisfaction in sinful courses. But when his heart is touched, he is ashamed ; for he finds, that instead of bread expected, he has got a stone ; instead of fish, a serpent. He finds, that he has been courting his own death and ruin ; and that from the wall he leaned on there has come forth a serpent and bit him. And hence is that reflection, Rom. vi. 21, "What fruit had ye in those things, whereof ye are now ashamed ? for the end of those things is death.

4. Discovering of one's reproach, Jer. ii. 26, "Sin is a reproach to any people." In the impenitent state the soul's reproach is hid to it; but when grace touches the heart, and the Lord brings the sinner's ways to mind, lays his sins in broad-band before him, how can he miss to be ashamed? In a special manner, a conviction of base ingratitude fills one with shame, as to be convicted of designs against him who had saved our life. And thus the goodness of God duly considered, fills the penitent with shame and blushing, while he thinks what an ungrateful wretch he has been: Jer. iii. 25, "We lie down in our shame, and our confusion covereth us: for we have sinned against the Lord our God, we and our fathers from our youth even unto this day, and have not obeyed the voice of the Lord our God.

Use. 1. Shamelessness in sin is a badge of impenitency, and therefore a forerunner of destruction, Jer. vi. 15. Phil. iii. 10. A forehead of brass is a sign the heart is of stone. Impudence in sin argues a filthy heart, an obstinate disposition, and a seared conscience. And such are a stage beyond others from the kingdom of God. What hopes can they have of the glory of heaven, that glory in their shame?

2. We see then that sin will bring shame sooner or later, here or hereafter. As for them that live and die without repentance, their shame is sure, and they will be covered with it, before the great congregation of heaven and earth at the last day, and they shall never recover their countenance: Dan. xii. 2, "Many of them that sleep in the dust of the earth shall awake, some to shame and everlasting contempt." And if people be recovered by repentance, they will be filled with shame before the Lord, even holy shame. But whatever shame men have, it is no holy shame that keeps them from glorifying God by taking shame to themselves when called thereto; for no grace of God keeps folk back from duty, Josh. vii. 19. Common discretion teaches, that one ashamed of an injury done to the honour of another, cannot look him in the face but with shame, till he has done what he can to repair that honour.

3. *Lastly*, The penitent soul is an ingenuous soul, and heartily at odds with sin. For such an one will be ashamed before God, of what the world cannot tax him with. Many may be sorry for sin before God, because of the terrible consequences of it which they apprehend, who yet are not ashamed before him, because they see not the evil that is in itself. But it argues a childlike disposition, to be heartily ashamed of secret sins before the Lord.

Fourthly, In true humiliation there is self-loathing and abhorrence : Ezek. xxxvi. 31, "Then shall ye remember your own evil ways, and your doings that were not good, and shall loathe yourselves in your own sight, for your iniquities, and for your abominations." The penitent not only loathes his sin, but himself for his sin. He cries out with Job, chap. xl. 4, "Behold I am vile, what shall I answer thee ? I will lay mine hand upon my mouth." Repentance sets a man at variance with himself. He sees his ugly face in the glass of God's law, Christ's sufferings, and the Lord's goodness, and he loathes himself. This self-loathing manifests itself,

1. In the low and mean thoughts the penitent justly entertains of himself. True penitents see such vileness in themselves, as makes them give a very mean account of themselves. Abraham owned himself to be dust and ashes; Jacob, less than all the mercies of God; David, a worm, and not a man; Asaph, as a beast before the Lord ; Agur, more brutish than any ; the centurion, unworthy that Christ should come under his roof : Paul, one born out of due time, the least of the apostles, nay, less than the least of all saints, nay, the chief of sinners ; and the prodigal son, Luke xv. 19, reckoned himself no more worthy to be called a son, but to be made a hired servant.

2. In the penitent's being heartily out with himself upon the account of his sin : Job xlii. 6, "Wherefore I abhor myself, and repent in dust and ashes." As one cannot with any pleasure touch himself, that has filth thrown on him, but his very heart stands at himself; so it is in spiritual self-loathing. He looks on himself as an ugly spectacle. He not only has nothing to say in defence of himself, but with indignation he rejects all the shifts and excuses for it, which he was satisfied with before : Luke xviii. 13. " The publican standing afar off, would not lift up so much as his eyes unto heaven, but smote upon his breast, saying, God be merciful to me a sinner."

3. In holy revenge, 2 Cor. vii. 11. He that was going on in sin before, is now divided against himself ; so that the devil's kingdom of sin in him must needs go to ruin. He acts the part of an accuser, advocate, and judge, against himself ; yea in some sort lashes himself for his sinful heart and life. Hence we find the humbled sinner,

1st, Smiting on his breast, Luke xviii. 13, as it were thereby declaring, that he deserves to be struck at the heart, and die for his transgression ; that within him is the cause of all his sin and sorrows, he may thank himself for all ; the source and spring of all is the corrupt heart.

2*dly*, Smiting on his thigh, Jer. xxxi. 19, as if he would thereby declare, that he would be willing to take vengeance on the feet that carried him out of the way of God; that he is filled with indignation against himself, for his unaccountable practices, saying, What have I done? what a wretched sinner have I been?

There are these five things that stir up this self-loathing especially, in the penitent soul.

(1.) The remarkable blots, and signal miscarriages in his way, that deeply wound and defile the conscience: like Peter's denying his Master, which made him weep bitterly, when he came to himself. These in a peculiar manner cover the soul with confusion, and fill it with self-abhorrence. And hence sometimes repentance begins at some such thing, from whence it spreads to the whole body of sin: Acts ii. 36, 37, "Let all the house of Israel know assuredly, that God hath made that same Jesus whom ye have crucified, both Lord and Christ. Now when they heard this, they were pricked in their heart, and said, Men and brethren, what shall we do?"

(2.) The fulness of sin seen in the soul: Is. lxiv. 6, "We are all as an unclean thing, and all our righteousnesses are as filthy rags." The penitent being made sensible of his soul's case, sees the leprosy spread over the whole man, his mind under much darkness, his will rebellious against the will of God, his affections disordered, his whole nature corrupted, the seed of every sin in it; so that he concludes, that his heart is full of iniquity, and that the lusts that are hatched there, their name may be Legion. His life is a loathsome spectacle of the outbreakings and workings of that corruption. So that he sees that "from the sole of the foot to the crown of the head there is no soundness; and therefore he loathes himself."

(3.) The pollution cleaving to his duties: Is. lxiv. 6. forecited. While he sees how the running sore of his natural corruption drops on all his holy things, and defiles them, how can he choose but loath himself? He sees his best works are like a moth-eaten garment, full of holes; never a prayer, nor confession made, but there are provocations against the Lord in them. His mournings for sin must be mourned over, because of the woful defects thereof; while he goes to mend one hole, still he is sure to strike out another. Thus the penitent is in his own eyes like Job, who had not whole fingers to dress his sores with; so he abhors himself.

(4.) The aggravations of sin, Luke xv. 18. A sight of these makes sin look like an opened stinking sore, wherein each of them contributes to make it more and more loathsome. When the penitent considers with what bent of affection he has sinned, the light, the many mercies, vows, and resolutions, &c. he has sinned against, he cannot but loath himself as a wretched self-destroyer, as an ungrateful miscreant, and as a beast before the Lord.

(5.) Instability in any thing that is good: Hos. vi. 4, "Your goodness is as a morning cloud, and as the early due it goeth away." Wavering hearts, and wavering hands, are very humbling to a soul truly touched. A good frame is a rare hour, and stays but a short while. How often are resolutions fairly taken up, and begin to bud in endeavours for practice, that yet are quickly let fall again? How often do men relapse into the same sins they have sometimes had made very bitter to them? There is nothing more apt than this to stir up self-abhorrence.

USE 1. Self-conceit is a need-nail to a state of impenitency: Rev. iii. 17, "Thou [the church of Laodicea] sayest, I am rich, and increased with goods, and have need of nothing; and knowest not that thou art wretched, and miserable, and poor, and blind, and naked." No repentance can be where there is no humiliation, and there can be no humiliation while people are puffed up with a conceit of themselves. Publicans and harlots will enter into the kingdom of heaven, before such self-conceited professors. Whenever the Spirit of the Lord takes a dealing with such persons, and discovers to them the signal miscarriages in their life, the fulness of sin, &c. that swelling conceit of sweet self will fall away, as ever the snow melts in a sunshine day. They that look on themselves as among the chief of saints, will see themselves the chief of sinners.

2. Look into yourselves, if ye would loathe yourselves and repent. Hence said Isaiah, chap. vi. 5, "Wo is me, for I am undone, because I am a man of unclean lips." Things may be going all wrong in the house, and the master not know it, while he is a stranger at home. Many a poor soul is pining away in its iniquity, and running with loathsome spiritual sores, threatening its ruin, while in the meantime they are mightily in love with themselves, and fond of their own condition, like a miserable man that is happy in a dream. But heavy will the awakening of such be.

3. *Lastly,* Sin must needs be a very loathsome thing in the eyes of a penitent, since it makes him loath himself. Alas! many times we love that in ourselves, which we loath in others. But when one loathes himself for his sin against a holy, gracious God, it is an argument that that soul is heartily out with sin.

Fifthly, and *Lastly,* In true humiliation there is a penitent confession of sin. Hence is that exhortation, Jer. iii. 13, " Only acknowledge thine iniquity, that thou hast transgressed against the Lord thy God," &c. This is the way that penitent sinners have always sought pardon and ease to their consciences in : Psal. xxxii. 5, " I acknowledged my sin unto thee, and mine iniquity have I not hid: I said, I will confess my transgressions unto the Lord ; and thou forgavest the iniquity of my sin." Confession of sin is the vomit of sin, whereby the sweet morsel is cast up again ; and it is the vent of real sorrow, shame, and self-abhorrence. And when the heart is loosed to it, the man becomes like the fish that is boiled in the water which it swimmed in.

This confession is to be according to the nature of the offence. If the sin be a secret one, a confession to God in secret is sufficient. If it be a private offence, the confession is to be so too : Jam. v. 16, " Confess your faults one to another." If it be a public offence, giving public scandal, the confession is to be public also : 1 Tim. v. 20, " Them that sin rebuke before all, that others also may fear." So penitent David left his confession on record, for the church's edification. And so did the apostle Paul, 1 Tim. i. 13. And the reason is evident, since by sin God's honour is impaired, and we can repair it no other way, but by confessing it with sorrow, shame, &c. the confession must be according to the nature of the offence, else the wrong done to the honour of God is not repaired by it. And in the private and public confession God is our party, and not men only, as well as in the secret one.

Now, confession is a necessary part of humiliation. If the hard heart be loosed to be truly humblied for sin, it follows of course, that the tongue will be loosed to confess it. Hence confession is put for the whole of humiliation, yea of repentance, Hos. v. 15, " I will go and return to my place, till they acknowledge their offence." 1 John i. 9. " If we confess our sins, he is faithful, and just to forgive our sins, and to cleanse us from all unrighteousness." Confession of sin hath two parts.

1. Self-accusing. God has given a law, the sinner has broke it ; the penitent confesseth his transgression with shame and sorrow, to the honour of the lawgiver. He cannot hide it, he dares not deny it ; his soul is humbled, and therefore he confesseth it : Psal. li. 3. " I acknowledge my transgressions : and my sin is ever before me." He approves of the law as holy, just, and good, and disapproves of the transgression. Thus the morsel that was sweet in the mouth, turning bitter in the belly is vomited up.

2. Self-condemning. Hence said the returning prodigal, Luke xv. 18, 19. " Father, I have sinned against heaven, and before thee, and am no more worthy to be called thy son." The penitent looks to the law, and the demerit of his sin, reads his own doom, and passeth sentence on himself. He owns that all the evil he smarts

under for the present, is just and righteous with God; Dan. ix. 14. "Therefore hath the Lord watched upon the evil, and brought it upon us: for the Lord our God is righteous in all his works which he doth: for we obeyed not his voice." If his broken bones pain him, he will own that it is just. If his sin find him, so that he read it in his punishment, he will acknowledge that it is a just contrivance; and that he deserves to sink under eternal wrath for it, saying with the afflicted church, "It is of the Lord's mercies that we are not consumed, because his compassions fail not," Lam. iii. 22. He will say, that God may justly take the filthy garments of his sin, cover them with brimstone, wrap him up in them, and cast him into the pit, Psal. li. 4.

Now, this confession should be sincere, full, very particular, free, and accompanied with forsaking.*

USE. 1. Hiding and covering sin, and refusing to confess it in the way that God calls for a confession, is a sign of an heart not humbled for it: Prov. xxviii. 13. "He that covereth his sins shall not prosper: but whoso confesseth and forsaketh them, shall have mercy." Many in our day, falling into public scandals by their works of darkness, put on a forehead of brass, and refuse to confess them for the glory of God, cheating themselves with that, that they will confess their sins to God but not to men. But little do they consider, that by that means they put a bar in their own way to pardon, while by resolute lying they cover one sin with another, and by refusing to honour God at his call. Nor do they consider the weight of that word standing in the way of their peace with God, while they refuse to remove the scandal, that so they may be reconciled to the church: Matth. xviii. 17, 18. "If he shall neglect to hear them, tell it unto the church: but if he neglect to hear the church, let him be unto thee as an heathen man, and a publican. Verily I say unto you, Whatsoever ye shall bind on earth, shall be bound in heaven: and whatsoever ye shall loose on earth, shall be loosed in heaven." It is true, it is but a word; yea but it is God's word, that will be more terrible to an awakened conscience than any punishment men can inflict.

2. They that shun to see their sins, that they may confess them, cannot repent of them: Jer. ix. 6. 7. "Thine habitation is in the midst of deceit, through deceit they refuse to know me, saith the Lord. Therefore thus saith the Lord of hosts, behold I will melt them, and try them; for how shall I do for the daughter of my people?" It is true, there are sins which we cannot so see in our-

---

* See Memorial concerning Fasting.

selves as to confess them particularly; but in that case the soul does not refuse conviction, as Psal. xix. 12. "Who can understand his errors? cleanse thou me from secret faults." But when one keeps the sweet morsel under his tongue, aud has no will to see the evil of it, lest he should be obliged to confess it before the Lord, this is quite another case, and speaks a deceit of the heart, holding fast sin, and refusing to let it go.

3. *Lastly* Labour to be sincere, full, free, &c. in confessing your sins. We are in debt to the justice of God, we cannot pay our debt; let us confess our debt, to prevent a pursuit, and that we may be capable to pray for forgiveness of it, which otherwise we cannot be. O, if we had a due sense and sorrow for our sins, this would, like an overflowiug flood, bear down before them all those things which now hamper us in confessing our sins.

Thus far of humiliation, the first part of repentance.

2dly, I come now to the second thing, viz. the returning of the soul unto God from sin. This is the completing of repentance. Whatever sense of sin, shame, sorrow, &c. for it one have, if it end not in returning to God, it is naught. It is under this notion that repentance is so often called for in the Old Testament, Return, Turn ye. And it may be well put for the whole of repentance: for,

First, The impenitent sinner is out of himself, out of his wits; but by repentance he returns and comes to himself. Hence we read, that the prodigal, Luke xv. 17. came to himself. There is never a soul that is brought to repentance, but there is as great a change upon him, as on a madman that is returned to his sound mind. He has quite other notions of things than he had before; he looks upon his sinful courses as the effects of spiritual frenzy. This is the first part of repentance, namely, humiliation.

Secondly, The impenitent sinner is out of his place, like a wandering bird: Prov. xxvii. 8, "As a bird that wandereth from her nest: so is a man that wandereth from his place." And so the soul is out of its rest, and out of its duty. Adam shook himself and all his race out of their rest, and out of that they wander up and down in the devil's common. Repentance is the sinner's returning to his place again, to take up his place again in God's house among his servants. This is the second part of repentance. And whenever the soul comes to itself, it will come to God again. The grace of God finds the sinner, as the angel found Hagar, Gen. xvi. 8, 9; and as Paul found Onesimus, Philemon ver. 10, 11, 12. Now, in this returning, according to the two terms,

I. There is a turning from sin: Ezek. xiv. 6, "Repent, and turn from your idols, and turn away your faces from all your abominations." 2 Tim. ii. 19, "Let every one that nameth the name of Christ, depart from iniquity." Psal. xxxiv. 14, "Depart from evil." The sinner changes his course, and gives up with his former lusts. The impenitent sinner is a misled traveller, who finding himself wrong, will go no farther on, but leave the wrong way, and seek the right one. To repent of sin, and yet continue in the practice of it, is a contradiction. No; the true penitent ceases from sin, he gives over his work in the service of sin and lusts, Is. i. 16. He forsakes his former ways, chap. lv. 7. And though sin remains in him, yet it reigns not as before. If the question be, How the penitent turns from sin, since he is daily offending, and sin abides in him, while he is here? I answer,

1. True penitents turn from it in their heart and affection. There is a bond in the impenitent state, whereby the sinner's heart is knit to his lusts, as ever the sucking child's heart is to the breast, which he can by no means want. Repentance looseth that bond: Rom. vii. 24, "O wretched man that I am! who shall deliver me from the body of this death?" So though sin cleaves to the soul, yet the soul cleaves not to it as formerly. It hangs on him, it is true, but only as the chains on the captive, which are his burden; as the grave-clothes on Lazarus raised, which he is working to put off. Thus repentance makes a change of the heart. And,

1st, His esteem of sin is turned to despite. His judgment is set against it: Is. ii. 20, "In that day a man shall cast his idols of silver, and his idols of gold, which they made, each one for himself to worship, to the moles and to the bats." What he approved before, now he condemns; for the scales are turned, and what was highest before is now lowest. Grace and holiness get the ascendant of sin and wickedness in his esteem. Those he counted most happy sometimes, because they took the greatest liberty in sinful courses, he now accounts most miserable, as slaves to sin, and in the road to destruction; and therefore takes up Joshua's resolution, chap. xxiv. 15, "As for me and my house, we will serve the Lord."

2dly, His love of sin is turned to hatred of it: Ezek. xiv. 6. fore-cited. Psal. cxix. 113, "I hate vain thoughts." Ver. 104, "I hate every false way." It was good in his eyes before, better than the favour of God, and communion with him. He knew nothing good or desirable but the world and lusts, and what might satisfy the corrupt cravings of the soul. But repentance turns his soul against it, and he hates it as an evil thing, as the worst of evils, worse than suffering and afflictions. Were he left to his choice without fear of punishment, he would never choose it; for he hates it for itself, its contrariety to God's nature and will.

3dly, His liking of sin is turned to loathing of it. Hence repentance is called a casting away of sin, Ezek. xviii. 31. as one would do some filthy thing that he cannot endure to have near him. For the penitent looks not only on sin as an ill thing, but as a loathsome thing which his heart stands at, Is. xxx. 22. And this is the ground of that self-loathing which the penitent is filled with.

Lastly, His cleaving to sin is turned into a longing to be rid of it, Rom. vii. 24. The man longs to be free from it, as ever the prisoner for the opening of his prison-doors, the captive for his being set at liberty, and the dropping off of his chains. It is a burden on his back, which he groans under; a sickness to his soul, that he would fain have the cure of. And therefore Christ with all his salvation is lovely in his eyes; his sanctifying Spirit, as well as his justifying blood.

2. They turn from it in their life and conversation. He that stood in the way of sinners before, now leaves it, when once the grace toucheth the heart, Is. lv. 7. The penitent not only has a pure heart, but clean hands. Repentance will make a visible change on one's life: for it sets men to mortify the members of the body of death, Rom. viii. 13; to refuse compliance with lusts and temptations, Tit. ii. 12; to starve the lusts of the flesh, Rom. xiii. 14; and to nail the body of sin with all its members to the cross of Christ, Gal. v. 24. And,

1st, They turn from the gross pollutions of the outward man, Psal. xxiv. 3, 4. An elect soul before conversion may be a habitual profane person, as well as others: but if he may be so after conversion, where is the difference betwixt Christ's sheep and the devil's goats? It is true, they may make gross slips, as David and Peter did: but they do not lie in them, they recover again by repentance. But a profane life is the mark of an impenitent state, Gal. v. 21. And it is a wonder how men can pretend to repentance, while they live in the habitual practice of drunkenness, swearing, sabbath-breaking, lying, dishonesty, and other gross pollutions of the outward man, where one would think the profane devil is not so much as gone out, far less cast out.

2dly, They become tender with respect to the sins of common infirmity, labouring to make conscience of their words and actions, Acts. xxiv. 16. What others account light of, they will stand at a distance from, as having felt the smart of sin; and that not only before the world, but even in secret where no eye sees but God's. They will stand aloof from temptations, and even from the appearance of evil: and wherein they are overtaken through the frailty of the flesh, they will mourn for it before the Lord.

3. In respect both of heart and life. They turn against sin to oppose and resist it, in the inner and outward man, as taking now the contrary side to the devil, the world, and the flesh. The spiritual combat is begun in the true penitent, Gal. v. 17. The war with sin is proclaimed and begun, which never ends till death. They revolt from, cast off the yoke, and stand up against their old masters, 2 Tim. ii. 19.

1st, They resist the motions of sin in their hearts, and endeavour after heart purity, as well as life purity : Psal. cxix. 113. " I hate vain thoughts : but thy law do I love." The Pharisaical professor may cleanse the outside of the platter, while he is little troubled about its being within full of ravening. But the hardest work a gracious soul has against sin, is with the heart, with what the world neither sees nor can see in him. And the guiding of the heart is the hardest piece of management in his religion.

2dly, They resist the outbreakings of sin in the life : Psal. xviii. 23. " I was also upright before him : and I kept myself from mine iniquity." They see they are in a world where snares are thick laid ; they see their own weakness, and how ready they are to be entrapped, and therefore labour to be on their guard, lest they be carried away with the stream. Hence they are afraid of temptations, and therefore labour to shut their eyes from beholding vanity ; sometimes fearing to fall one day by the hand of temptation, and therefore longing to be beyond the reach of sin.

4. And *Lastly*, Because their turning from sin is never perfect till death, therefore so long they are ay turning, and renewing their repentance, John xiii. 10, They are not true penitents who look on it as the work of some days or weeks, at the soul's first conversion to God. A true penitent will ay be repenting, as long as he is sinning. He sees that he is often falling into the mire, and therefore must be often washing ; daily contracting new debt, therefore must be daily crying for forgiveness. And the more heinous his after miscarriages be, the longer he lies secure, his repentance will be the more bitter when he riseth up again.

Now, this turning from sin has these properties.

1. It is voluntary, as springing from an inward principle set up in the heart against sin : Job xlii. 6. " I abhor myself, and repent in dust and ashes." The penitent does not only cast away sin as a live coal out of his bosom, that would burn him, but as some loathsome thing, that would defile him. Some turn from their sins against their will ; they part with their sin as Phaltiel did with his unlawful wife Michal, 2 Sam. iii. 15. They dwell in the tents of sin, till the rigging-tree break, and there is no abiding longer there

for them; they part with their sins, as the covetous man with his riches at death, when, nill he will he, he must let it go. But true repentance is a turning from sin out of choice: and forced reformation neither is sincere nor will last, Psal. lxxviii. 34.

2. It is sincere, as being a turning from sin as sin, a turning from it because it is a turning away from God, a turning from it for its contrariety to God's holy nature and law, Luke xv. 18. The man leaves his sin, not for the inferior motives only of danger to himself by it, but from the higher motives, namely, because it is offensive to God, dishonours his Son, grieves his Spirit, transgresses his law, and defaces his image. If your turning from sin proceed not from these motives, God will never regard it as acceptable in his sight. It is done for self not for God; and God will never be the reward of that work whereof he is not the end.

Question. What should one do with respect to those sins he has turned from, from these lower motives of self, or those sins that have left him, before he left them? *Answer.* Do not turn back to them; but do with them as they use to do with those that die by their own hands, bury them disgracefully, and throw stones on their grave. Look on them and loathe them, rise higher in your motives to forsake them than before. Ye left them for your own sake, put them further away for the sake of God's honour. Set them before your eyes again, and see how provoking they have been to a holy God, how dishonouring to his Son, &c; repent and mourn over them on these accounts. And then your turning from them will be sincere.

3. This turning from sin is universal: Psal. cxix. 104, "I hate every false way." Ezek. xviii. 31, "Cast away from you all your transgressions." Whoever turns sincerely from one sin, turns from all known sin whatsoever; because the reason that moves the true penitent, is to be found in all as well as any one. Partial reformation is not sincere; for God requires the whole heart, and will not be served by halves. Every sin is a deadly wound to the soul; and therefore though many be cured, if but one remain uncured, the man is a dead man by that one: Matth. v. 29. "If thy right eye offend thee, pluck it out, and cast it from thee: for it is profitable for thee that one of thy members should perish, and not that thy whole body should be cast into hell." A drop of poison will make a whole cup of good win edeadly, and one sin retained will render all other reformation naught; as Abimelech the son of Jerubbaal's concubine was the death of all his seventy sons by his wives except one.

4. It is speedy, without delays: Psal. cxix. 60, "I made haste, and delayed not to keep thy commandments." As long as a man is

undetermined to turn from his sin, or delays to do it, his repentance is not sincere. It is an evidence that the lance of humiliation has not gone deep enough, when the filthy matter does not presently spring forth. A man whose heart is truly touched with a penitent sense of sin, will delay as long the flinging a burning coal out of his bosom, as the casting away of his sin. No: when it goes to the quick, it must off presently; though it were an offending right hand, it must be cut off presently; though it were an offending right eye, it must be presently plucked out.

5. *Lastly*, This turning from sin is thorough; it makes complete work evangelically, though not legally. It was a flaw in Judah's repentance, that she turned not unto the Lord with her whole heart, but feignedly. Jer. iii. 10; and in Ephraim's that he mixed himself among the people, and was a cake not turned, Hos. vii. 8. Men turn thoroughly from sin in these four respects.

1*st*, The true penitent sticks at no known sin, but turns from all without exception, even those sins that are dearest and nearest to them, and which they have been most easily beset with, Heb. xii. 1, "I kept myself from mine iniquity," Psal. xviii. 23. This turning from sin is never thorough, till it reach the sin that is the sin of one's constitution, the sin that is the sin which most attends his calling, stations, and relations wherein he stands; the sin that he has most frequent and strongest temptations unto. That is the predominant evil which the heart must be loosed from, the right hand and right eye sin, the one thing lacking, which mars all other things, Mark vii. 21. Unless there be a turning from, a warring with this, it is all wrong; though indeed they may sometimes lose as well as win in the battle.

2*dly*, He turns from that which is the ensnaring hook in any of his sins, the handle whereby it caught hold of him, Psal. cxxxi. 2. Pharaoh would have been content to let Israel go, so be they would have left their little ones, which he was sure would have brought them back again. And Satan will let people turn from sin for a time, while they retain a reigning love to the bewitching thing that is in a sinful course. For while it is so, the tree is indeed cut, but the root is left in the ground, and will grow again.

3*dly*, He turns from the occasions of sin, Ezek. xiv. 6. Wherefore David prays, "Turn away mine eyes from beholding vanity;" and Solomon gives advice in case of drunkenness, Prov. xxiii. 31, "Look not thou upon the wine when it is red, when it giveth his colour in the cup, when it moveth itself aright. It is vain to pretend to repent and turn from sin, while men do not watch against the occasions of it, and wrestle against them, as against the sin itself. They that in a siege mind really to defend the town, they will defend the outworks as long as they can; wilfully to let the enemy in there, speaks treachery. Much lies in this point for reformation: Prov. iv. 14, 15, "Enter not into the path of the wicked, and go not in the way of evil men. Avoid it, pass not by it, turn from it, and pass away."

Lastly, He turns from the enjoyment of the fruits of his sin. To pretend to turn from sin, and yet to feed sweetly on the fruits of it, is an absolutely vain pretence. When sin itself is truly quit, the profit of it is given up with. This the prophet teacheth, Is. xxxiii. 15, "He that walketh righteously, and speaketh uprightly, he that despiseth the gain of oppressions, that shaketh his hands from holding of bribes, that stoppeth his ears from hearing of blood, and shutteth his eyes from seeing evil," &c. This is so evident, that even Judas in his repentance, such as it was, could no longer brook the reward of his iniquity, Matt. xxvii. 3. A philosopher had bought a pair of shoes, but had not paid the price of them; the tradesman died; the philosopher thought the money was gained; but his conscience caused him bring back the money, and throw it into the shop. "Take it," says he, "thou art alive to me, while dead to all the world besides." Hence two things belong to this part of repentance.

(1.) Restitution, or restoring the thing again, which has been sinfully and wrongously taken away from others. He that can do it, and will not, cannot repent of that sin; for he wilfully feeds on the fruit of his sin; and that is a continuing in it inconsistent with turning from it. And since there is no pardon of that sin which a man does not repent of, it is a maxim in divinity, *Non remittitur nisi restituitur,* namely, to a person that is able, but unwilling to do it. Hence Zaccheus proves himself a true penitent by restitution, Luke xix. 8. And one may as well think a thief may repent in the time he is feeding on what he has stolen from his neighbour, as that one may repent of what in other cases he has unjustly taken from his neighbour, and can, but will not restore. When lovers part, they give back their tokens; and so when a sinner parts with his sin, he restores all that he had unjustly taken from others.

(2.) Reparation as far as may be, in those cases wherein proper restitution cannot be made: as in the case of unjust wounding our neighbour's honour, reputation, peace, quiet, and contentment, &c. Hence is that exhortation, Jam. v. 16, "Confess your faults one to another, and pray one for another, that ye may be healed." One may as well pretend to repent and go on in sin, as wilfully to refuse this and repent of the sin. The like reparation is necessary in those scandalous sins, whereby the honour of God is impaired before the world, religion wounded, and exposed to the contempt and scorn of profane men, and the hearts of the godly saddened. To repent of such sins, and yet wilfully to refuse the way whereby the honour of God, and the credit of religion, might in some measure be repaired, is impossible. One may as well pretend to repent of his wounding a man, while he stands looking on him bleeding to death, and will not, though it is in his power, bind up his wounds.

Use. 1. Hence we may see what is the proper way to follow out the design of our congregational fast; namely, to turn from our sins which have provoked the Lord to wrath against us. For humiliation without reformation can do little service. Let each of us lay our hands to our heart, and consider what has been the coal that we have cast in to raise this flame, and heartily turn from these things. If so, we would readily wear with thankfulness the blessings obtained by prayers.

2. All the trouble, grief, and sorrow that men have for their sin is little worth, if it issue not in turning from sin. For men to be sighing, but still going backward, is not repentance, but of that sort which may be carried on in hell, through eternity. If turning be not joined to mourning for sin, it is unsanctified sorrow, that will neither be acceptable to God, nor profitable to our souls.

3. Turning from sin outwardly, while the heart remains glued to it, is not repentance either. It is an easy thing to reform outwardly; but the great business lies in getting the heart weaned from the world and lusts. If we would be satisfied as to the truth of our repentance, we must likewise examine the motives prevailing with us to turn from sin; for the mean and low motives that rise no higher than ourselves, our own advantage, ease, safety, &c. will never denominate us true penitents.

4. Repentance is not the work of a day or a year, but the work of our whole lives. For so turning from sin is. Sin follows us, while we flee from it; often does it overtake us, and so we must renew our flight. The whole life of a Christian is a war; in that war are many battles, sometimes-the Christian gains the day, and sometimes he loses. If he lose, he must renew the battle; if he win, he must pursue the victory, and lay his account with a new engagement. The great comfort is, that though he may lose a battle, yet he shall be victorious in the war: "The God of peace shall bruise Satan under his feet shortly," Rom. xvi. 20.

5. *Lastly*, See here the necessity of turning from sin. "Except ye repent," says the text, "ye shall all likewise perish." Now, if ye do not turn from sin, ye do not repent; therefore if ye turn not

from it by repentance, ye shall perish. Our sins or our souls must go. Turn, or burn in the fire of God's wrath, is the choice. Let us then return speedily and thoroughly from all our iniquities, so shall they not be our ruin.

II. In repentance there is a returning unto God: Hos. vi. 1, "Come, and let us return unto the Lord." This is the term to which the sinner comes back. Sin is a departing form God, repentance is a coming back to him again. It is a coming back, like that of a runaway servant to his master, returning to his place and duty in the family. Sin carried away mankind from God two ways.

1. Sin carried men away from God as a portion wherein to rest. He is all-sufficient to himself and to his creatures, and none but he is so. Sin carried man away from God to the creatures for happiness and satisfaction: hence says Jehovah, Jer. ii. 13, "My people have committed two evils: they have forsaken me the fountain of living waters, and hewed them out cisterns, broken cisterns, that can hold no water."* There he seeks a rest to his heart. By faith man returns to God as a portion, unites with him again through Christ, and takes up his everlasting rest in him. Thus he returns as the dove to the ark, Is. lx. 3, "Who are these that fly as a cloud, and as the doves to their windows?"

2. Sin carried man away from God as a Lord and Master, to whom he owes obedience. In this respect man returns to God by repentance, returning to his duty, Psal. cxix. 59, "I thought on my ways, and turned my feet unto thy testimonies;" as Hagar was by the angel sent back to Sarah, Gen. xvi. 9. Men turning from God, turn their backs on his laws, and make their own lusts their laws; but the repenting sinner turns back to the laws of God, Psal. cxix. 59, forecited. He has slipt his neck out of the yoke of the commands of Christ, but he comes and takes it on again, never to throw it off more, Matth. xi. 29. He has gone off the road, the strait way; but he comes back, and bids an eternal farewell to the broad way. And there is here,

1st, A return of the soul to God himself, 1 Kings xviii. 37, consisting in the heart's turning to the loving and liking of the Lord as a Lord and Master. Sinners departing from God, not only mislike their service, but the Master and his house: Luke xix. 14, "His citizens hated him, and sent a message after him, saying, We will not have this man to reign over us." They are filled with prejudices against him, there is a natural aversion in the heart to him, they cannot away with subjection to him. Hence "they say unto

* See the author's sermons on this text, vol. 2.

God, Depart from us; for we desire not the knowledge of thy ways,"
Job xxi. 14. But in repentance that aversion is cured, and the soul
inclines and moves towards him in heart and affections. This con-
sists in three things.

(1.) The soul is brought to esteem the Lord worthy to be served
and pleased in all things. The name of God is to the penitent a
worthy name, Jam. ii. 7. The soul sees the transcendent glory and
excellency of God, worthy of all adoration and obedience; and so
slights and disdains all other masters, as unworthy of the service of
an immortal soul.

(2.) The soul chooseth him as its only Lord and Master, saying,
as in Is. xxvi. 13, "O Lord our God, other lords besides thee have
had dominion over us: but by thee only will we make mention of
thy name." This was Joshua's choice, chap. xxiv. 15, "As for me
and my house, we will serve the Lord." The enlightened mind
beholds his glory, the glory and excellency of himself, his image,
laws, ordinances, and service; and the renewed will consents and
cleaves to him. It has tried many masters, "serving divers lusts,"
Tit. iii. 3; but could never have satisfaction in the service of any of
them, and therefore says, as Hos. ii. 7, "I will go and return to my
first husband, for then was it better with me than now."

(3.) The soul looks upon the service of God as its great happiness. Hence said the prodigal, when he came to himself, "How
many hired servants of my father's have bread enough and to
spare, and I perish with hunger? Luke xv. 17. And therefore the
saints are found declaring them happy who are most employed in
his service, as the queen of Sheba said of Solomon's servants: Psal.
lxv. 4, "Blessed is the man whom thou choosest, and causest to
approach unto thee, that he may dwell in thy courts." And
lxxxiv. 4, "Blessed are they that dwell in thy house: they will be
still praising thee." And till the soul come to this, to account the
Lord's service the only true freedom and happiness, though they
may take up his service, they will not abide with it, because they
do not like their Master.

2dly, There is in this returning a return of the soul to its duty to
God. Hence said Saul, "Lord, what wilt thou have me to do?"
Acts ix. 6. Whoever returns to God, comes home as a servant to
enter to work: for idlers about God's house may be nominal
servants, but real ones they cannot be. God's servants have higher
relations which they stand in to him; but all of them have duty
annexed to them. Are they married to Christ? they must bring
forth fruit, Rom. vii. 4. Are they friends? they must do whatsoever he commands them, John xv. 14. See Mal. i. 6. Now, the
penitent returns to his duty in these two respects.

(1.) The penitent returns to his duty in his heart. He is (1.) reconciled to the whole law of God, and the whole yoke of Christ, so far as it is known to him to be his law and yoke, Psal. cxix. 6. " I have respect unto all thy commandments." He has a love and liking of the duties of piety towards God, and righteousness towards men. Though there remain in him a contradicting principle, yet he can say, as Rom. vii. 22, " I delight in the law of God, after the inward man." The heart-enmity against the law and the power of godliness is removed, and nothing is so desirable to him as to be holy as God is holy. (2.) He has a full and fixed purpose of new obedience: Psal. cxix. 57, " O Lord, I have said, that I would keep thy words." Ver. 112, " I have inclined mine ear to perform thy statutes alway, even unto the end." He returns with a purpose never to be what he has been; to pursue holiness, to enter upon and keep the way of duty, whatever be the hardships and difficulties he may meet with in it. And this purpose is for to-day, not for to-morrow only; not to delay a minute, but presently to fall in with every known duty, as knowing there is no time for delaying.

(2.) The penitent returns to his duty in both heart and life. He is brought to sincere endeavours after new obedience: 2 Cor. vii. 11, " Behold, this self-same thing, that ye sorrowed after a godly sort, what carefulness it wrought in you, yea, what clearing of yourselves, yea, what indignation, yea, what fear, yea, what vehement desire, yea, what zeal, yea, what revenge! in all things ye have approved yourselves to be clear in this matter." Purposes without endeavours are but fair blossoms without fruit, which will never prove a penitent. If the lame man be cured, though not perfectly cured, he will rise and walk as he can. It is true, while here we can do nothing perfectly well; but the true penitent will endeavour to do all, and aim at no less than perfection. Hence said Paul, " I press toward the mark, for the prize of the high calling of God in Christ Jesus," Phil. iii. 14. So the penitent returning to his duty,

[1.] Returns to the practice of every known duty. Hence said David, " I have respect unto all thy commandments," Psal. cxix. 6. He labours to know what is duty, and is willing to know it; and when known, endeavours to perform it. He puts hand to external and internal obedience; to serve God in heart and life too; to perform his duty to God and to his neighbour; personal and relative, secret, private, and public.

[2.] Returns to spirituality in every duty: Phil. iii. 3, " For we are the circumcision, which worship God in the Spirit, and rejoice in Christ Jesus, and have no confidence in the flesh."* The true penitent will not sist in the carcase of duties, but will endeavour to get in to those unseen things where lies the life and soul of duties; namely, to have his heart imbued with love to God as the principle of his obedience, touched with regard to the honour of God as his end, raised above selfish ends and designs, and performing all in faith, leaning on the Lord for strength.

Now, this returning to the Lord is,

1. A sincere returning, not feigned and hypocritical, with the whole heart, Jer. iii. 10. Hypocrites are said to have a heart and a heart, a divided heart, one for God, and another for their lusts. But the Lord says in this case, If ye take me, let these go away. For no man can serve two masters. It is a returning to him to abide with him for ever, as Onesimus to Philemon, ver. 15. The penitent, like the servant under the law, his ear is nailed to God's door-posts, to serve him for ever. To return for a time is naught.

2. A voluntary return. The penitent comes back with heart and good-will, Psal. cx. 3, "Thy people shall be willing in the day of thy power;" as one that is going back to a good and honourable master, and will serve him with gladness: Psal. c. 2, "Serve the Lord with gladness." They that are only driven back to God, by heavy rods or sharp convictions, will come away again; yet people may be driven at first to God, who seeing his glory and excellency, and the desirableness of his service afterwards, do voluntarily and heartily yield themselves to him.

3. A speedy return: Psal. cxix. 60, "I made haste, and delayed not to keep thy commandments." They that are sincere will not delay for a moment; they will make no truce with sin. The moment wherein true repentance touches the heart, is the precise term of going home to God; for they know that if they delay a moment longer, that moment may be the fatal moment to them.

4. A thorough return. The soul sticks at no known duty, but embraces all, be it ever so hard, and unpleasant to flesh and blood. Hence said the Lord of David, Acts xiii. 22, "I have found David the son of Jesse; a man after mine own heart, which shall fulfil all my will." The penitent puts a blank in God's hand, saying, "Lord, what wilt thou have me to do? Speak, Lord," says he, "thy servant heareth." He is for the will of God, without disputing. For God is an absolute master, and is therefore to be obeyed without reserve.

USE of this point. It lets us see, that negative reformation

---

* See the author's sermons on this text, in this volume.

is not sufficient for repentance. One must not only turn from sin, but turn unto God. We must not only put away evil, but take in to us the contrary good: Is. i. 16, "Wash ye, make you clean, put away the evil of your doings from before mine eyes, cease to do evil, learn to do well," &c. We must not only give up with such and such lusts, but be endued with the contrary graces. Some people reform from the evils of their life, but they do not go forward to the positive ways of holiness. They satisfy themselves, with the proud Pharisee, that they are not unjust, no extortioners, &c.; but, alas! they do not consider, that when the house which the devil goes out of is empty, he returns with seven spirits more wicked than himself, and so the last state of such a person is worse than the first, Matt. xii. 44, 45.

THE APPLICATION.

I come now to the application of the whole. And here I would sound the alarm in the ears of impenitent sinners, to repent, and turn from their sins unto God. O sinners, repent, repent; ye are gone away to your lusts and idols, turn from them; ye have turned your back on God, turn to him again. In prosecuting this call to repentance, I shall,

1. Endeavour to convince you of the need you have to repent.
2. Lay before you a train of motives to repentance.
3. Shew you the great hindrances of repentance. And,
4. Give directions in order to your obtaining repentance.

I. I shall endeavour to convince you of the need you have to repent, to make way for the motives to it. There are three sorts of persons that will readily stave off all our calls to repentance.

1. One says, I repent of my sins daily. Well were it with thee, if it were so. Surely there is need for it. But none are so ready to pretend to this, as those that never yet knew what it is to repent. If ruing the ill thou hast done, a sigh for it, and a short-winded wish for mercy, be repentance, it is easy work. But it is not so. Thou canst not repent with a hale heart: that heart of thine must be rent for sin, and rent from it; thou must turn from sin unto God in all known duties of obedience. If ye pretend then to repentance, bring forth fruits meet for it. But to such pretended penitents we may say, as Samuel to Saul, 1 Sam. xv. 14, "What meaneth then this bleating of the sheep, and the lowing of the oxen?"

2. Another says, I have repented already. But O consider, repentance is not the work of a day, but of thy whole lifetime,

2 E 2

since thou art never free of sin, Jer. viii. 6. New provocations require new repentance; nay, old sins are not to be forgotten. Hence said Moses, Deut. ix. 7, "Remember, and forget not how thou provokedst the Lord thy God to wrath in the wilderness." And hence prays the Psalmist, Psal. xxv. 7, "Remember not the sins of my youth, nor my transgressions." And if thou repent of them thoroughly, thou wilt be ashamed, and the wound will bleed afresh at the remembrance of them. Hence said the apostle, Rom. vi. 21, "What fruit had ye in those things, whereof ye are now ashamed?"

3. Another sees no need of repentance for him; for such persons are of that blinded generation that are pure in their own eyes, and yet is not washed from their filthiness, Prov. xxx. 12. They deny their sin instead of mourning over and confessing it, saying as ver. 20. "I have done no wickedness." They possibly keep free from the gross pollutions of the outward man; and for the positive duties of religion, they either see no need of them, or if they do perform them too, they are blind to the corruption of their nature, and to heart sins, and the spirituality of the law of God. But ye need repentance as much as the proud Pharisee, Luke xviii. and as the Apostle Paul, Rom. vii. 9. compared with Tit. iii. But O consider,

1st, Are there not many of us that never got a sound awakening all their days? They had lived under the sound of the gospel, but it never broke their rest effectually in a sinful course. I will read the mystery of your case, Luke xi. 21. "When a strong man armed keepeth his palace, his goods are in peace." Repent then, else ye are undone.

2dly, Are there not many whose awakening has produced a partial change on them, but it has ended in a fearful apostacy from the way of God? 2 Pet. ii. 22. "It is happened unto them according to the true proverb, The dog is turned to his own vomit again; and, the sow that was washed, to her wallowing in the mire." Their fair blossom they once had, has gone up as dust. Repent, or your backsliding will be your ruin.

3dly, Are there not many sleeping virgins at this day, who are in a course of departing from God? The life, vigour, and tenderness they sometimes had, is gone; and death has settled down on their eyelids, and they are turned to be of the colour of the earth. To these we must say, as Rev. ii. 5. "Remember therefore from whence thou art fallen, and repent, and do the first works."

4thly, Are there not many living in known sin? They know the particulars wherein they are wrong, and yet on they go, as an ox to the slaughter. Their corruptions are too strong for conscience. Ye must repent, or ye will perish. Profane courses will make a miserable end, and one sin retained will ruin the soul.

5thly, Look and see whether thou canst perceive the footsteps of Christ's flock, or of the devil's drove, on the way which thou art going, Cant. i. 8. Is your case the case wherein the fair company walked with displayed banners to Cannau, or that wherein many have slept and slipped away to the pit ?

6thly, Canst thou deny but that there are many foul steps thou hast made and art making ? O then repent. Go no farther on; one step more may put you beyond returning, Luke xiv. 24. Little knows the sinner how soon God may take the foot from him, either by clapping a withering curse on him, as on the fig-tree, Hos. iv. 17. or by taking him red-hand in his sin, and sending him to the pit, Prov. xxix. 1. "He that being often reproved, hardeneth his neck, shall suddenly be destroyed, and that without remedy."

II. I will lay before you a train of motives to repentance

MOTIVE 1. Consider the obligations that lie on you to repent. Sit down and consider how ma nifold ties are on you to it.

1. The command of God obligeth you to it: Acts xvii. 30. "God commanded all men every where to repent." And will ye not have regard to the sovereign authority of him that made you ? The command to repentance is one of the two great commands of the gospel, Acts xx. 21. "Testifying both to the Jews, and also to the Greeks, repentance toward God, and faith toward our Lord Jesus Christ." This is the command which the prophets of old did so often inculcate, Ezek. xviii. 30. "Repent, and turn yourselves from all your transgressions; so iniquity shall not be your ruin." This our Lord Jesus and the Baptist preached, and his disciples, saying, "Repent, for the kingdom of heaven is at hand." This the Apostles preached, Acts ii. 38. "Repent, and be baptized every one of you in the name of Jesus Christ, for the remission of sins." And this all along is the joint sound of the preachers of the gospel. So it is an old and new command too. No command is more peremptorily laid on, as in the text. As ye regard then God's authority, repent.

2. Your baptism obligeth you: Mark i. 4. "John did baptize in the wilderness, and preach the baptism of repentance, for the remission of sins." It is a solemn tie laid upon you to return to and serve God the Father, Son, and Holy Ghost; to die unto sin, to live unto righteousness. Ye have then taken on the Lord's badge; how dreadful must it be to continue runaways from your Great Master ? Repent, then, and return, as ye would not be treated as runaways from your colours, as rebels that cast off your allegiance sworn to the King of heaven.

3. Your mercies oblige you in point of gratitude; Rom. ii. 4, "Despisest thou the riches of his goodness, and forbearance, and long-suffering; not knowing that the goodness of God leadeth thee to repentance?" your common mercies, and special ones, preventing, restraining, &c. Every mercy is forfeited by sin; yet ye are still in God's debt, and every day a new load of favours is laid on, and these are strong ties to repentance.

4. *Lastly,* Your profession obligeth you. Ye profess yourselves Christians. If ye will name the name of Christ, then depart from iniquity, 2 Tim. ii. 19. Why do ye call God Father, if ye will needs do the works of the devil, (John viii. 44.) which Christ came to destroy? Do ye profess Christ your Redeemer, the Holy Ghost your Sanctifier? why then do ye continue in bondage to your sin, in unholy courses? Do ye believe every sin deserveth God's wrath? what madness is it then to be treasuring up wrath againt the day of wrath? Quit your profession then, or quit your sinful courses.

MOTIVE 2. Seriously consider what sin is, that ye are so fond of, prefer to Christ, and for the enjoyment of it forfeit the favour of God. What do you see in it, that does so powerfully charm you? If you are taken with the profit of it, ye would consider that no advantage will quit the cost of the soul's ruin brought about by it: Matt. xvi. 26, "For what is a man profited, if he shall gain the whole world, and lose his own soul? or what shall a man give in exchange for his soul?" Job xxvii. 8, "For what is the hope of the hypocrite, though he hath gained, when God taketh away his soul?" If you are taken with the pleasure of it; that is dear bought, being purchased at the rate of eternal flames, which sin will bring men to without repentance. The pleasures of sin are but momentary, Heb. xi. 25. And there is far more in God's service, even in this world: Psal. iv. 6, 7, "There be many that say, Who will shew us any good? Lord, lift thou up the light of thy countenance upon us. Thou hast put gladness in my heart, more than in the time that their corn and their wine increased." Consider, I pray you,

1. Has not every bait a hook with it? Prov. xxiii. 31, 32. Is there not a trap, gin, and snare in them all for you? How often have ye seen there has been death in the pot, when ye have sit down to feed your corruptions? Ye have snatched at the bait, but have ye not in the meantime felt yourselves wounded with the hook? ye have smelled the rose, but have not the prickles meanwhile annoyed you? And how can it be otherwise? for "he that diggeth a pit, shall fall into it; and whoso breaketh an hedge, a serpent shall bite him," Eccl. x. 8.

2. Is there any solid rest in a sinful course? No, surely: Is.

lvii. 21, "There is no peace, saith my God, to the wicked." Do not your consciences witness, that the sting of guilt in the conscience is like a dead fly in the ointment, causing all to be unsavoury? Is there not always a worm at the root of every sinful gourd you sit down under the shadow of? Do not the very maybees of conscience suck the sap out of your lusts many times? Will any man say, that ever he found rest to his soul in a course of departing from God? No, no; ten thousand worlds will not satisfy an immortal soul.

3. Do not ye find sin to be an insatiable tyrant, like the grave and the barren womb, never saying, It is enough? Is. lvii. 20. "The wicked are like the troubled sea, when it cannot rest, whose waters cast up mire and dirt." O but they have a hard task, that have living raging lusts to feed! James iv. 2, 3, "Ye lust, and have not: ye kill, and desire to have, and cannot obtain: ye fight and war, yet ye have not, because ye ask not. Ye ask, and receive not, because ye ask amiss, that ye may consume it upon your lusts." Psal. lxxviii. 18, 19, "And they tempted God in their heart, by asking meet for their lust. Yea, they spake against God: they said, can God furnish a table in the wilderness?" The more they are indulged, the more they grow rampant: the more their thirst is cared for, the greater thirst is created. Hence men in a sinful course go from evil to worse.

4. Is not a sinful course a most foolish course? No man is unfaithful to God, but he is unfaithful to himself, and his own interest and happiness. The Lord offers to reason the matter with you, and to make your consciences judge; Isa. i. 18, "Come now, and let us reason together, saith the Lord: though your sins be as scarlet, they shall be as white as snow; though they be red like crimson, they shall be as wool." It stands betwixt you, and temporal and eternal happiness. It is a poisonous cup, bringing death along with it. And how foolish is it for men to hug a serpent in their bosom, when called to throw it out; to drink a cup of poison, when called to throw it away; to take coals in their bosom, when it is told they will burn them; to court their own death and ruin?

5. Is not sin the separation wall betwixt God and you? Is. lix. 2, "Your iniquities have separated between you and your God, and your sins have hid his face from you, that he will not hear." Does it not mar your comfort from the word, your confidence in the Lord, and your access to God in duties? does it not make as it were a gulf betwixt Heaven and you, that whatever communion others have with Heaven, your unrepented-of sins lets you have none? Shall this be your choice? Sure, then, ye need not wonder, if ye will not

come back to God, he bid you at last depart from him, "into ever-lasting fire, prepared for the devil and his angels."

6. *Lastly*, Consider what will be the end thereof. Surely it will be bitterness in the end: Jer. ii. 19, "Thine own wickedness shall correct thee, and thy backsliding shall reprove thee: know there-fore and see, that it is an evil thing and bitter, that thou hast for-saken the Lord thy God, and that my fear is not in thee, saith the Lord God of hosts." However pleasant the cup seem to be at the brim, the dregs of it will be bitter: Prov. ix. 17, 18, "Stolen waters are sweet, and bread eaten in secret is pleasant. But he knoweth not that the dead are there; and that her guests are in the depths of hell." However taking the entertainment be, the reckoning will be dreadful.

MOTIVE 3. Consider ye must die: Heb. ix. 27, "It is appointed unto men once to die." Death is certain, and therefore repentance is necessary. O if men would realize death to themselves, sinners would soon find it necessary to turn a new leaf. One hearing Gen. v. read in the church, was so impressed with the thoughts of death, that he presently betook himself to a new course of life, that he might die well. We must all meet with death, lie down in the grave; let us view it aforehand, and see how it calls us to repent. Look to thy dying hour, and to thy grave, O impenitent sinner, and consider these few things.

1. Wouldst thou be content to die as thou livest? Thou livest in thy sin, without God; wouldst thou desire to die so? Many indeed entertain Balaam's wish, for the death of the righteous, while they care not for their life, Num. xxiii. 10, "Let me die the death of the righteous, and let my last end be like his." But remember he did not get it, chap. xxxi. 8, "Balaam also the son of Beor they slew with the sword." And while death is so uncertain, it is the hanging of an eternal weight on a hair, to look to get matters mended then, that are not mended now.

2. Consider, what will a sinful life look like on a death-bed? How will ye be able to look your unrepented-of guilt, and a long eternity in the face together? Ezek. xxii. 14, "Can thine heart endure, or can thine hands be strong in the days that I shall deal with thee? I the Lord have spoken it, and will do it." Sin sits easy now on a sleepy conscience, while health and strength lasts, and death appears not. But when death stares thee in the face, and the awakened conscience flies upon thee, it will cut thee to the heart, that thou hast not repented before.

3. What will it be to die, and go to another world with a load of unrepented-of guilt on thy back? Look to your grave aforehand;

think with yourselves, how will it be to lie down there with your bones full of your iniquity? Is it not best now, to shake off and cast away your transgressions, as knowing that however ye may live with them, ye cannot die with them well.

4. At a dying hour ye must part with the world, and the enjoyment of your lusts. The foul feast ye sit at now, death will overthrow the table, and the sad reckoning for it comes in then, and continues for ever. O rise up now, and leave it by repentance. Part with these things at God's call, which ye must part with ere long, whether ye will or not.

5. *Lastly*, There is no repentance in the grave, Eccl. ix. 10. Ye must repent, or ye perish; and it is now or never. Mar matters now by an impenitent life, and let death catch you there, ye shall never be able to mend them more. The working time, and time of trial is over then. If the brittle thread of life were broke, which may be snapt asunder in a moment, then ye are beyond the line of mercy. The candle burnt to snuff, shall be as soon brought to burn again, as time shall be recalled.

MOTIVE 4. Take a view of the tribunal of God, before which thou must appear: 2 Cor. v. 10, 11, "We must all appear before the judgment-seat of Christ; that every one may receive the things done in his body, according to that he hath done, whether it be good or bad. Knowing therefore the terror of the Lord, we persuade men." O sinner, knowest thou not that there is a judgment to come, and how this calls thee to repent? Acts xvii. 30, 31, "God commandeth all men every where to repent: because he hath appointed a day, in the which he will judge the world in righteousness, by that man whom he hath ordained: whereof he hath given assurance unto all men, in that he hath raised him from the dead." Were men to lie for ever neglected, without a future reckoning, as the beasts that perish, they might live as they list, the hazard of condemnation for an eternity would not press them. But it is not so: Heb. ix. 27, "It is appointed unto men once to die, but after this the judgment." Consider,

1. While thou art going on in sin, thy debt to the divine justice is increasing, the accounts are swelling; and the reckoning for them before the tribunal will be terrible, however little ye think of them now, Eccl. xi. 9. They may fall out of thy memory, but they will not fall out of the book of God's remembrance, Hos. xiii. 12. But now is the time to get them laid over on the cautioner's score.

2. Though thou wilt not seek them out now to mourn over them, and turn from them, they will find thee out before the tribunal of God. Happy would the sinner be, if his sins would part with him

at the grave ; but they " shall lie down with him in the dust," Job
xx. 11 : or if they would lie down with him there, if they would lie
still and never rise again ; but " God shall bring every work into
judgment, with every secret thing, whether it be good, or whether it
be evil," Eccl. xii. 14.   The Judge is omniscient, nothing can be hid
from him, he is not capable to forget the least injury which the sinner has done to his glory ; all must come into the account.

3. When thou seest Christ come again, and his throne set for
judgment, when the trumpet shall blow, and the dead arise, and
made to compear before that tribunal, when the heavens and earth
shall pass away, what will be thy thoughts of staving off repentance ?

4. *Lastly,* Thy state for eternity will be determined there according to thy deeds done in the flesh.   Impenitent sinners will get a
long eternity to rue their obstinacy in, while those that repented in
time shall be happy for ever.

MOTIVE 5. To move you to repentance, consider the sufferings of
Christ.   A Roman senator intending to provoke the people to revenge the death of Cæsar killed by Brutus, brought forth his bloody
robe, and cried, " Here is the robe of your late emperor."   And O
will ye look to the bloody robe of Christ, hung up on the pole of the
gospel, to move you to repentance ? Zech. xii. 10, " They shall look
upon me whom they have pierced, and they shall mourn for him,"
&c.   And learn here,

1. How dreadful must God's indignation against sin be, which is
written with the blood of Christ, pierced with the sword of justice.
Is it not " a fearful thing to fall into the hands of the living God ?"
And shall we continue in sin, against which such indignation appeared ?

2. Sin appeared terrible in Sodom when in flames, but yet more
terrible in mount Calvary, where the justice of God pursued the Son
of God with the sword of vengeance.   A spectacle of amazement,
the Son of God set up for a mark to the arrows of God !   Do ye
not ask into the cause of all this ?   It was sin.   The children ate
the sour grape, and the father's teeth were set on edge.   They contract the debt, justice lays hold on him, and he " restores what he
took not away, Psal. lxix. 4.   The elect took on the debt jovially,
but he is put to tears and strong cries in the paying of it.   And will
we not hate and loath sin ?

3. Many waters cannot quench love, neither can the floods from
above nor from below drown it.   " Behold how he loved you."   He
might have been happy in his Father's love, though mortals had
never shared of it with him.   But such was his love to sinners, as made

him lay down his life for them, that so a way might be paved for the egress of his Father's love towards them. And will ye not hate and loathe sin which was the cause of his death? Is this your kindness to your friend?

4. When Christ suffered, the earth quaked, rocks rent, the dead arose, the sun was struck blind with the sight, and hid his face for shame: and how can we stand unmoved, who were the first movers of the bloody tragedy, whose sins furnished a Judas to betray him, a Pilate to sentence him? &c. Look here, and mourn for, and turn from sin.

5. *Lastly*, Did he not suffer enough? must he suffer more still, even in his state of exaltation? will ye grieve his Spirit, trample on his laws, yea and his blood, continuing impenitent in your sins?

MOTIVE 6. Consider the wrong done to God by your sin, in which ye may see the ugly picture of it. This kept Joseph from yielding to a strong temptation, Gen. xxxix. 9; and pierced David's heart with repentance for his sin, Psal. li. 4; and lay heavy on the prodigal son, Luke xv. 18. Every sin reacheth the throne of God in heaven, and him that sits on it. It is true, the malice of sinners against God is impotent malice, and can do him no real prejudice, do their worst. They cannot make him less happy, they cannot disturb his peace, Job xxxv. 6—8. But the sinner is like the beggar full of sores lying on a dunghill, venting his spite against the prince on the throne. He wrongs the honour of God, his declarative glory, though he can do nothing against his essential glory. Sinner, thou wrongest God by thy sin,

1. By setting thyself in opposition to his nature and will. What is sin continued in without repentance? "A walking contrary to God," Lev. xxvi. 21; an interpretative aim to throw him down from his sovereignty, Psal. xiv, 1, "The fool hath said in his heart, There is no God." Thou mayst put what fair colours thou pleasest upon it; but it is a throwing out the flag of defiance against the God that made thee. For dost thou not thereby in effect disregard his allseeing eye, and presence every where, bid defiance to his justice, and call in question his truth, despise his goodness and mercy, and run counter to his holy nature and will, while thou runest still on that of which he has said, Jer. xiv. 4, "Oh do not this abominable thing that I hate!" And is this a course to be insisted in?

2. Thou wrongest God by trampling on his laws, Is. xxxiii. 22. He has given thee a law to be the rule of thy life, he has stamped it with his own sovereign authority, fenced it with punishments threatened, suitable to his infinite greatness: but thou makest no more of these than if they were cobwebs fit only to catch flies.

Thou breakest through the fences, and in contempt of his authority, will be over into the forbidden ground. Thus thou affrontest the God that made thee: will he sit with it think ye? No, he can avenge the affront, James iv. 12, "There is one lawgiver, who is able to destroy;" and he will do it, Luke xix. 27, "Those mine enemies which would not that I should reign over them, bring hither, and slay them before me."

3. Thou wrongest God by despising his Son, John v. 40. Ye wrong God at the rate heathens cannot do, and therefore your condemnation will be greater than theirs, John iii. 19. God has sent his Son into the world, by his death to procure reconciliation betwixt God and sinners; he has "exalted him to give repentance," Acts v. 31: but by your continuing in sin, ye slight his death, and the purchase of his blood: you love your disease so, as you loathe the Physician. What will be the end of these things? Acts xiii. 41, "Behold, ye despisers, and wonder, and perish."

4. Thou wrongest God by grieving his Spirit, Eph. iv. 30. Hear God's complaints of impenitent sinners, Ezek. vi. 9, "I am broken with their whorish heart which hath departed from me, and with their eyes which go a whoring after their idols." Amos ii. 13, "Behold, I am pressed under you, as a cart is pressed that is full of sheaves." How often has the Spirit of the Lord been at work with you to turn you from your sins, speaking to you by the word, providences, the secret checks of your own conscience, and secret motions and whispers within your own breast, but all to no purpose? This will not last: Gen. vi. 3, "And the Lord said, My spirit shall not always strive with man, for that he also is flesh." And it will have a doleful end, if ye do not repent: Is. lxiii. 10, "They rebelled, and vexed his holy Spirit: therefore he was turned to be their enemy, and he fought against them." If sinners continue to be a burden to the Spirit of God, and do not take off the burden by repentance, God will throw it off to their cost: Is. i. 34, "Therefore saith the Lord, the Lord of hosts, the mighty One of Israel, Ah, I will ease me of mine adversaries, and avenge me of mine enemies."

5. Thou wrongest God by defacing the remains of his image in your own soul, "God made man upright, after his own image." Adam's sin ruined his image in us. But the more we go on and sin, we render ourselves still the more unlike God, and the more contrary to him. How fearful is this, to be still blotting out any appearance of the traits of God's image in us?

6. *Lastly,* Thou wrongest God by the ill influence your example has on others. Hence says our Lord, Matth. xxiv. 12, "Because iniquity shall abound, the love of many shall wax cold." Every

impenitent sinner is an agent for the devil, and invites and encourages others to despise God and his ways, and so will be made to reckon for the mischief his sin does that way. The rich man in hell was sensible of this, though it would seem not before, Luke xvi. 27, 28, " I pray thee, father," said he to Abraham, " that thou wouldst send him [Lazarus] to my father's house : for I have five brethren ; that he may testify unto them, lest they also come into this place of torment."

Now, will ye go on, thus wronging God by your sin, and not turn from it unto him ? Consider, I pray you,

1. He is your Creator, Eccl. xii. 1. He gave you a being, and brought you out of the womb of nothing, and will ye not be for him ? will ye be against him ? Has not he that made you a right to rule you ? does not reason itself say, that God's creating us gives him a sovereign dominon over us ? O why will the creature thus set itself against the Creator ? Will the potsherds strive against the potter.

2. He is your Preserver, Heb. i. 3. Acts xvii. 28. You live on his earth, feed on his good creatures, breathe in his air, and will ye not hearken to his voice ? Who was it that preserved thee in the womb, that brought thee out of it, so that it was not made thy grave ? Who has kept the brittle thread of thy life from being broken hitherto, and fed thee all thy life long ? Is it not the Lord ? And wilt thou fight against him with his own benefits which he has bestowed on thee, yea, is bestowing on thee while thou goest on in thy sin ? Shall the life, strength, comforts of life, time, &c. which he has given thee, be employed to the grieving of his Spirit ? What will the end of these things be ?

3. He can destroy you, and that when he will, Matth. x. 28. Your life and breath is from him, and he can stop it when he pleaseth. He does not suffer you to go on to your sin, because he cannot help it, nay, the moment thou provokest him, he can strike thee dead, or send thee down alive into the pit. But he waits to be gracious. And this one consideration might determine sinners to repent, if madness were not in their hearts, setting them to provoke him, who in a moment can destroy them, and make them silent in the grave.

4. He is your Witness, Psal. li. 4. Luke xv. 18. Sinners that like not to retain God in their knowledge, do in effect please themselves with the notion that God is closed up in heaven, Ezek. ix. 9. " For they say, The Lord hath forsaken the earth, and the Lord seeth not." But the day comes when they will see themselves miserably deceived. No ; he is a witness, though many times a

silent witness; but he will speak in due time, Psal. l. 21, 22. The opening of the book of conscience, and of God's remembrance, will clear his being a witness of your whole way and every step of it.

5. *Lastly*, He will be your Judge, 2 Cor. v. 10. And he is an omnicient one, from whom nothing can be hid; a just one, that will reward every one according to his works; an omnipresent one, from whose presence there can be no escape; an omnipotent one who can without fail make his sentence take effect. Will men pretend to believe a judgment to come, and yet be at no pains to make the judge their friend aforehand, but keep up the war against him, and not break it off by repentance? Alas! horrid unbelief is at the bottom of impenitency.

MOTIVE 7. God is calling you to repentance. Be not deaf to the calls of God, lest the Lord pay home your rebellion, by refusing to hear you when ye call to him, Prov. i. 24. and downwards. God is calling you to repentance,

1. By the mercies wherewith he is daily loading you. *Quot beneficia, tot ora.* Rom. ii. 4. "Despisest thou the riches of his goodness, and forbearance, and long-suffering; not knowing that the goodness of God leadeth thee to repentance? These are the cords of a man wherewith God is drawing you. That you are spared on God's earth, that you are kept out of hell, that he gives you daily bread, and does not lock up heaven and earth that they may not help you, call aloud to you to repent, and turn to him. And he takes notice how little these prevail, Jer. v. 24. "Neither say they in their heart, Let us now fear the Lord our God that giveth rain, both the former and the latter in his season: he reserveth unto us the appointed weeks of the harvest."

2. God is calling you to repentance by the crosses and afflictions, either laid on you, or threatened. Every cross providence is a messenger from Heaven calling you to repentance: Mic. vi. 9. "Hear ye the rod, and who hath appointed it. They meet you in the way of sin, as the angel did Balaam; they bid you halt, and go no farther on; nay, they bid you return to the Lord. God is speaking to the land this way, to this church, and to the congregation, and to every one of us at this day.

3. God is calling you to repentance by the preaching of the word, Acts xvii. 30. This is the great scope of all our preaching, that ye may repent and turn from your sins unto God. And while God continues his gospel with us, it is a sign he is waiting for our repentance: but to continue in sin over the belly of all warnings, will have a fatal end to take us from the gospel, or the gospel from us; which we have ground to fear at this day on more accounts than

one. Hence says Christ to the church of Ephesus, Rev. ii. 5, "Remember from whence thou art fallen, and repent, and do the first works; or else I will come unto thee quickly, and will remove thy candlestick out of his place, except thou repent."

MOTIVE ult. Consider the text, "Except ye repent, ye shall perish." There are two things in this to press you to repentance.

1 If ye repent not, ye shall perish. Sin unrepented of, brings ruin upon kingdoms, churches, congregations, families. And that is like to be the ruin of our land, and of our church, at this day. For, alas! the face of all at this day is like that described, Jer. viii. 6. "I hearkened and heard, but they spake not aright: no man repented him of his wickedness, saying, What have I done? every one turned unto his course, as the horse rusheth into the battle." God has threatened us with desolating strokes, and is yet threatening but the generation is like to those scoffers spoken off, 2 Pet. iii. 4. saying, where is the promise of his coming? And because God does not speedily execute the sentence, therefore men cast off fear, and go on in their sins, in defiance of heaven. But that concerns us nearly: Jer. ix 9. "Shall I not visit them for these things? saith the Lord: shall not my soul be avenged on such a nation as this?"

Sin unrepented of will ruin your souls; Except ye repent, ye shall perish. Consider, your life, your souls lie at stake. Sinner, thou hast gone away from God, thy soul is left in pawn that thou shalt return by repentance. If thou return not, thy pawn, thy soul is lost, lost for ever. Heaven's gate is too narrow to let you in there with a burden of unrepented-of sin on thy back. Nay, heaven thou canst never see; hell thou canst not escape, if thou repent not. The gospel calls you to repent; if not, the Lord Jesus shall be revealed from heaven, with his mighty angels, in flaming fire, taking vengeance on you that know not God, and that obey not the gospel of our Lord Jesus Christ," 2 Thess. i. 7, 8. Have pity therefore on your souls, Ezek. xviii. 31, 32, "Cast away from you all your transgressions, whereby ye have transgressed, and make you a new heart, and a new spirit; for why will ye die, O house of Israel? For I have no pleasure in the death of him that dieth, saith the Lord God: wherefore turn yourselves, and live ye." To this narrow point the matter is brought, Repent, or perish eternally; quit your sins, or quit heaven.

Now, I pray you consider here,

1st, The certainty of your ruin in an impenitent state. Ye have it from the mouth of the Lord himself, in most plain and peremptory terms, that "except ye repent, ye shall perish." If it were but a may-be, it were sufficient in all reason to determine us to repentance; for it is unaccountable to put the soul in hazard of everlasting destruction, for all the profit or pleasure of a sinful course; a thousand times more than for one to put himself in hazard of drowning to catch a fly. But it is not a may-be, but certainly it shall be.

2*dly*, All other grounds of hope are cut off, if ye repent not. Tell me, O impenitent sinner, that will not turn from thy sin, what wilt thou trust to for salvation from the wrath of God? Wilt thou trust to the mercy of God? I tell thee thou art a despiser of mercy, Rom. ii. 4; and thou canst not have it in this case, but over the belly of the truth of God; for he has said, " Except ye repent, ye shall perish." Pray consider, if thou wouldst have mercy, thou must seek it in God's way: Is. lv. 7, " Let the wicked forsake his way, and the unrighteous man his thoughts: and let him return unto the Lord, and he will have mercy upon him, and to our God, for he will abundantly pardon."

Wilt thou trust to Jesus Christ, his blood and merits? Do not deceive yourself. Is not this Christ's own word, " Except ye repent ye shall perish?" does not the Saviour tell thee this? *Q. d.* None of my blood shall ever be wared on a sinner to save him from wrath, that will not repent and turn from his sin. Why does any body at all perish that hears the gospel, if folk may continue impenitent, and yet share of Christ's blood? No, no; to whom Christ will be a Saviour from wrath, he will be first a Saviour from sin, Matth. i. 21. He will first give repentance, before he give access to heaven; for Christ's blood was never shed to bring in dogs and swine into his Father's house, but shed, " that he might redeem us from all iniquity, and purify unto himself a peculiar people, zealous of good works, Tit. ii. 14.

3*dly*, Where will the fruit of sin be, when this dear reckoning begins? Heb. x. 31, " It is a fearful thing to fall into the hands of the living God." Thou mayst get a time to run thy course: but at length thy eye-strings will break, the last pulse beat, and the soul will take wing and go to another world, and because of unrepented-of sin, be condemned to everlasting flames. And when thou enterest there, what will abide with thee of all the satisfaction thou hast had in thy sinful courses? No; then thou must bid an eternal farewell to all satisfaction, ease, or delight whatsoever, either in God or thy lusts.

4*thly*, How wilt thou be able to stand under the load of wrath in the pit of destruction? Is. xxxiii. 14, " The sinners in Zion are afraid, fearfulness hath surprised the hypocrites: who among us shall dwell with the devouring fire? who amongst us shall dwell with everlasting burnings ? How wilt thou be able to grapple with vengeance, the Mediator's vengeance, while God shall hold thee up with the one hand, and punish thee with the other ? Think in time on the worm that never dies, and the fire that is never quenched : for either thou must repent now, or that worm will gnaw thee, and that fire scorch thee for ever.

Lastly, Consider the eternity of this state. The pleasure, profit, and ease of sin are but for a moment; but the destruction for sin unrepented of is for ever, 2 Thess. i. 9. O madness! to run the risk of everlasting pain for a moment's pleasure ! If ruing, sorrow, remorse, rage against one's self for sin, were repenting, there would be repentance enough in hell. Men stave off repentance now for the bitterness of it; but there is a sweet in it too: but then ye shall have the bitterness of it in full measure, but never taste of the sweetness of it; for then the hopes of mercy are razed; and a fearful sight of an everlasting continuance of misery, without end.

Have pity then on your own souls, and throw them not away for that which cannot profit.

2. If ye repent, ye shall never perish. Repentance is the way to keep off the wrath of God from nations, churches, &c. Repentance is the way for each of us to escape the wrath of God: Ezek. xviii. 30, " Repent, and turn yourselves from all your transgressions ; so iniquity shall not be your ruin." Acts ii. 38, " Repent, and be baptized every one of you in the name of Jesus Christ, for the remission of sins." All the threatenings of wrath are summons to repent, and have always that clause understood in them, " Except ye repent, ye shall perish :" Rev. ii. 22, " Behold, I will cast her into a bed, and them that commit adultery with her into great tribulation, except they repent of their deeds." Though ye have sinned with the world, if ye repent with God's elect, ye shall not perish with the world. Consider,

1st, It is not falling into sin, but lying in sin without repentance, that ruins folk to whom the gospel comes, John iii. 19. For there is a remedy provided; and it is for all diseases of the soul, even the worst and most desperate : and so nothing can be fatal to those that are willing to employ the Physician, and to undergo his method of cure. They are in glory this day, whose sins have been of the first magnitude, as David, Paul, Manasseh, Peter, &c.; but they were repenting sinners.

2dly, There is mercy for thee, if thou wilt repent, and come to Christ. Good news, O sinners, If ye repent, all your sins shall be blotted out, ye shall be embraced in the wide and warm arms of mercy; if, as ye have gone away from God, so ye will come back again: Is. lv. 7, "Let the wicked forsake his way, and the unrighteous man his thoughts: and let him return unto the Lord, and he will have mercy upon him, and to our God, for he will abundantly pardon." Rev. iii. 20, "Behold, I stand at the door, and knock: If any man hear my voice, and open the door, I will come in to him, and will sup with him, and he with me." O sirs, will not bowels of mercy draw you? God is now on a throne of mercy; he stretches out the golden sceptre to you for peace, if ye will have it in his own way: and in his name we proclaim mercy to all poor sinners that desire to turn from their sins unto God. O will not the proclamation of the indemnity touch the hearts of rebel sinners, and cause them to relent?

OBJECTION 1. But my sins are many and great sins. ANSWER. God's mercies are many, Psal. li. 1. and great too, Psal. lxxxvi. 13; and his mercy is magnified in pardoning of such. If thy sins were as great as mountains, as many as the catalogue of them would reach from heaven to earth, there is mercy for thee, if thou wilt repent: Is. i. 18, "Come now, and let us reason together, saith the Lord: though your sins be as scarlet, they shall be as white as snow; though they be red like crimson, they shall be as wool." There are riches of mercy, Eph. ii. 4. abundance of pardoning grace, Is. lv. 7.

OBJECTION 2. I have relapsed, gone back with the dog to the vomit, and with the sow that was washed, to the wallowing in the mire. ANSWER. There is mercy for backsliders too: Jer. iii. 14, "Turn, O backsliding children, saith the Lord, for I am married unto you." Ver. 22, "Return, ye backsliding children, and I will heal your backslidings." If it were not so, who could be safe? Men must forgive in that case, and much more God will, Luke xvii. 4. For as the heavens are above the earth, so are God's thoughts above ours: Jer. iii. 1, "They say, If a man put away his wife, and she go from him, and become another man's, shall he return unto her again? shall not that land be greatly polluted? but thou hast played the harlot with many lovers; yet return again to me, saith the Lord."

OBJECTION 3. But I have despised and slighted mercy, and the remedy of sin. ANSWER. They had gone all that length, who had so far despised mercy, and the remedy of sin, as they had murdered the Lord of glory, and yet they obtained mercy, Acts ii. 36, 37, 38. Despise and slight it no more, and your former sins shall not be remembered.

OBJECTION 4. I have so long gone on in sin, that I can have no hope. ANSWER. The longer the greater is your sin; yet God has not discovered to us any particular time, beyond which he will not wait. There are some called at the eleventh hour; and those that come in then, are not rejected. So was the thief on the cross. See Ezek. xxxiii. 10, 11; Luke xiv. 22; Joel iii. 21.

OBJECTION 5. But there is no body's case like mine. ANSWER. Consider the case of Manasseh, 2 Chron. xxxiii. and of Paul, 1 Tim. i. 13. Such instances are designed to encourage sinners to repent in hope of mercy, Eph. ii. 7. Adam's case was more hopeless, who had sinned against more light and mercy, than ye were capable to do. But suppose your case is a non-such evil, the mercy of God and the blood of Christ are non-such remedies. And ye may be sure, since he has said, John vi. 37, "Him that cometh to me, I will in no wise cast out," that he will work a new thing on the earth, rather than that your case be unhelped, if ye will put it in his hand. So I conclude that there is mercy for you, if ye will repent.

Lastly, Thou shalt certainly be saved for ever, if thou dost repent: Ezek. xviii. 30, "Repent, and turn yourselves from all your transgressions; so iniquity shall not be your ruin." No true penitents go to hell. Heaven is the landing-place of all true penitents. They that turn from their sins now, and turn unto God, shall for ever be with the Lord in another world.

O look to the glory that is above, and let your souls be moved to repentance by it. Cast not away the hope of eternal happiness for what does not profit.

Now, sinners, consider these things, and be stirred up to repentance, and do not adventure over the belly of fair warning to go on in a course of impenitency. Impenitency under the gospel is a sin of a deep dye; beware of it.

1. It is a continuation of sin; it draws out the thread of a God-provoking course, adding sin to sin, till God cut the thread of life. And O are there not enough of items standing in God's accounts against you already? why will ye be still adding more, instead of diminishing and breaking off the course by repentance?

2. It seals sin and guilt on your soul. Impenitency keeps all the rest of your sins fast on your souls: John iii. 19, "This is the condemnation, that light is come into the world, and men loved darkness rather than light, because their deeds were evil." If you would repent, no sins whatsoever you are guilty of should ever be able to ruin you: but if you do not, that one will keep all the rest in life and vigour, to your utter ruin.

3. It flies in the face of the gospel, of Christ himself, his apostles

2 F 2

and ministers, who with one voice call sinners to repentance. If ye do this, ye do all; if ye do not this, ye do nothing; ye receive the grace of God in vain; it will be in vain to you that ever you heard the gospel, that Christ died for sinners, &c.; for ye will have no benefit by any of these things.

4. *Lastly*, It is a bloody sin, that will involve you in everlasting misery. For there is no escaping of the wrath of God; if ye do not repent, ye are undone for ever. For "except ye repent ye shall perish."

Now, ye have had a message from the Lord, what answer shall I return to him that sent me? I think I may rank up all in these six sorts of sinners.

1. The brutish sinner, that hears as if he heard not. The word makes a noise in their ears, because they are capable of hearing; but, alas! they are no better than the beasts, in so far as they make no reflections on it, with respect to their state and case. What shall I say to you, but that the time comes when these souls of yours, drowned in a moss of flesh and blood, will be separate from your bodies, and get a long eternity to reflect on the calls ye have had to repent? Is. i. 3, "The ox knoweth his owner, and the ass his master's crib: but Israel doth not know, my people doth not consider." Psal. xxxii. 9, 10, "Be ye not as the horse, or as the mule, which have no understanding : whose mouth must be held in with bit and bridle, lest they come near unto thee. Many sorrows shall be to the wicked."

2. The sullen, desperate sinner, whose answer will be that, Jer. ii. 25, "There is no hope. No, for I have loved strangers, and after them will I go." Their hearts are glued to their sins, they have no will to part with them, and they have no hope that ever they shall be made willing, or if they were so, that God would receive them; and therefore they are resolved to take their time. But O consider, they have been reformed that have been as mad on their idols as you, as Manasseh and Paul. If that cannot draw you, pray answer that question, Is. xxxiii. 14, "Who among us shall dwell with the devouring fire? who amongst us shall dwell with everlasting burnings?

3. The crafty, subtile sinner, whose answer will be that of Saul to Samuel, 1 Sam. xv, 13. "Blessed be thou of the Lord: I have performed the commandment of the Lord." But let the return to them be that of Samuel to Saul, ver. 14. "What meaneth then this bleating of the sheep in mine ears, and the lowing of the oxen which I hear?" What means your continuing in sin, your not wrestling and striving against it in heart and life, if it be so?

4. The presumptuous sinner, whose answer will be that, Deut. xxix. 19. "I shall have peace, though I walk in the imagination of mine heart." There are some who have a heart of adamant, and put on a forehead of brass, that nothing of this sort can affect them. Let the messengers of the Lord be saying what they will, they will be doing. They will have their course, and persuade themselves all shall be well. To such I would say, as vers. 20, 21. "The Lord will not spare him, but then the anger of the Lord, and his jealousy shall smoke against that man, and all the curses that are written in this book shall lie upon him, and the Lord shall blot out his name from under heaven. And the Lord shall separate him unto evil, out of all the tribes of Israel, according to all the curses of the covenant, that are written in this book of the law." See Is. xxviii. 16. and downwards.

5. The slothful sinner, whose answer will be that of Felix to Paul, Acts xxiv. 25. "Go thy way for this time; when I have a convenient season, I will call for thee." They are convinced that they must repent, and resolve to do it, but not yet. Young folk put it off to old age; old folk delay it till a death-bed. Every one puts it off from time to time. But O sirs what certainty have ye of an hour, much less of a year? How many are there that never see old age? How many drop into eternity ere ever they are aware?

6. *Lastly*, The convinced sinner, who being awakened, says, "What shall I do to be saved?" For which reason I shall,

III. Show you the great hinderances of repentance. And,

1. Thoughtlessness is a great hinderance of it: Jer. viii. 6. "I hearkened and heard, but they spake not aright: no man repented him of his wickedness, saying, What have I done? every one turned to his course, as the horse rusheth into the battle." Men do not consider their souls' state, case, and way. They sleep away their time carelessly without due reflection; and therefore their spiritnal state goes to wreck and they pine away in their iniquity, and are not aware of the same.

2. The love and cares of the world are great hinderances of repentance, Luke viii. 14. These take up men's hearts so, as that they have neither heart nor hand for the case of their souls. How many are there, whom the world keeps in a constant hurry all their life long, that they never come to consider their way till death stare them in the face?

3. Prejudices against religion and seriousness are great hinderances of repentance. Some see no profit in it; but "godliness is profitable unto all things, having promise of the life that now is,

and of that which is to come," 1 Tim. iv. 8.   Some see no pleasure in
it ; but " wisdom's ways are ways of pleasantness, and all her paths
are peace," Prov. iii. 17.   Some think that it is needless to be at all
that pains, for less will serve : but, alas ! they do not consider what
a holy jealous God the Lord is, and how many shall seek to enter
in, and shall not be able.

4. Presumption is a great hinderance of repentance, Deut. xxix.
19.   They hope still all shall be well, however they take their
liberty in a sinful course.   They abuse the mercy of God as a screen
to their lusts ; not remembering that he will by no means clear the
guilty.

5. Unbelief, the not embracing of Christ, and apprehending the
mercy of God in him, is likewise a great impediment in the way of
repentance.   And,

6. *Lastly*, Slothfulness, whereby the business is still put off from
time to time.

IV. I shall give directions in order to your obtaining repentance.
Supposing what I have said before of the way to gain repentance
by believing, I offer further these following directions.

1. Labour to see sin in its own colours, what an evil thing it is.
Jer. ii. 19.   What makes us to cleave to sin, is false apprehensions
we have about it.   To see it in itself would be a means to make us
fly from it.   For this end consider,

1*st*, The majesty of God offended by sin.   Ignorance of God is
the mother of impenitency, Acts xvii. 30.

2*dly*, The obligations we lie under to serve him, which by sin we
trample upon.

3*dly*, The wrath of God that abides impenitent sinners.

4*thly*, The good things our unrepented-of sins deprive us of.

Lastly, The many evils which are bred by our sin against the honour of God, our own and our neighbour's true interest.

2. Be much in the thoughts of death.   Consider how short and
uncertain your time is.   Hopes of long life bring many into a hopeless case.   And who knows when he may have outlived his day of
grace, when the moment comes that God shall say, " My Spirit shall
not strive any more with this man, for that he also is flesh ?"

3. Dwell on the thoughts of a judgment to come, where ye shall
be made to give an account of yourselves.

4. Meditate on the sufferings of Christ.

5. Pray for repentance and believingly seek and long for the
Lord's giving the new heart, according to his promise, Ezek. xxxvi.
26. " A new heart will I give you, and a new spirit will I put within
you, and I will take away the stony heart out of your flesh, and I

will give you an heart of flesh." Ver. 32. "Not for your sakes do I this, saith the Lord God, be it known unto you : be ashamed and confounded for your own ways, O house of Israel."

6. *Lastly,* What ye do, do quickly. The sooner you begin, the easier will the work be.

Take the three following marks of true repentance.

1. Sorrow for sin, as offensive to a good and gracious God, Zech. xii. 10,

2. Hatred of sin, as the most abominable thing, Rev. ii. 6. This will be, 1. universal, against all known sin ; 2. constant, without intermission ; 3. implacable, without reconciliation ; and, 4. vehement, without tolerating it.

3. A fixed purpose and desire of eschewing sin, and following duty ; guarding against present sins, and the occasions of these we are in hazard of ; honestly endeavouring after it in the use of means, and labouring to remove the hinderances to a holy life.

THE DANGER OF DELAYING REPENTANCE.

Prov. vi. 10, 11.

Yet a little sleep, a little slumber, a little folding of the hands to sleep. So shall thy poverty come as one that travaileth, and thy want as an armed man.

I HAVE been pressing sinners to repentance from the former text, and I hope by this time all of you may be convinced of the necessity of it. But, alas ! delays in this matter kills their ten thousands. Men put off the work from time to time, till time be gone, and they are surprised into ruin, as we may learn from this text. Where,

1. We have the sluggard's picture drawn in reference to his eternal concerns ; which is the main thing here aimed at. He is one that puts off his great work from time to time, " Yet a little sleep, a little slumber, a little folding of the hands to sleep."

In the 6th verse the slothful sinner is set to school to learn a lesson of the emmet ; which though she has not the advantages that he has, yet has so much natural sagacity, as to provide for winter, in the time of summer and harvest, when meat is to be got. In the 9th verse there is a rousing call to the sinner to follow that example. But behold how he entertains it ;. as a person that is loath to arise, he begs "a little more sleep, a little more slumber, a little more folding of the hands to sleep." Here is,

1*st*, Something supposed; and that is threefold.

(1.) The sleeper convinced that he has slept, and neglected his work. There are many who see themselves wrong, yet have no heart to endeavour to get right. They are convinced that their great work is far behind, yet have no heart to stir to set it forward.

(2.) The sleeper convinced that he must awake, and set to his work. Slothful sinners may see that the case they are in, is not a case they would venture to die in: they see that it is necessary to turn over a new leaf, to mind their salvation at another rate than they have done, or are doing.

(3.) The sleeper resolved to awake, and mind his business. He would fain sleep, but he does not design to sleep long, to sleep always. No; he designs but a little sleep, if ye will believe him, and afterwards to awake; though, poor soul, he does not consider that he is sleeping within the sea-mark, and may be swallowed up ere he awake out of his little sleep.

2*dly*, Something expressed; and that is threefold too,

(2.) A delay craved: "Yet a little sleep," &c. He is not thinking never to waken, never to repent, but only he cannot think on doing it as yet. However long a sleep he has taken in sin, yet he must have more. For as men, the more they sleep, the more they would sleep; so the more they continue in sin, the more they would continue. And the more they put off repentance, they are the more unfit for it.

(2.) The quantity of this delay: it is but a little in the sluggard's conceit. Though the Spirit of the Lord be grieved and wearied with waiting on his awakening, yet he thinks that all is but little. If the sluggard considered that his whole time is but little in comparison of eternity, the least time he spends in his sleep would appear very great. But, alas! he considers it not.

(3.) The mighty concern he is in for this delay. Though his ruin be wrapt up in it, he is fond of it, his heart is set upon it; and he pleads for it, as a starving man for bread. Ease is sweet to him; and so he speaks, "A little sleep, a little slumber." There are three things here which he craves, each less than the other; which shews how loathe he is to bestir himself. (1.) "A little sleep;" not a dead sleep, but a moderate one. (2.) If that cannot be granted, let him have but "a little slumber;" a napping, as it were, a middle betwixt sleeping and waking. (3.) If he cannot get that, yet he would have "a folding of the hands to sleep;" (Heb.) to lie a-bed. Let him but lie still loitering, and embracing his sweet self, and not presently be obliged to rise to put hand to work. Love to folded hands goes deep with him.

Observe, how the hearts of sinners are glued to their sins, and carnal security. When conscience begins to draw them out of their bed of sloth, they will not yield, they will dispute every foot of ground with it. And they will take very little ere they want all. O were we as nice in the point of our salvation, as in the state of blindness, in the point of our ruin, how happy might we be?

2. We have the fatal issue of this course. Delays are dangerous, but most of all in matters of eternal concern. The issue of these delays is, the man is ruined, he never awakes till it is out of time. His little sleep, &c. spends all his little time, and throws him out quite unprovided into a long eternity. Here consider,

1st, What ruin comes upon him: Poverty and want. It is held forth under these notions, to answer to the provision the ants make for themselves. They provide for themselves in summer and harvest: so that when the winter comes, when they cannot stir out of their holes, they live on the provision they have laid in. There is a winter abiding us, a time wherein no man can work, when there will be no access to God's grace and favour. Death brings in this. This time is our summer and harvest, wherein matters may be secured for eternity: but, alas! the sluggard sleeps in working time; and so when it is over, he must starve and perish for ever.

2dly, How this ruin comes upon him. It comes on,

(1.) Swiftly and speedily. So the word rendered one that travaileth, imports: one that walketh vigorously, as a man in a haste upon the road. Though the sinner lies at ease on his bed of sloth, yet his ruin hasteth on apace, 2 Pet. ii. 3. The sun stands not still, though the sluggard's work goes slowly on. Every breath he fetches in his spiritual sleep, draws his destruction a step nearer.

(2.) Silently and surprisingly; "Thy poverty shall come as one that travaileth." If we send one on an errand, we will be looking for him again at the time appointed; but we know nothing of the traveller, till he come at us. So ruin comes on the delaying sinner ere he is aware; destruction is at his bedside ere he is awakened, Prov. xxix. 1.

(3.) Irresistibly: "Thy want shall come as an armed man;" (Heb.) a man of a buckler, who may hurt thee; but not thou him, for his buckler defends him. Were this traveller unarmed, the danger were not so great; or were the party attacked watching, and armed too, he might possibly come off safe. But alas! the poor man is naked, and sleeping too; how then can he make his part good against his enemy? He cannot; he must fall a sacrifice to his own sloth. Which brings me to consider,

3*dly*, What all this is owing to : " So shall thy poverty come as one that travaileth," &c. It is all owing to the cursed love of ease, to sloth, to the delays and put-offs, wherewith precious time is squandered away, and the precious soul is irrecoverably lost. They delay and delay on, till the golden opportunity is lost, and they are swept away into the pit, with all their good resolutions for the time to come, which they never see.

The point I intend to speak to from these words, is,

DOCTRINE, The delaying and putting off of repentance or salvation-work, is a soul-ruining course among gospel hearers.

In discoursing this doctrine, I shall shew,
I. Why it is that gospel hearers delay and put off repentance.
II. That this delaying is a soul-ruining course.
III. *Lastly*, Make application.

I. I shall shew why it is that gospel hearers delay and put off repentance. There is a generation that are not resolved never to repent, never to ply salvation-work ; but only they are not for it yet. They hope to mend and reform afterwards, but for the present they have no heart to it : so by cheating themselves out of their present time, they put a cheat on themselves for ever. They are called by the word, and by their own consciences, to make ready for another world, to work out their salvation ; but their hearts say, " Yet a little sleep, a little slumber, a little folding of the hands to sleep ;" and their practice is conformable thereto. Why is it so ?

1. Satan has a great hand in this. If he cannot hold out the light altogether from disturbing them, he will do what he can to lull them asleep again, before they be fully wakened : Luke xi. 21. " When a strong man armed keepeth his palace, his goods are in peace." Thus he did with Felix, Acts xxiv. 25, who, " as Paul reasoned of righteousness, temperance, and judgment to come, trembled, and answered, Go thy way for this time ; when I have a convenient season, I will call for thee." When the soul begins to think on making its escape, all the art of hell will be employed to hold it fast ; and it is easier to get one to put off salvation-work till afterwards, than downright to refuse it altogether. And thus Satan is always on one of the two extremes, urging either that it is too soon, or else that it is too long a doing.

2. The cares and business of the world contribute much to this. Hence our Lord explained " the seed which fell among thorns, to be those, who when they have heard, go forth, and are choked with cares and riches, and pleasures of this life, and bring no fruit to perfection," Luke viii. 14. How often are people in such an un-

sanctified throng of business, that they cannot find a convenient season for putting their salvation-work to a point? They have so many other cares upon their hands, that they jostle out the care of their souls. They find themselves wrapt up in a cloud of cares; but think with themselves, that were they but once through that, they shall ply their main work. Well, but they are no sooner out of that, than they are in to another; and so on, till the work being put off from time to time, is quite neglected. The truth is, persons in such a case will hardly find a time for that work, till they be resolute that they shall take it as they can find it.

3. The predominant love of carnal ease: Prov. xxvi. 15, "The slothful hideth his hand in his bosom, it grieveth him to bring it again to his mouth." We are all naturally like Issachar, who saw "that rest was good, and the land that it was pleasant; and bowed his shoulder to bear, and became a servant unto tribute," Gen. xlix. 15. Could people get sleeping to heaven on the sluggard's bed, would drowsy wishes carry them thither, many would be the passengers in that way. But that will not do. Men must labour, strive, and wrestle; and that is hard in the eyes of carnal men; and therefore, if it cannot be altogether refused, it is put off as long as may be. And hence never will a soul ply salvation-work in earnest, till it be effectually roused out of its lazy disposition.

4. The predominant love of sin. Why do persons stave off repentance, but because they are like those who entertaining their friends whom they have no will to part with, do therefore put off their departure from day to day? The parting with sin is like the cutting off of a member of the body, Matth. v. 30; which one will never yield to, unless he be very resolute. No man will delay a minute to throw a burning coal out of his bosom; but they will love to keep a sweet morsel under the tongue, who yet know that they must spit it out at length. And hence it is, that no purpose of reformation, which is only for afterwards, can be sincere; because it argues a love to, and loathness to part with sin.

5. A natural aversion and backwardness to holiness: Rom viii. 7. "The carnal mind is enmity against God: for it is not subject to the law of God, neither indeed can be." The heart will never be reconciled to the yoke of Christ, till grace make it so, Psal. cx. 3. But like as the bullock unaccustomed to the yoke is loath to stoop to it, and therefore still draws aback; so will the heart of man do, till overcoming grace reach it, Jer. xxxi. 18. Hence, when light is let into the mind, but the aversion still remains in the will, what can be expected, but that the business of repentance, which they dare not absolutely refuse, will be delayed?

6. The hope of finding the work easier afterwards. The sluggard thinks with himself, that a little more sleep, a little more slumber, a little more folding of the hands to sleep, would make it easier to him to get out of his bed; though, on the contrary, the more he sleeps unseasonably, the more he would sleep; and the longer persons delay the work of repentance, it is the harder to go through with it. For sin is a disease, which, the longer it lasts, gathers the more strength, and is harder to cure. And he that is not fit to-day to repent, will be less fit to-morrow.

7. A large reckoning on the head of time that is to come: Hence the rich man reckoned, " I will say to my soul, Soul, thou hast much goods laid up for many years; take thine ease, eat, drink, and be merry." But let us hear the judgment of God concerning this speech: "But God said unto him, thou fool, this night thy soul shall be required of thee: then whose shall those things be which thou hast provided?" Luke xii. 19. 20: God has given no man a tack of years, no nor hours; yet every body is ready to tell what they will do to-morrow, next month, or next year. The young people think they have a great deal of time before their hand for repentance; the old people think they have enough before them for that too: and in people's conceit there is always enough, till their time be gone quite, and they be wakened out of their dream. Hopes of long life have ruined many a soul. O to be wise! James iv. 13. 14. " Go to now, ye that say, to-day or to-morrow we will go unto such a city, and continue there a year, and buy, and sell, and get gain: Whereas ye know not what shall be on the morrow: For what is your life? It is even a vapour that appeareth for a little time, and then vanisheth away." But what folly is it to venture eternity on such uncertainty!

8. A fond conceit of the easiness of salvation-work. There is a generation that please themselves with the thought, that it is but to believe and repent, and that is soon done. What persons can do with a touch of their hand, they think they need to be in no haste with. But O how contrary is this to the whole strain of Scripture, and the saint's experience? Matth. vii. 14, " Strait is the gate, and narrow is the way, which leadeth unto life, and few there be that find it." Luke xiii. 24. " Strive to enter in at the strait gate: for many, I say unto you, will seek to enter in, and shall not be able." Eph. i. 19, 20, "The apostle speaks of the exceeding greatness of God's power toward them who believe, according to the working of his mighty power; which he wrought in Christ, when he raised him from the dead. 1 Pet. iv. 18. " If the righteous scarcely be saved, where shall the ungodly and the sinner appear?" Did men believe

this, that there is such a difficulty in getting to heaven, they would not dare delay for a minute entering on the way.

9. A conceit of sufficient ability in ourselves to turn ourselves from sin unto God. That the doctrine advancing the power of natural reason and ability in spiritual things, does take so much with the world, is no wonder, since man naturally is such a stranger to his own spiritual impotency. Hence it is observed, that the first question with the awakened is, "What shall I do to be saved?" It is worth observing how the carnal heart turns itself into different shapes, to retain its sinful lusts. Sometimes the man says, that he is not able to do any good; but when his sin cannot find shelter under this covert but he is pursued hot with conviction, he puts off his reformation and repentance to another time; thereby in effect declaring that he can do it, if he had but a season for it. He that is to use his oars may row at what hour he pleases; but he that must sail by the help of the wind must set off while it blows, because he cannot command it.

II. I shall show that this delaying is a soul-ruining course.

This is evident if ye consider,

1. It is directly opposite to the gospel call; which is for to-day, not for to-morrow: Heb. iii. 7, 8, "To-day if ye will hear his voice, harden not your hearts." All the calls of the gospel require present compliance, and do not allow sinners to put off till another day. It is true, salvation-work must be deliberate work; but ye are not allowed a time to deliberate whether ye will come to Christ and be holy or not. It is like the call to quench fire in a house, that must presently be done, yet done deliberately, so as the work be not marred in the making. How then can it be but a soul-ruining course?

2. It is threatened with ruin. The text is very express, "So shall thy poverty come as one that travaileth, and thy want as an armed man." And one with a thousand times more safety might venture on a sword-point, than the edge of such a divine threatening. See Prov. xxiii. 21; Eccl. x. 18. And this threatening has been accomplished in many, whom their slothful delays have caused to perish; as in the case of Ephraim, Hos. xiii. 13. and of Felix, Acts xxiv. 25. Many have been not far from the kingdom of God, who yet never came to it.

3. Whenever grace touches the heart, men see that it is so. Hence says the Psalmist, Psal. cxix. 60, "I made haste, and delayed not to keep thy commandments." When men are in earnest to get into Christ by faith, and to get back to God by repentance, they dare linger no more in the state of wrath, they flee out of it,

as one fleeing for his life, Matt. iii. 7. Their eyes are opened to see their danger, and therefore they are presently determined.

4. It has a native tendency to soul-ruin, which inevitably over-takes them, if they do not at length break off all delays, and come away. This is evident, if ye consider,

1*st*, The state of sin is a state of wrath, where ruin must needs compass a man about on every hand: John iii. 36, "He that believ-eth not the Son, shall not see life; but the wrath of God abideth on him." To have staid in Sodom that day it was to be burnt, was dangerous; but to abide a moment in the state of wrath, is far more dangerous. Who would venture into a house that is about to fall? who would not presently leave it? And will men venture "yet a little sleep, a little slumber, a little folding of the hands to sleep," in a state of enmity with God? Surely such persons know not God's greatness, nor the worth of their own souls.

2*dly*, The longer ye continue in sin, your spiritual death advan-ceth the more upon you. Every sin sets you a step farther from God, is a new bar in the way of your peace with him, strengthens your natural enmity against him, and alienates you more from the life of God. And where can this natively end, but in your souls' ruin? Ah! are we not far enough on in that way already? why delay more, that we may go yet farther off from God?

3*dly*, While ye remain in this state, there is but a step betwixt you and death, which you may be carried over by a delay of ever so short a time. All that is your security in this case, so far as ye can see, is the brittle thread of your life, which may be broken with a touch, and then ye are ruined without remedy. So that every delay, shorter or longer, of repentance, is a venturing of eternity on that uncertain life of yours, which in a moment may be taken from you.

Use I. For Information. This lets us see,

1. That delayers of repentance are self-destroyers, self-murderers. Well may it be said to such, as Ezek. xviii. 31, "Why will ye die?" Should a man wilfully neglect a remedy for his disease, which puts him in hazard of his life, he could not be guiltless of his own death; more than one who being called to rise and quench the fire in his house, and yet would lie still till it were consumed to ashes, would be blameless of its ruin. Self-love, that is, love of sinful self, is the source of the greatest cruelty; whereby lusts are spared to the destruction of the life of the soul.

2. By delays the interest of hell is advanced; where many are this day who had resolved to repent, but death did not wait their time, and so they were disappointed. No wonder new grounds of

delay be still laid to persons' hands, for it is Satan's great drift to get men entangled in the wilderness, that they may not make forward to Canaan's land. And every new entanglement sets the soul a step nearer to destruction: and who questions but Satan has art enough to coin new pretences for delays?

3. No wonder Satan is most busy to ply the engine of delays, when a sinner is somewhat awakened by conviction; as he did with Felix, Acts xxiv. 25. " A soft answer turneth away wrath;" and delays will blunt the edge of convictions, as much as a peremptory refusal. Under convictions, at a sermon, or on a sick-bed, the sinner is awakened out of his sleep; but then nothing can serve Satan's purpose better, than yet a little sleep: which if they get, they sleep off the edge of convictions.

4. They are sinners' best friends, that give them least rest in a sinful course. And whatever men think of them now, they will think so afterwards, Prov. v. 11, 12, 13. Every body loves ease, and therefore faithful preaching and dealing with souls, is a torment to those who love to be undisturbed in their rest in sin, Rev. xi. 10. But what suits best with our sinful inclinations, is worst for our souls, and will in the end be found so. Flattery has ruined many, when plain dealing and fair warning has brought many out of the snare.

USE 2. Of Lamentation. We may lament here the case of many, nay of most that hear the gospel. They put off their work from time to time, and so their spiritual case is going to wreck day by day. This is the case in natural things: Eccl. x. 18. " By much slothfulness the building decayeth, and through idleness of the hands the house droppeth through." They are in a dying condition, the physician comes to their bed-side, and offers them a remedy; they do not absolutely refuse it, only they put off the taking of it. In the mean-time their distemper increases, and death is advancing apace. The market of free grace is opened, and they are called to come and buy: they see they need to buy, yet they are not like to stir till the market be over. O madness and folly to be lamented with tears of blood! Poor slothful creature, that is yet for a little sleep, a little slumber, a little folding of the hands to sleep, there are four things thou knowest not.

1. Thou knowest not the worth of a precious soul, which thou art throwing away for what will not profit. Will the sweet sleep in sin quit the cost of the soul's ruin? No, no: " For what is a man profited, if he shall gain the whole world, and lose his own soul? or what shall a man give in exchange for his soul?" Matth. xvi. 26. Christ left the bosom of the Father, and shed his precious blood to

redeem the soul. He was wise that paid the price; and if less would have done, he would not have been at needless expense of blood: he was a Father that received it; and would not have put his Son to that if it had not been necessary. Satan goes about without intermission to ruin it. But what low thoughts dost thou entertain of it, that wilt not break thy rest to save it from ruin?

2. Thou knowest not the excellency of precious Christ; sleep locks up thine eyes that thou canst not see the ravishing sight, John i. 10. The eyes of saints and angels are fixed on him, as the glory of the upper house: the eyes opened here by grace, are arrested by his overcoming glory. Hence are these rapturous expressions in Scripture, Psal. lxxiii. 25. "Whom have I in heaven but thee? and there is none upon earth that I desire besides thee." Cant. i. 3. "Because of the savour of thy good ointments, thy name is as ointment poured forth, therefore do the virgins love thee." Zion's crowned King is making his progress through the city where thou dwellest; the cry to come out and behold him, reaches thine ears, Cant. iii. ult; but while he goes by, thou must have "yet a little sleep, a little slumber, a little folding of the hands to sleep," and so thou losest the sight. The royal Bridegroom stretches forth his hand unto thee, to espouse thee, saying, Behold me, behold me: thou openest thy drowsy eyes, and beginnest to stretch forth the hand; but sleep overcomes thee, thine eyes close, and thy hand falls down again, and the match is marred. The chariot of the covenant that is driving on to his Father's house halts at thy door, and thou art called out: the ship is to sail to Immanuel's land, thou art called to come aboard: but "yet a little sleep, a little slumber, a little folding of the hands to sleep," and all is lost.

3. Thou knowest not the worth of precious time. The Apostle will have time redeemed, Eph. v. 16; but thou squanderest it away as a thing of no value; and working time is turned by thee into sleeping time. Precious moments slip away, and thou regardest not; though once gone, they can never be recalled. What would those who are past hope, give for an hour of that time, whereof thou lettest days, months, and years slip, without any improvement for eternity? O unhappy soul, who "knowest not in this thy day, the things that belong unto thy peace!"

4. Thou knowest not the weight of the wrath of God. It is true none can have a full comprehension of it, Psal. xc. 11. "Who knoweth the power of thine anger?" But all the elect of God get such a notion of it, as rouses them up to fly from it, 2 Cor. v. 11. "Knowing the terror of the Lord," says the Apostle, "we persuade men." And if thou hadst tolerable apprehensions of it, it would

break off thy sleep and slumber, and cause thee put forth thy hands to work. Didst thou consider what a fearful thing it is to fall into the hands of the living God, and how when thou fallest down again into thy bed of sloth, thou art truly in hazard of it, it would give thee such a gliff as would keep the waking.

There are three things thou dost not observe.

1. Thou dost not observe what speed thy ruin is making, while thou liest at ease; how thy judgment lingereth not, "and thy damnation slumbereth not," 2 Pet. ii. 3. The avenger of blood is pursuing thee, though thou art not fleeing from the wrath to come. Thou art like a man sleeping in a leaky ship, which is drawing water every moment, and within a little it will be full, and sink to the bottom of the sea, if he do not awake and help it. Every hour thy debt is growing, the cup of wrath is filling, and fills so much the faster, as thou art secure.

2. Thou dost not observe how near thy destruction may be. Thou art like the old world, who " were eating and drinking, marrying and giving in marriage, until the day that Noe entered into the ark, and knew not until the flood came, and took them all away," Matt. xxiv. 38, 39. Thy spiritual lethargy and dead sleep hinders thee from hearing the sound of the feet of the approaching stroke. Thou liest open to the most terrible surprise, to sleep the sleep of death, which thou mayest never awake out of till in hell, Luke xii. 19, 20. and xvi. 23. And O how sad is it for men to be past hope, ere they begin to fear; to have the house falling, ere they get over their bed!

3. Thou dost not observe how utterly unable thou art to ward off the blow when it comes: Is. xxxiii. 14, "The sinners in Zion are afraid, fearfulness hath surprized the hypocrites: who among us shall dwell with the devouring fire? who amongst us shall dwell with everlasting burnings?" Ezek. xxii. 14, "Can thine heart endure, or can thine hands be strong in the days that I shall deal with thee? I the Lord have spoken it, and will do it." Can worm man stand before the almighty God, whose patience may be worn out ere thou awake? And if mercy and patience quit the field, justice will succeed into their room; and then there shall be no more sleeping, nor ease for ever.

USE 3. Of Reproof to delayers of salvation-work. Why do ye go on in this soul-ruining course? Have ye no respect to the calls of the gospel, none to your souls, none to eternity? Why do not ye with all your might whatever your hand findeth to do? I would apply myself here,

1. To delaying saints.

2. To delaying sinners.

1. To delaying saints; for such there may be, and of such there are many at this day, Caut. v. 2, 3; and our text is a general truth and warning. Spiritual sloth is so interwoven with our corrupt natures, that it will never be quite rooted out, till the corrupt nature be perfectly expelled. And as it remains in great measure in the saints, so it is fruitful of delays. There are these five delays incident even to the saints.

1. A delay of righting their case when matters are wrong, by renewing their repentance, and the actings of faith. Sometimes their case is quite out of order: their graces are not in exercise; they are strangers to the Spirit's influences, and to access to and communion with God in duties. They have a secret dissatisfaction with this, and are resolved to get to their feet again; but sloth masters them, and the work is put off from time to time; as was the case with the spouse, Cant. v. 2, 3, "I sleep, but my heart waketh," says she, "it is the voice of my beloved that knocketh, saying, Open to me, my sister, my love, my dove, my undefiled: for my head is filled with dew, and my locks with the drops of the night. I have put off my coat, how shall I put it on? I have washed my feet, how shall I defile them?"

2. The delaying to give up with some bosom-idol that mars their communion with God, Cant. iii. 1; Psal. lxvi. 18. They are convinced, that the harbouring of it does much harm to their souls' case, and many resolutions they have to put the knife to the throat of it, but still they draw back their hand. And from one time to another the crucifying of it is put off; so that still it lives, like a waster in the candle, causing the soul's case go to wreck.

3. The delaying to clear their state before the Lord. They see need to have marches rid, and to be brought to a point whether they be in Christ or not, whether in a state of grace or not. They have resolutions to put it to a solemn trial, to examine themselves, and search what evidences they have for a title to heaven: but still the heart draws back, and the trial is put off.

4. The delaying of some particular duty, or piece of generation-work, which they are convinced God calls them to. They have often thoughts of setting about it in earnest; but still some one thing or other intervenes, and it is put off. They begin perhaps sometimes; but it is broken off again, and they must yet have "a little sleep, a little slumber, a little folding of the hands to sleep."

5. *Lastly,* The delaying of actual preparation for eternity; like the virgins, Matt. xxv. 5, who, "while the bridegroom tarried, all slumbered and slept." They see that it is no easy thing to die;

they resolve to labour to put themselves through grace into a case for it; but day after day it is delayed. The lamps are not trimmed for meeting the Bridegroom. Though they be in a good state, they have not a dying frame.

To all such I would say, as Jon. i. 6, " What meanest thou, O sleeper? arise, call upon thy God, if so be that God will think upon thee, that thou perish not." Let me expostulate with you upon this head, O delaying saints.

1. Do ye find yourselves any thing the nearer your purpose by all your delays? Nay the longer ye delay, do not ye find yourselves the farther from it? Does not your aversion and backwardness to duty grow upon you the more? and is not your confidence in the Lord still the more lessened? Yes; the more ye give yourselves to spiritual sleep, the more ye will desire to sleep.

2. Do not ye find this the way to rank poverty and want? Your consciences will witness the truth of that, that where the diligent shall abound with blessings, the idle soul shall suffer hunger. Is it with you as in months past? Have ye that sense and gust of religion, that access to God in duties, which ye have had when ye were doing with your might what your hand found to do?

3. Has not your poverty come upon you as one that travaileth? Have ye not been sometimes like Samson awaked out of Delilah's lap, and found your strength gone from you when you had most to do with it? Perhaps thou hast spent many days in estrangement from God, with much ease; but at length some strong temptation, or piercing trial has overtaken you; and then you have sucked the bitter sap of your slothful delays.

4. A little more sleep, a little more slumber, a little more folding of the hands to sleep, and the occasion may be lost, the opportunity for doing neglected duties may be lost. Either they may be taken from you, or ye from them. No man has a tack of his life, nor of occasions of doing good; and therefore " as we have opportunity, let us do good unto all men, especially unto them who are of the household of faith," Gal. vi. 10. And though the soul that is in Christ shall be saved surely, yet this will make the salvation to be so as by fire.

5. *Lastly*, The long delayed work is hard work when it comes to the setting too, Cant. v. 5—8. When the awakening comes, there may be little time, much opposition, and less strength than otherwise thou wouldst have had, and yet more to do with it than otherwise. The longer thy hand is from thy case the more ravelled will it be. And it will readily occasion much fear, darkness, and perplexity in a dying hour.

II. I would apply myself to delaying sinners, to those that are yet out of Christ, and have all to do for eternity still. They are living in a state of wrath, and yet they linger, and put off their removal from Sodom. They delay repentance, and go on in their sin. I would say to you, as Prov. vi. 9, "How long wilt thou sleep, O sluggard? when wilt thou arise out of thy sleep?" I must expostulate with you on this head.

First, Ye young people, why do ye delay repentance? why are ye like the wild asses' colts, untractable and unteachable? No doubt, ye think it is too soon for you; that it may be time enough several years after this. Ye think repentance and seriousness suits best with the wrinkled brows, the pale face, and hollow eyes, &c.; that it is pity to spoil the bloom of youth with such work. When do ye mean to repent then? It is like, it is when ye are settled in the world, or when ye grow old; at least the days of youth must be over first. But, poor fool,

1. Is the debt of sin so small upon thy head, that thou must run thyself deeper in the debt of God's justice? Dost not thou know that thou wast born a child of wrath? Eph. ii. 3; that thou broughtest that into the world with thee, that will damn thee, if thou repent not, and come to Christ? And will not that sink thee deep enough in destruction, though thou add no more to it, unless thou repent?

2. Is not the same holy law binding on thee, since thou couldst discern betwixt good and evil, that is binding on the oldest alive? Have the young a liberty to sin, and to cast off the fear of God and religion, more than the old? See Gal. iii. 10, " For as many as are of the works of the law, are under the curse: for it is written, Cursed is every one that continueth not in all things which are written in the book of the law to do them." Here there is no exception. The follies of youth men may pass; but assure yourselves, God will not pass them: Eccl. xi. 9, " Rejoice, O young man, in thy youth, and let thy heart cheer thee in the days of thy youth, and walk in the ways of thy heart, and in the sight of thine eyes : but know thou, that for all these things God will bring thee into judgment." And I doubt not, but if ye saw your sinful thoughts, words, and actions, whether vain or vile, laid before you, as you must reckon for them at length, how few soever your years have been, you will see them to be more than the hairs on your heads. And I must tell you, that being yet unrenewed, and strangers to the life of grace, all your actions have been sin : Prov. xxi. 4, " An high look, and a proud heart, and the ploughing of the wicked, is sin." And is it not then time to repent?

3. Who has assured thee, that ever thou shalt see the age thou speakest of? Go to the churchyard, and ye will see graves of all sizes, of your length and under. There are far more young corpses, than there are of those that carry gray hairs, ten to one.* Most men and women are cut off before they come to old age. What has befallen others as young and flourishing as you, may befal you too. And therefore, since ye know not but ye may die young, repent while ye are young, lest in the end ye find yourselves miserably disappointed.

4. Who has best right to your youth and strength? God or the devil? God is courting you for his own gift: Eccl. xii. 1, "Remember now thy Creator in the days of thy youth." Satan will labour to keep his possession. God is the first and last; and he required the first and best, the first-fruits, the first-born, the morning-sacrifice; and he requires the first of your days, and he takes pleasure therein: Jer. ii. 2, "I remember thee, the kindness of thy youth, the love of thine espousals, when thou wentest after me in the wilderness, in a land that was not sown." And will ye devote the first and best to sin and Satan, reserving the last and worst to your Creator?

5. Great is the advantage of those that get a gripe of religion while they are young, beyond others, in many respects. (1.) Readily their passage in the pangs of the new birth will be easier than that of others. In none is that scripture fulfilled more, Mark iv. 27. of the seed's springing and growing up, none knoweth how, than where grace joins with good education in young persons. The nail lately driven, draws easily in comparison of that which has been long rusted in. Where grace catches persons before they begin to dip into the gross pollutions of the world, it frees them of much remorse that these must occasion to those that have been led away with them. (2.) Young people's affections are easiest moved; and as they move easiest, so they move most vigorously, whatever way they be set. Hence they lie most fair for tasting the sweet of religion: Hos. ii. 14, "I will allure her, and bring her into the wilderness, and speak comfortably unto her." God sometimes dandling young converts upon the knees, and giving them sensible tastes of the pleasure of religion, is agreeable to the particular promise made for their encouragement, Prov. viii. 17, "I love them that love me; and those that seek me early shall find me." (3.) They are in the fairest way to have most access to serve God in their generation.

* It is observed, by those who have accurately examined the records of the dead, that one half of mankind die before five years of age, and near a third more before twenty. How few then must arrive at old age?

Suppose a man to be converted when he is old, his salvation will be secure; but, alas! his time for serving God's honour in the world is almost gone ere he puts hand to work.

6. *Lastly*, God commands you to repent presently, and therefore it is on the peril of your soul, that ye venture to delay a moment longer: Heb. iii. 7, 8, "To-day if ye will hear his voice, harden not your hearts." Remember that word, Eccl. xi. 9, 10, "Rejoice, O young man, in thy youth, and let thy heart cheer thee in the days of thy youth, and walk in the ways of thy heart, and in the sight of thine eyes: but know thou, that for all these things God will bring thee into judgment. Therefore remove sorrow from thy heart, and put away evil from thy flesh: for childhood and youth are vanity." A sinful youth will at length make a sad soul. Ye know not how soon God may be provoked against you to cut you off, if you delay. Monuments of the Lord's anger have been set up in childhood and youth, as well as in old age. Witness the children at Bethel, 2 Kings ii. 23, 24.

Let not Satan deceive you, as if there were no pleasure in religion. No, Wisdom's "ways are ways of pleasantness, and all her paths are peace," Prov. iii. 17. There is a sweet in religion a thousand times preferable to all the pleasures and vanities youth gades after.

Secondly, Ye middle-aged people, why do ye delay repentance? why do not ye think with yourselves seriously, where ye are like to take up your eternal lodging, and prepare for eternity by repentance? No doubt ye think ye have time enough too; but no time at present, for ye have another thing ado, the care of a family upon your heads, Luke xiv. 20. When is your term-day of repentance? It is like it is when ye shall have more time than now, or when ye grow old. But, O sirs,

1. What know ye that ever you shall see old age? Yea what dost thou know, but, as Luke xii. 20, "this night thy soul shall be required of thee"? Alas! shall men thus from time to time venture their eternal state upon a mere uncertainty? Thy life is but a day, a short day, a winter day, and thou hast a long journey to go; thy forenoon is past already, and wilt thou sleep on till the evening that will soon be upon thee? The declining sun calls thee to awake.

2. What reason is there, that thy business in the world should shuffle out thy business for eternity? Remember they had as good excuses as you, who upon the sending of them were rejected, and it was declared their day of grace was past, Luke xiv. 18, 19, 20, 24. Oh hast thou not a soul to provide for, thy eternal state to look after? Can ye wonder, if, as ye prefer the world to Christ now, he

give you your portion in this life; and if ever the time come that thou set thyself to repent, he deny thee his grace, and bid thee go to the gods thou hast served?

3. Consider the advantages thou hast now for seriousness, when the foam of youth has settled, and the infirmities of old age have not yet drawn on. O consider, and shew yourselves men. Ye have spent your youth in vanity,.and will ye spend this age too that way? What is it ye design for God, the dregs of thy years, that age that is the sink of infirmities? and ye will part with sin, when ye can follow it no longer. O sirs, what confidence can ye have, that God will accept that off your hand? Mal. i. 8. "And if ye offer the blind for sacrifice, is it not evil? and if ye offer the lame and sick, is it not evil? offer it now unto thy governor, will he be pleased with thee, or accept thy person? saith the Lord of hosts."

4. Suppose ye should live till ye grow old, O how few are there that get grace to repent when they are old? I shall not say, there are none such; but truly though they be, they are very rare. Be not ye encouraged to delay, because some were called at the eleventh hour, Matth. xx. 6; for if ye mark the text, these were others than those that were standing there at the third, sixth, and ninth hour. We set no bounds to sovereignty; but as for those that live under the gospel, and spend their best days in sin and estrangedness from religion, common observation tells us, that it is God's ordinary way to plague them with hardness of heart, when they grow old: Job xx. 11. "His bones are full of the sin of his youth, which shall lie down with him in the dust." About three hundred years after Christ, there was one that had lived a pagan till he was an old man; when he told Simplicianus that he was a Christian, he would not believe him: but when the Church saw that he was really so, their was great shouting and gladness, saying, Caius Marius Victorius is become a Christian! They wondered to see a man when he was old born again.

5. *Lastly*, Will ye see the deceit of delays. When ye were young, did ye not put it off to this time? and now when that is come, ye are as unready as before. Delay no more then lest ye sleep the sleep of death.

Thirdly, Old people, why do ye delay repentance: why is not your heart bowing to God's call, when ye are begun to bow to meet the grave? Ye that have always thought ye had time enough all your days, ye will think there is time enough yet. But when is your term-day for repentance? a death-bed, it is like. And when ye come there, ye will hope it will be but a sick-bed, and so drive off your work till the utmost point. But, O sirs,

1. May not the time past of your life suffice to have wrought the will of the flesh? Must ye have "yet a little sleep, a little slumber, a little folding of the hands to sleep?" Well, when ye have taken it over the belly of God's call to you all your days, what confidence can ye have to look for grace or mercy then? Sin, Satan, and the world shall have all your time, and ye will look to God, and seek his favour, when ye can do no more. O, are ye not afraid, that that be accomplished on you? Prov. i. 24. &c. "Because I have called, and ye refused, I have stretched out my hand, and no man regarded; but ye have set at nought all my counsel, and would have none of my reproof: I also will laugh at your calamity, I will mock when your fear cometh; when your fear cometh as desolation, and your destruction cometh as a whirlwind; when distress and anguish cometh upon you," &c. I trow, if your conscience were awakened just now, ye should have enough ado to fasten your feet on a promise of mercy.

2. How do you know, that ye will get a death-bed or sick-bed? What do ye know, but that in a moment ye may drop into eternity, as many have done? Mind him who used to say, three words would do his turn at death. Death does not always send messengers to warn us of its approach. Nay, see what our Lord says expressly, Matth. xxiv. 48—51. " If that evil servant shall say in his heart, My Lord delayeth his coming. And shall begin to smite his fellow-servants, and to eat and drink with the drunken: the Lord of that servant shall come in a day when he looketh not for him, and in an hour that he is not ware of; and shall cut him asunder, and appoint him his portion with the hypocrites: there shall be weeping and gnashing of teeth."

3. *Lastly*, And is dying such an easy business, that ye must be laying up other work, yea your main work, for a dying time? I should think, that dying itself, with the pains, throes, and sickness that ordinarily attend it, were enough of themselves. Surely, if we were rightly exercised in health, we would endeavour, that when we come to die, we should have nothing ado but to die. But I pray you remember, you may come to die roving, without the exercise of your reason. But though ye should have it to the last, I pray you consider, is the work of repentance such an easy work as to leave it till the time you can do nothing else? Will ye put off turning to God, till ye are not able to turn yourselves on a bed, but as ye are lifted? taking heaven by storm, till your strength be gone? crying to God, till ye are not able to speak two sentences at once? making ready for death, till it be come to your bed-side?

Use ult. I exhort you all to delay repentance and salvation-work no longer.

MOTIVE 1. Consider ye do but mock God, and cheat yourselves by your delaying. For it is inconsistent with a sincere purpose to repent and turn from sin, 1 Pet. iv. 1, 2, 3. For he that sincerely minds to turn from sin, will presently turn from it.

MOTIVE 2. Repentance is not in your power; it is God's gift, which he gives when he will, Acts v. 31. "God hath exalted Christ with his right hand, to be a Prince and a Saviour, to give repentance to Israel." The time of God's grace is limited: a time wherein he will be found, and when not: Is. lv. 6. "Seek ye the Lord while he may be found, call ye upon him while he is near." Death certainly puts a period to it. But it seems to be clear, that men may outlive their day of grace: Luke xiv. 24. "I say unto you, that none of those men which were bidden, shall taste of my supper." Time was when Esau might have had the blessing, but then he despised it; but the time came when he could not have it: Heb. xii. 17. "Ye know how that afterward when he would have inherited the blessing, he was rejected: for he found no place of repentance, though he sought it carefully with tears." Strike in then with the occasion; for if wind and tide fail, there can be no setting to sea.

MOTIVE 3. Though we knew certainly, that our day of grace were far from the end; yet it is a most unworthy thing so to deal with God. Shall men abuse mercy and grace because the Lord waiteth to be gracious? Will men abuse the divine patience, because it suffers long? What a folly is it to stand off as long as we can from him to whom we must needs submit ourselves at length?

MOTIVE 4. The time is short, the work great, and so is the opposition. Salvation-work is a great work; it is no easy thing to be a Christian; ye must lay your account with all the opposition the devil, the world, and the flesh can make you; ye have but an age that is an handbreadth, as nothing to do it in.

MOTIVE 5. Your life is most uncertain. We are tenants-at-will, we have no tack for to-morrow, Jam. iv. 13, 14. forecited. We are agreed about the necessity of repentance; the only question is, When shall it be done? God says, To-day; and to morrow is not yours, but God's. How then can ye destinate for this use the time that is not yours? Return to God one day before thy death, say the Jewish doctors. Wisely said; return then to-day, for it may be ye shall die to-morrow.

MOTIVE 6. The longer ye delay, the work will be the harder. For sin becomes stronger, as the waters, the farther from the head, the greater they grow. And the arrow that going from the bow strays from the mark, how far wide will it be ere it come to the utmost point? It is observed, that Christ groaned at the raising

of Lazarus four days dead; but not so at the raising of the young
man of Nain, or Jarius' daughter. Jer. xiii. 23. "Can the Ethiopian change his skin, or the leopard his spots? then may ye also
do good, that are accustomed to do evil." Their number increaseth;
the devil who comes alone at first, at length his name is Legion.
The heart grows harder, the mind blinder, the will more perverse,
the affections more carnal.

MOTIVE 7. A moment's delay may be an eternal loss, because thou
knowest not any moment that may not be thy last.

MOTIVE ult. God commands you to repent presently, Heb. iv. 7.
Therefore upon your peril it is, if ye delay any more.

OBJECTION. The thief on the cross repented at the last gasp.
ANSWER. His repentance was one of the miracles at Christ's death;
and he glorified God more at his death than ye could if ye had been
a penitent all your days. But though there was one that none might
despair, yet there was but one that none might presume. The other
thief even died as he lived.

THE EXTRAORDINARY CASE OF THE THIEF ON THE CROSS NO
ARGUMENT FOR DELAYING REPENTANCE.

Two Sermons preached, at Ettrick, in June, 1717.

LUKE xxiii. 42,

*And he said unto Jesus, Lord, remember me when thou comest into thy
kingdom.*

THE love that sinners bear to their lusts, and the conviction men
generally have of the necessity of repentance, each of them putting
in for a share, do natively produce a delay. And Satan and the
corrupt heart join to support the delaying temper, both by pretended reasons, and abused examples: amongst which last none is
more so than this of the thief who repented on the cross.

My great design being to convince you, that this instance can be
no encouragement to delay repentance, I need not here lay for a
foundation the proof of this man's sincerity, which the text and
context put beyond all doubt; nor insist on explaining this his
prayer, full of faith and repentance, which had a most gracious
answer.

Every body knows the story; and they that know very little of the Bible, will be found acquainted with this instance of the penitent thief on the cross; and they abuse it to their own ruin, drawing encouragement from it to put off repentance till they come to a death-bed.

We need not much wonder, that this becomes a stumbling-stone to many, on which they are ruined. Hearing the thief was converted near the last gasp, and having led a sinful life, the thread was suddenly broken, and he died happily; his day was a dark day all over, till in the evening, the sun broke out with a bright though short glimpse, and then set; That this, I say, is abused and turned to a stumbling-stone by impenitent sinners, is no great wonder, if ye consider the following things.

1. As a vicious stomach corrupts the best of meat; so impenitent sinners abuse the best things to their own ruin: so that what raises up others taught of God, is an occasion of falling to them. The altar of God, and the whole law was so to the unbelieving Jews, Rom. xi. 9. Is not the very gospel, and the preachers thereof, a savour of death to some? 2 Cor. ii. 16. Nay, Christ himself is a stumbling-block to them. 1 Pet. 7, 8.

2 There is a particular disposition in the hearts of impenitent sinners to abuse and wrest the Scriptures. Hence Peter, speaking of Paul's epistles, says, " In them are some things hard to be understood, which they that are unlearned and unstable wrest, as they do also the other scriptures, unto their own destruction," 2 Pet. iii. 16. The Scripture is a light, and a rule of divine authority; and it may well be expected, that if sinners can persuade themselves of a shelter there for their sins, it will be the most effectual one. This is the most feasible means for stilling the clamours of an ill conscience, and cheating men into their own ruin.

3. Abused Scripture is one of the chief pieces of Satan's armour, wherewith he maintains and promotes his kingdom among those that have the Scriptures. Thus Satan said to Christ, Matt iv. 6. " If thou be the Son of God, cast thyself down: for it is written, He shall give his angels charge concerning thee, and in their hands they shall bear thee up, lest at any time thou dash thy foot against a stone." Hence unclean persons still their consciences with the example of David, swearers with that of Joseph by the life of Pharaoh, or Peter's, &c. Men that are mere moralists screen themselves with that, Mic. vi. 8, " He hath shewed thee, O man, what is good; and what doth the Lord require of thee, but to do justly, and to love mercy, and to walk humbly with thy God?" And others satisfy themselves with good meanings and desires, because

of that, Matt. v. 6, " Blessed are they which do hunger and thirst after righteousness : for they shall be filled." Others think, they may repent at any time, from that Scripture, Ezek. xviii. 27, " When the wicked man turneth away from his wickedness that he hath committed, and doth that which is lawful and right, he shall save his soul alive." And thus it becomes harder to convince men that have some notional knowledge of the Bible, than those that never knew it.

4. Reigning love to sin makes people very dexterous to find out shifts to preserve their lusts; as in Saul's speech to Samuel, 1 Sam. xv. 15, " They have brought them from the Amalekites : for the people spared the best of the sheep and of the oxen, to sacrifice unto the Lord thy God, and the rest we have utterly destroyed." What people would fain have to be true, it is easy to persuade them of : and what they are loathe to part with, it is not hard to invent shifts to hold it still. Were men willing to be the Lord's, they would be so presently; and they would be loathe to delay one moment, lest they should never see another.

To come to this particular instance in the text, I must tell you, That though here is ground of hope for poor trembling sinners, that they may be brought to repentance, and be accepted of God ; yet there is no ground here for crafty delaying sinners to put off repentance, in hopes to go through with it afterwards, especially in a dying hour.

I. There is ground of hope for trembling sinners. And we may learn from this instance these following lessons.

1. They may go long on, and far on in the way to hell, whom yet God may bring home to himself. Here is a man, a thief, whose course brought him to an ill end, to a violent death, and yet grace reaches him. See the following remarkable passage, 1 Cor. vi. 9, 10, 11, " Know ye not that the unrighteous shall not inherit the kingdom of God ? Be not deceived : neither fornicators, nor idolaters, nor adulterers, nor effeminate, nor abusers of themselves with mankind, nor thieves, nor covetous, nor drunkards, nor revilers, nor extortioners, shall inherit the kingdom of God. And such were some of you : but ye are washed, but ye are sanctified, but ye are justified in the name of the Lord Jesus, and by the Spirit of our God." From this it appears, that some of the Corinthian converts had been formerly the vilest of wretches, and guilty of the most enormous lewdness and impiety ; and yet became famous monuments of the triumphs of sovereign efficacious grace. What a length did Manasseh and Paul go ; and yet what illustrious penitents did they afterwards become ? The latter justly acquired the

character of the greatest of saints, and the most eminent of all the apostles.

2. Grace sometimes catches them that in appearance, and to the eyes of the world, are farthest from it. It passeth by the most likely, and pitches on the most unlikely objects. While chief priests, scribes, and elders mock Christ, the thief on the cross is converted. The Lord loves to set up the trophies of his victory in the midst of the devil's kingdom. Hence is that promise, Is. lv. 5, " Behold, thou shalt call a nation that thou knowest not, and nations that knew not thee, shall run unto thee, because of the Lord thy God; and for the holy One of Israel; for he hath glorified thee."

3. Grace makes a vast difference betwixt those betwixt whom it finds none. Here are two thieves, both on the cross: grace touches the heart of the one, but passeth by the other; and makes the one a convert, while the other dies hardened. So true is Paul's observation, Rom. ix. 16, " So then it is not of him that willeth, nor of him that runneth, but of God that sheweth mercy."

4. *Lastly,* While there is life there is hope. Here is one converted when near the last gasp; while his last sand was running, grace overtakes him, opens the eyes that before were closed, wins the heart that had been all along hardened. But I stay not on these things. Only the use that is to be made of this, is,

1. Let those that seek God early be encouraged from this, that they shall find him: Prov. viii. 17, " I love them that love me, and those that seek me early shall find me." Was he so ready to receive a penitent soul coming in at the last hour, then surely he will be very ready to receive thee that comes in before that time. He rejected him not because he was long a-coming; but received him because he came. Come then forward with assured hope of thy acceptance upon thy early return.

2. Let not those whose day is almost gone, before they have begun their work, despair. Who knows but that may be done in the evening, that was neglected the whole day before? A gale for heaven may blow, that may put life in an old sinner, and make his flesh fresher than that of a child. The door of the vineyard stands open for labourers to come in even at the eleventh hour. Sovereignty is not pent up to times and ways, but takes a latitude in both.

3. *Lastly,* Let us sow beside all waters, in the morning and in the evening. It depends on the working of free grace, which shall prosper. We are ready to be hopeless of success, where persons have long stood out against the Lord. But God's heavy hand on a

man, and a view of eternity, may afford a season wherein the wild ass may be caught.

II. But there is no ground here for the crafty delaying sinner to put off repentance, especially till a dying hour. To set this matter in a true light, consider these following things.

1. It is a most rare example. There is not an instance like it in all the book of God, unless it be that of Achan, Josh. vii. 20, 21. Yet the Lord has left that case of Achan's much under a cloud; so that it is not positively determined as this is, though we may charitably hope the best in his case too. Now, here I would have you to consider,

1*st*, What less could there have been to have cleared a possibility of acceptance with God, for a sinner at the last, after he has spent all his days in sin? If we had not had this instance, what could have been said to shew such wretched misspenders of time, that ever any that was so long a setting off in their journey to heaven did get in? And because this says, that none should despair; must it therefore import, that they may safely delay? The sun once stood still in the days of Joshua; which says it is possible such a thing may be: but will any man delay his work in hope of such an extraordinary cast again? And why will ye?

2*dly*, As one swallow makes not spring, so neither can this one event make a general rule that you or I may trust to. The ordinary rule is, that as men live, so they die; a holy life, a happy end; a graceless, careless life, an unhappy and miserable end. Because Providence may go off the ordinary road, and do that in a few minutes with some, that ordinarily costs many years to others; can you venture eternity on that, that he will do so with you? Moses fasted forty days and nights, Exod. xxxiv. 28: yet who will venture on that in hopes of having his life preserved without food?

3*dly*, Are there not eminent instances to the contrary, wherein men living in their sin have been struck down in a moment, getting no time to repent of them, but fiery wrath has put an end to their days? Consider the case of Nadab and Abihu, Lev. x. 1, 2, of whom it is thought they had erred through drink, ver. 9; Korah, Dathan, and Abiram, Numb. xvi. 31, &c.; Ananias and Sapphira, Acts v., who died instantly with a lie in their mouth. But why do I instance in particular persons? Did not millions die together in their sins, by the deluge that swept away the old world, the fire and brimstone that burned up Sodom, Gomorrha, Admah, and Zeboim? What multitudes were there there, who, being warned, put off to the day they never saw? And shall this one instance encourage you to delay, over the belly of the dreadful example of millions on the other hand?

4thly, The most that this so rare an example can amount to, is a possibility. It is not to so much as a probability or likelihood. That is a probable event, which though it does not always fall out, yet for the most part it does so; as that the husbandman shall get more than his seed again. But from what is said it appears, that for the most part it falls out otherwise, namely, that people even die as they live. So that it is probable, that if thou do not repent before, God will deny thee grace to repent at the last. How then can a man that has any belief of a God, a heaven, and a hell, venture his salvation on a mere possibility, while the probability lies the other way?

2. Though there were two thieves on the cross at that time, yet it was but one of them that got grace to repent. The one indeed was a true penitent; but the other died as he lived, hardened in his sin ; nay, perhaps worse ; for he died blaspheming the Son of God, before whose tribunal he was to appear, ver. 39. Now, upon this I would make these rational reflections.

1st, Is it not possible that thou mayst die blaspheming, if thou do not repent now in time ? Thou canst not deny the possibility of it, when there is such a plain instance of it in the case of one of these thieves. Thou thinkest it may be thou may die a penitent with the good thief; and I say, it may be thou mayst die blaspheming with the other. The one is even as certain, as to us, as the other. Thou livest impenitent all thy days ; when thou comest to a death-bed, God may withhold his grace from thee which thou hast all along refused; he may let thee see thy case hopeless for ever, and thou mayst be filled with despair ; and in that case it is more than possible that both tongue and heart may rise against God.

2dly, It is at least an equal venture, that thou mayst die impenitent, as that thou mayst die a penitent. Thou hopest to repent at the last; why? because the thief on the cross repented. And I must say, that delaying repentance till then, thou runnest the risk of dying impenitent; for the other thief died so. And who has told thee, whether thy lot shall be with the one or with the other ? Now, to repent presently, makes thy salvation certain ; to delay it, does at best leave it to a venture. And consider with yourself seriously, if salvation and damnation be such trifling things, as to be left to an uncertainty, you do not know how it may fall.

3dly, It is inconsistent with common sense, to leave that thing to a venture, which may be made sure, where a hit or a miss is of the utmost concern. Suppose a rebel might certainly have his life by a willing submission to his prince, should he choose to stay till he were apprehended by the officers, he would act most unreasonably, and put his life in hazard where there is no need; as in the case of Shimei, 1 Kings ii. 42. A thousand times more unreasonable art thou in such delays of repentance, for now thou mayst make heaven sure: but if thou delay, thy soul is left to a dreadful venture; and if thou miss when it comes to the point, thou art ruined for ever.

4thly, Nay but the venture is very unequal; for it is far more likely that delaying thou mayst die impenitent, than that thou mayst die penitent. Few took part with the good thief amongst all the crowd of spectators; the multitude went the other thief's way, mocking, ver. 35. And what casts the balance here in case of likelihood, is,

(1.) Common observation, that tells us, that most people even die as they live. Repentance is a flower rarely seen springing up from a death-bed. A melting of heart for sin, because of the dishonour done to God by it, is seldom seen in such as have lived a graceless, careless, presumptuous life; but that disposition even hangs about them to the end.

(2.) It is certain that few are saved, in comparison of them that are left: Matt. vii. 14, " Strait is the gate, and narrow is the way, which leadeth unto life, and few there be that find it." As to what some say of the infants of all mankind; all that are saved must go by the strait gate, and still these are few. It is evident, that most men live impenitent; yet all must die; and therefore it follows, that few get grace to repent at their last, but most of those that live impenitent even die so too.

(3.) The sad threatenings denounced against sinners going on in their sin, with respect to their latter end: Prov. i. 24—27, " Because I have called, and ye refused, I have stretched out my hand, and no man regarded; but ye have set at nought all my counsel, and would none of my reproof: I also will laugh at your calamity, I will mock when your fear cometh; when your fear cometh as desolation, and your destruction cometh as a whirlwind; when distress and anguish cometh upon you." Ezek. xxiv. 13, " In thy filthiness is lewdness: because I have purged thee, and thou wast not purged, thou shalt not be purged from thy filthiness any more, till I have caused my fury to rest upon thee." Now, show me one promise in all the Bible, promising the grace of repentance to those that delay, for to balance this. It is true, the gospel-offer is general, and excludes none while in this world: but O what a hazard is there, that these threatenings be accomplished to the denying the grace to lay hold on them then.

(4.) Corrupt nature sticks fast in thee; and it will harden thee in the face of death as well as it does now, unless thou get grace from above. Now, that corruption has possession long continued already, thou art sure of it; but thou hast no certainty for the grace of God to break it in thee, and work repentance in thy so long impenitent heart. And therefore I must conclude the venture to be very unequal.

(5.) Repentance is not to be wrought by the sinner's being brought to an extremity, as you may possibly imagine. Here was a man that was hanging on a cross, bleeding to death in great torment, having a present prospect of eternity before him, who could have no more pleasure in the world. But did that humble him? No, no. His heart remains obdured to the last gasp. He is going into eternity; yet he is adding sin to sin, and going out of the world as he lived in it, if not worse. We find from Matt. xxvii. 44, that after the chief priests, scribes, and elders had mocked and railed on Christ, it is added, that "the thieves also which were crucified with him" joined in the railing. Whence some think, that even the other too joined in this railing on Christ, till grace broke in upon him and overcame his nature.

(6.) The most powerful and likely means of grace will not prevail, unless accompanied with a special operation of the Spirit. This blaspheming thief was near Christ himself, and might hear his words and groans. He had the example of his companion moving him to repent. Grace was at work working wonders upon his neighbour. He had a dying preacher to call him to repent. The sun's light was eclipsed, the earth quaked, the rocks rent, the graves opened: yet for all these he died impenitent, and hard-hearted. Think on this, ye that deem it so easy to repent, if ye were come to your last.

(7.) They that delay repentance till a dying hour, readily find they have another thing to do then, than to repent; as is evident from the case of the other thief on the cross, ver. 39. "And one of the malefactors which were hanged, railed on him, saying, if thou be Christ save thyself and us." Death is the destruction of nature, and therefore nature wrestles against it, though there be no hope. This man was more concerned to get his body saved than to get his soul saved. And, alas! is not this the case of the most part at that time? They have so much ado with the disease, that they can hardly get a due concern for their souls, or a composed thought.

3. There is no evidence that this thief had before such means of grace as you have. Who can say, that ever he heard the gospel preached by Christ or any of his disciples? It is most likely he was a rake; that if he heard any thing of God, it was from the

Scribes and Pharisees at times; and may be, when he might have heard either them, or Christ and his disciples, he was about his thievish trade. Now,

1*st*, It is unreasonable to think, that it should fare at the last with those who have had means of grace all their days, and despised them, as it may do with those who never have such means till they come to die. One would think it no wonder at all, to see a man converted at his last, who gets the first notice of Christ and the way of salvation when on his death-bed. But what is that to thee, who hast all along been invited to repent, and come to Christ, but wouldst not? The former is no wonder in comparison of the latter.

2*dly*, This conversion of the thief doubtless was a perfect surprise to him, a thing he was not looking for. But thou art setting tryst with repentance at thy last hours. Can you believe, that ever this thief delayed repentance in hopes of what he met with, namely, to die on a cross with Christ, and then to feel the power of his grace? Nobody can believe it. What is his example then to thee? Is it rational for thee to expect that favour which one has sometimes been surprised with, and got when he was not looking for it?

4. This thief was converted, when by the hand of public justice he was to die. When he was made a public example to the world, and as a malefactor brought to an untimely end for his crime, he got repentance at the gallows, not on a death-bed. He was cut off perhaps in the midst of his days; at least he died not by the course of nature, nor by any sickness, but was executed for his evil deeds. And it is observable, that the one other case which looks likest to this in the Bible, was of the same sort, namely Achan's. Now,

1*st*, It is evident, that wicked men who are running on in such courses as will bring them to an untimely death, by the laws of the land, such as thieves, robbers, murderers, &c. have a fairer ground from this to delay repentance till they come to the scaffold, than you have, who are looking for a death-bed, and delay repentance till you come there. For their case is nearer akin to this than yours. But are not they most foolish if they so do, even in your eyes? No doubt they are. And so are ye in the eyes of others, whose eyes God has opened.

2*dly*, If we compare the case of this thief put to death for his crimes, and of other malefactors so dying, with the case of men that have lived impenitently dying in their beds; though grace is alike free to both, yet, humanly speaking, there is more hope of the repentance of the former than of the latter. And this I say on these three grounds.

(1) It is more easy to convince a malefactor upon the scaffold, of

his crime, and the evil of it, and of those other sins that have been the inlets to it, than to convince another of his sin upon a death-bed, as common observation sheweth. Hence our Lord says, "that the publicans and harlots go into the kingdom of God before the self-righteous Pharisees," Matth. xxi. 31. Many a time is sabbath-breaking, disobedience to parents, drunkenness, neglect of the means of grace, confessed and regretted on a scaffold, while there is not one word of them from a death-bed, in cases where there is perhaps as good ground for it. When the corruption of nature breaks out in some atrocious crime that brings a person to an untimely end, there is more access to convince them of it, than others who have the same plague in them, but it has not so appeared.

(2.) The view that the thief had of eternity upon the cross, and that other malefactors have in such a case, is more certain than what impenitent sinners generally have on a death-bed. The one see they must die without peradventure, the other have some hopes of life generally while they have breath. And so the terror of death must needs be more operative in the one than the other; forasmuch as there is such a difference in the certainty of the view of it.

(3.) If we except the time wherein both are actually grappling with death, the one with a violent death, the other with a natural one; the former have less hinderances from the body to prepare for death than the latter; forasmuch as the one is tossed with bodily sickness and indisposition, the other commonly is not.

5. The conversion of the thief on the cross was an extraordinary manifestation of our Lord's power, made for special reasons. And therefore though it shows what the Lord can do; it does not show what ordinarily he will do. Consider here, to evince this, that,

1st, It was done in such a juncture of time, as the like never was, and the like never will be again; namely, when the Lord of glory, the Saviour of the world, was actually hanging upon the cross, paying the ransom for the lost elect world; Rom. vi. 9, "Christ being raised from the dead, dieth no more; death hath no more dominion over him."

2dly, It was a wonder wrought in a time allotted in a particular manner beyond all times, for God's working wonders. The time of the Lord's giving the law on Mount Sinai, was a time of wonders; but not comparable to this. The leading wonder there was God's making his voice to be heard, and speaking forth a holy law; and it was attended with other wonders, namely, thunders, lightnings, a thick cloud upon the mount, smoke, and fire, and the sound of a terrible trumpet waxing louder and louder, Exod. xix. 16, &c. But the leading wonder on Mount Calvary was yet greater, namely, the Son of God, and Saviour of the world, hanging, groaning, dying on a cross : and therefore the attending wonders were proportionably greater. For,

(1.) The sun was under a dreadful eclipse, for the space of not a few minutes, but three hours, Matth. xxvii. 45. The eye of the visible world was struck blind at the sight.

(2.) The vail of the temple was, without hands, rent from the top to the bottom, Matth. xxvii. 51 ; to shew that by this death an end was put to the ceremonial law, and the way unto the holiest of all made open.

(3.) The earth quaked at the dreadful fact of crucifying the Lord of glory, Matth. xxvii. 51.

(4.) The hard rocks rent, upbraiding the spectators and guilty multitude with the hardness of their hearts, Matth. xxvii. 51.

(5.) The graves were opened, and many of the dead saints arose, to shew that Christ by his death had overcome the power of death over his people, Matth. xxvii. 52.

(6.) The spectators of those strange things smote their breasts, being struck to the heart, Luke xxiii. 48.

(7.) *Lastly*, The centurion and his soldiers were convinced, that he whom they had crucified was the Son of God, Matth. xxvii. 54.

Now, upon all these I would make these reflections.

[1.] Is it reasonable, because the thief was converted at the last hour, in a time that the like never was, nor will be, for thee to expect that it shall fare so with thee ? Thou mayst as well throw thyself into a burning fiery furnace, and hope to come forth safe, because Daniel and his fellows were once so delivered. Were Christ to come again, and to be crucified a second time between two malefactors, and thou wert one of them to be crucified with him, it might be that thou mightst be converted at thy last hour. And yet thou couldst not be sure ; for it might be thy lot to be the hardened one, as it was the other thief's. But since it is not so, how darest thou trust to such a late repentance ?

[2.] Is it any wise strange, that amongst all these wonders of justice, power, and faithfulness, there was one wonder of mercy upon the thief on the cross ? that the same power that was rending the rocks, did mercifully open the heart of one of those thieves to receive Christ and his grace ? But how canst thou think, that the time of thy departure will be a time of such wonders ? And if not, how canst thou deceive thyself into a delay of repentance, in expectation of receiving such a signal display of divine grace and mercy ?

[3.] Was it not very becoming the divine wisdom, that when the divine glory of the Son of God was veiled upon the cross, a ray of it should break forth in the conversion of one of two that were hanging there with him? that when his judges, and the rulers and people had got him on the cross as a malefactor, he should have his glory owned by one of those crucified with him: but what is that to thee in a day wherein it is long since Christ was set down at his Father's right hand, and his glory published through the world by the gospel?

[4.] Is it any thing strange, that when our Lord was triumphing over principalities and powers, he set up one trophy, one sign of his victory, in the field of battle? Col. ii. 15. Was it not very natural, that he who when he should be lifted up, was to draw all men after him, should actually at the time draw one after him? But what encouragement can that be to thee to delay to the last, when that nick of time is over long ago? And now there are thousands of visible monuments of Christ's conquest by his death set up, so that thou wilt never be missed, though thou die as thou livest, impenitent.

6. *Lastly*, The penitent thief on the cross was not only sincere, but he glorified Christ more in his late repentance, than thou art capable to do by thine, nay more than if thou hadst lived a penitent all thy days. For consider,

1*st*, When our Lord was in his lowest step of humiliation, he professed his faith of his divine nature, and his being King of the other world: "Lord," says he, "remember me when thou comest into thy kingdom." What wonderful faith was this, that while Christ was so low as hanging on a cross, he owns him King of heaven; that dying, he was going to receive a kingdom; that he has all power there; that he is full of mercy, compassion, and faithfulness; so that the very remembrance of him would be sufficient to secure his eternal welfare! thou mayst believe and profess all this, but never at such a time. He is now the exalted Redeemer, who has ascended far above all heavens, and sits on the right hand of God. But what is that to the glorifying of him in his lowest humiliation?

2*dly*, When others had crucified him as a malefactor, and were mocking him, and railing on him, as one that deserved not common compassion, he was praying to him, as Lord of the other world. If thou shouldst now do so too; yet remember how small a thing is that in comparison of what the good thief did in these circumstances.

Lastly, All this he did, and more, publicly before a multitude of spectators, which thou art not likely to have when thou comest to a death-bed. He justifies God before them all; he condemns himself; he does what he can to convince and convert his poor graceless companion, who possibly sinned with him as he did suffer; he condemns those that crucified Christ, and gives his public testimony against them, as men that feared not God.

To conclude this matter: Repent ye timeously, and trust not to a late repentance. Let not this example of the thief on the cross, or any thing else, make you to delay. Many a call ye have had to return to the Lord; but, alas! to the most part they have been ineffectual. God is giving us a providential call to repentance, at this time: he is saying to us, as he did to the church of Ephesus, Rev. ii. 5, "Remember therefore from whence thou art fallen, and repent, and do the first works; or else I will come unto thee quickly, and will remove thy candlestick out of its place, except thou repent." God knows what our present trial may end in. But in that dark dispensation we may clearly see that God is a jealous God, and makes people's sins to find them out. Repentance would be the most feasible means to extricate us out of our difficulties. If there were a spirit of prayer and mourning for the causes of the Lord's controversy with us, it would be a token for good. But, alas! the work of repentance for the most part is put off from time to time, till it be put off to a death-bed; and who can secure the tryst to be kept there?

There are three things I would say of death-bed repentance.

1. If it be got, it is the most unuseful repentance for God, and the most uncomfortable for one's self. Unuseful; for then men begin their work for God, when their time is ending; and so though they may be saved, yet God gets little honour from them. And uncomfortable to persons themselves; for being saved, they are saved so as by fire; they must go to heaven by the brink of hell; while they see their last sand running, and get their consciences awakened, eternity must be to them a dreadful spectacle.

2. Death-bed-repentance is seldom sincere. The king of terrors may make a Pharaoh say, I have sinned. But what sincerity is in the most part of those things that begin on death-beds, may be learned from the case of many, who being past hopes of recovery from their sickness, either as to themselves or others, do yet recover, and turn just the old men and women they were before. When the best appearances of death-bed repentance are, it is hard to make sure conclusions; but as Augustine said in such a case, *Non dico damnabitur, non dico salvabitur; sed tu, dum sanus es, pœnitentiam age.**

* *i. e.* I don't say, that such a person shall be damned, or that he shall be saved; but do thou, whilst thou art in health, mind the business of repentance.

3. *Lastly,* Many trust to deathbed repentance that never see it. Some are surprised into eternity; some are tossed so with sickness that they cannot have a composed thought; some quickly lose the use of their senses and reason; and most part die as they live: Therefore repent ye in time, and delay no more, lest ye bring the ruin on your souls that will never be recovered.

GOD'S DELAY OF EXECUTING THE SENTENCE OF CONDEMNATION AGAINST UNGODLY MEN, OFTEN MISERABLY ABUSED BY THEM.

Several sermons preached at Ettrick, in summer, 1728.

Eccl. viii. 11.

Because sentence against an evil work is not executed speedily; therefore the heart of the sons of men is fully set in them to do evil.

This book of Ecclesiastes is in a particular manner a book of providence, wherein Solomon gives his observations upon it. It is a subject that has puzzled the best of men, how to reconcile it with the being and attributes of God: but there is no inconsistency; all odds will be made even at length.

He had observed some set on high to their ruin, made rulers of others to their own destruction, to the feeding of their own lusts, and so aggravating their own condemnation, ver. 9. He had observed them live prosperously in their wickedness, die in honour, and buried magnificently, ver. 10. He opens the secret of this dispensation in the text, namely, That a reprieve is no pardon. In the words we have,

1. God's patience with, and forbearance exercised towards ungodly sinners: "Because sentence against an evil work is not executed speedily." (1.) It is supposed that sentence is passed in their case. There is a righteous sentence standing against an evil work, and the evil worker for what he has done: it is not overlooked, nor forgotten. (Heb.) doing of the evil; by which is meant an ungodly course. This is plain from 1 John iii. 8, 9, "He that committeth sin, is of the devil; for the devil sinneth from the beginning. For this purpose the Son of God was manifested, that he might destroy the works of the devil. Whosoever is born of God doth not commit sin; for his seed remaineth in him: and he can-

not sin, because he is born of God. See the sentence, Rom ii. 9, "Tribulation and anguish upon every soul of man that doth evil." (2.) The execution is oft-times delayed; it is not speedily execute. Though the word is gone out of the mouth of the Judge, he does not presently bring on the blow; he spares the criminal a while for holy ends. (3.) It supposeth, that though the execution be slow, yet it is sure, if the sentence be not got reversed, and a pardon obtained. Saying, that it is not speedily executed, he intimates that it will be executed at length.

2. The wretched abuse sinners make of this patience of God with them. "Therefore the heart of the sons of men is fully set in them to do evil." Because sentence is not executed speedily, they think it will never be executed; and so they give themselves the loose. "Their heart is fully set in them to do evil." They find providence gives them head, does not check and strike them down in their course: and so they even run away with themselves. Their impunity fills their heart for their sinful courses, that they drive on like a ship with a full sail before a brisk gale.

Three doctrines may be deduced from the words thus explained.

DOCTRINE I. There is a sentence passed in the court of heaven, and standing, against ungodly men, evil-workers, however easy they be under it for a time.

DOCTRINE II. The Lord oftentimes does not soon come to the execution of the sentence against ungodly men, evil-workers; but delays it for a time.

DOCTRINE III. God's delay of execution is often miserably abused by sinners, to the filling of their hearts to do evil, and sinning more and more.

I shall handle each of these doctrines in order.

DOCTRINE I. There is a sentence passed in the court of heaven, and standing, against ungodly men, evil-workers, however easy they be under it for a time.

In prosecuting this doctrine, I shall,

I. Shew, that there is a sentence passed in the court of heaven, and standing, against ungodly men, evil-workers.

II. Explain the nature of this sentence.

III. Make some practical improvement of the subject

I. I shall shew, that there is a sentence passed in the court of heaven, and standing, against ungodly men, evil-workers.

1. They are already judged and condemned of God: John iii. 18, "He that believeth not, is condemned already, because he hath not believed in the name of the only begotten Son of God." Ungodly

men, evil-workers, are unbelievers; and being unbelievers, they have not the benefit of absolution by Christ: so they are under condemnation of the law for their evil works. For whom the gospel doth not absolve, the law doth condemn.

2. Only those that are in Christ, are not under condemnation; and their freedom from it is of no older date than their believing: Rom. viii. 1, " Their is no condemnation to them which are in Christ Jesus." But evil-workers are not in Christ, 1 John iii. 8, 9, fore-cited. If they were in Christ, they would be new creatures; 2 Cor. v. 17, " For if any man be in Christ, he is a new creature." Therefore they are still under condemnation.

3. They are in a state of death, dead in sin, Eph. ii. 1. They who are morally dead in sin, being without a principle of spiritual life, Eph. iv. 18, are legally dead too; they are dead men in law, under a sentence of death, John v. 24. Hence they are called children of wrath, of hell, &c.

4. The power that Satan has over them, proves this. They are close prisoners, bound hand and foot, Is. lxi. 1. Satan is the keeper of the prison, Heb. ii. 14; and they are under his power, Acts xxvi. 18. What gives him the power over them, but that they are condemned in law? Let the sentence be reversed, and he has them no more under his power, 1 Cor. xv. 56.

5. *Lastly*, The spirit of bondage witnesseth the truth of this, convincing the sinner that he is a dead man, Rom. vii. 9, and that he stands in need of a remission, chap. iii. 19. This testimony is true; for it is the testimony of the Spirit of God, whereby he brings sinners to see their need of Christ.

II. To explain the nature of this sentence, consider,

1. Every evil work is a breach of God's law; and every sinful thought, word, or action is an evil work: 1 John iii. 4. " Whosoever committeth sin, transgresseth also the law: for sin is the transgression of the law." No man is lord of himself but is answerable to God for every action of his life: and being guilty, if out of Christ, he is liable to vengeance, under the curse; if in Christ, he is liable to temporal strokes. So all ungodly ones, evil-workers, are liable to the curse for their sins.

2. The law is the accuser, that accuseth the sinner of rebellion against God, and demandeth vengeance on him, John v. 45. Every command broken by the sinner accuseth him before God; and as many breaches as he has made of it, as many articles there are of the libel against him. And though these be innumerable to men, and many of them unknown to them; they are not so unto an omniscient God.

3. God is the judge that judgeth and passeth the sentence against the guilty, Psal. l. 6. And he is a judge whom no artful conceal-ment can beguile. He cannot be blinded, bribed, or biassed, 1 Pet. i. 17. His sentence, hower severe, is always righteous, Rev. xvi. 7. And there lies no appeal from his tribunal; for there is none above him who is the Most High. Only, while the sinner is, in this world, there is access to a remission in Christ.

4. The sentence is a sentence of death, Gen. ii. 17; death in its full latitude, comprehending all miseries of soul and body; eternal death, in which the gnawing worm never dies, nor is the fire quenched. The sentences of men are at most the death of the body: but his sentence adjudgeth the soul to die eternally. The reason is, the infinite dignity of the divine Majesty offended by sin.

5. The grounds of this heavy sentence, are the transgressions of God's holy law: Gal. iii. 10. " Cursed is every one that continueth not in all things which are written in the book of the law to do them." The holy law is a transcript of the purity of the divine na-ture; in it he hath set forth his own image. That image the sinner does what he can to deface, by violating the law: but God will magnify the law; and make it honourable, though in the destruction of the sinner.

The grounds of it more particularly are,

1*st*, The sin of nature, original sin imputed, Rom. v. 12; and ori-ginal sin inherent, that corrupt frame of soul that is natural to us, whereby we are prone to evil and averse to good, Gen. vi. 5. By reason of this we come into the world under the sentence of death. And as serpents and vipers are objects whose destruction men seek on the first sight of them, because of their poisonous nature; so it fares with men, the very first sight of whom, in respect of their original sin, is loathsome unto a holy God, and thereby they become objects fit only for destruction.

2*dly*, The sins of the heart, Psal. xxiv. 4; Matt. v. 28, 29. Heart-sins are not liable to man's judgment: but how can they escape the judgment of God, to whose all seeing eye our hearts are just as open as our lives? He sees the rottenness that is within the whited sepulchers, and passes his sentence against lusts of covet-ousness, uncleanness, malice, revenge, &c. burning within the heart, as well as against the same defiling the conversation.

3*dly* The sins of the tongue, Matt. xii. 37. It is a channel by which the heart vents much of its inbred corruption, contempt of God, &c. Jude 15, in his mocking, maligning, and running down seriousness, and agenting the cause of irreligion; and contempt of our neighbour, in railing, reproaching, obscenity, lying, &c.;

which may shew why the rich man in hell is represented as seeking water to cool his tongue.

4*thly*, The sins of the life, wicked actions, whether of impiety against God, unrighteousness against men, or intemperance against ourselves, Jude 15. None of all these will escape the judgment of God, however craftily they be managed, whatever fair colours be drawn over them: Eccl. 12, ult "For God shall bring every work into judgment, with every secret thing, whether it be good, or whether it be evil." Sinners may forget them, and let them slip out of mind : but "the Lord hath sworn by the excellency of Jacob, Surely I will never forget any of their works," Amos viii. 7.

5*thly*, Omissions of duty, Matt. xxv. 41, &c. Men will find sentence passed on them by a just God, not only for the ill they have done, but for the good they were obliged to have done, but did it not. The man that hid his talent, and improved it not for his Lord, is doomed to outer darkness, Matt. xxv. 24, 30.

6. This sentence against the ungodly is openly pronounced in the word : Rom. ii. 8, 9, "But unto them that are contentious, and do not obey the truth, but obey unrighteousness : indignation, and wrath ; tribulation and anguish upon every soul of man that doth evil." God speaks from heaven to men, Heb. xii. 25; not by a voice coming through the clouds, but by his voice in the written word, 2 Kings xxii. 19, compared with ver. 11. The Bible is God's word to us, whereby he is speaking to us, and will speak to men unto the end of the world, either absolution or condemnation according to their state.

7. It is registered there too; Gen. ii. 17, "In the day that thou eatest thereof, thou shalt surely die." Ezek. xviii. 4, "The soul that sinneth, it shall die." The Scripture is the records of the court of heaven, where the ungodly may read their doom, and see the sentence standing against them. And that certainly is one of the causes of the neglect of the Scriptures in our day; for in it "the wrath of God is revealed from heaven against all ungodliness, and unrighteousness of men, who hold the truth in unrighteousness," Rom. i. 18. Ahab hated Micajah, because he never spake good of him. The Scripture never speaks good of a man that is wedded to his lusts, and has no will to part with his beloved liberty in the way of sin ; and therefore he hates or neglects it.

8. It is secretly intimated by the conscience sometimes, 1 John iii. 20. Conscience is God's deputy within the man ; and when his corruption drives him full to do an ill work, and when he has done it, to defend it; conscience will be condemning it, and him too, from the holy law, Rom. ii. 15. And when it is thoroughly

awakened, it will so pronounce the sentence against the man as will fill him with the greatest terror.

9. It will be openly pronounced before all the world at the last day: Matt. xxv. 41, "Then shall he say also unto them on the left hand, Depart from me, ye cursed, into everlasting fire, prepared for the devil and his angels." Where it is observable, that they are declared cursed and condemned ones, before that solemn publishing of the sentence against them. For none will be condemned then, but such as are in this world before that in this life condemned already.

10. *Lastly,* Howbeit, the time of the execution of the sentence, in particular, is not now intimated to the sinner. The Lord keeps that a secret, that sinners may not adventure to live a moment in the state of condemnation; but not knowing but it may be executed next moment, they may not put off a moment the suing for a remission.

USE 1. Of Information. Hence learn,

1. The state of every ungodly person, worker of iniquity, and all unbelievers, is a miserable state, a state of condemnation. They are as really under a sentence of death, as ever any malefactor was: John iii. 18, "He that believeth not, is condemned already; because he hath not believed in the name of the only begotten Son of God." Think on this, ye young and old ungodly ones: though the sentence is not executed against you, it is passed on you; look into your Bible, and see it.

2. As silent as God sits on heaven, while sinners on earth are neglecting and affronting him, he is no idle spectator of their way and manner of life: Psal. l. 21, "These things hast thou done, and I kept silence: thou thoughtest that I was altogether such a one as thyself: but I will reprove thee, and set them in order before thine eyes." He has sentenced them, and "sees their day is coming," Psal. xxxvii. 13. They have their sinning day, and God sees their day of count and reckoning is coming on, wherein every item shall be distinctly charged on them: Eccl. xi. 9, "Know thou, that for all these things God will bring thee into judgment." They laugh at the evil day, because they do not see it come; God laughs at them, because he sees it coming; and his will be when theirs is done, Prov. i. 26, when he will laugh at their calamity, and mock when their fear cometh.

3. It is not strange, that the world is filled with the noise of men's lusts and ungodly lives. If ye were gone into a prison filled with condemned men, ye would think it melancholy indeed, but not strange to hear the iron chains rattling in every part of the room.

This world is such a place, crowded with condemned people; unmortified lusts are the chains on them: and that is the reason of
the grating noise which the serious godly hear from every corner.
And the jailor, the devil, is going among them.

4. *Lastly*, No wonder that most men love this life, so as to loath
exchanging it for another; Psal. lv. 23, "But God shall bring them
down into the pit of destruction." The prison is a heavy place to
the condemned man; but to go out of it is more so, for that is to go
to execution, Jer. xvii. 11. Death brings the execution of the
sentence.

USE 2. Of trial. Try whether that sentence is standing against
you, or whether it is reversed, and ye justified.

To move you to put this to the question, consider,

1. One thing is sure, that once it was passed and standing against
you: Eph. ii. 3, "And were by nature the children of wrath, even
as others. Gal. iii. 10, "Cursed is every one that continueth not in
all things which are written in the book of the law to do them."
Compared with Rom. iii. 19, "Now we know that what things
soever the law saith, it saith to them who are under the law; that
every mouth may be stopped, and all the world may become guilty
before God." Now, what course have ye taken to get this sentence taken off? and if you have been aiming at it, have ye carried
it?

2. As your state is in this life, condemned or justified, so it will
be determined at death and judgment: Eccl. ix. 10, "Whatsoever
thy hand findeth to do, do it with thy might; for there is no work,
nor device, nor knowledge, nor wisdom in the grave whither thou
goest. Now, there is access for a remission; but when death comes,
there will be no more for ever.

3. Men are apt to mistake in this point. Many draw an absol-
viture from the sentence for themselves, which God will never set
his seal to: Luke xvi. 15, "Christ said unto them, Ye are they
which justify yourselves before men; but God knoweth your hearts:
for that which is highly esteemed amongst men, is abomination in
the sight of God." Is xliv. 20, "He feedeth on ashes: a deceived
heart hath turned him aside, that he cannot deliver his soul, nor
say, Is there not a lie in my right hand? The foolish virgins
called themselves the Bridegroom's friends; but he shut the door
on them as his enemies.

4. *Lastly*, A mistake here is very fatal. By it men let the time
of obtaining a remission slip. The oil might have been got for the
lamps, if they had missed it timely. It brings a ruining surprise:
dreaming of peace, they are awaked with the noise of war for ever.

MARK 1. They that never saw themselves in a state of condemnation, are under it to this day. For they are strangers to the very first work of the Spirit, conviction, John xvi. 8, "The law is our schoolmaster, to bring us unto Christ, that we might be justified by faith, Gal. iii. 24. They that have never been at the law's school, to learn that they are cursed and condemned sinners by nature, are not Christ's disciples.

MARK 2. They only are absolved, who laying hold on Christ in the covenant of grace have applied to the law's sentence of condemnation against them, the righteousness of Christ wrought by him, and offered to and accepted by them. Hence says the apostle, Phil. iii. 7, 8, "But what things were gain to me, those I counted loss for Christ. Yea, doubtless, and I count all things but loss, for the excellency of the knowledge of Christ Jesus my Lord:—and do count them but dung that I may win Christ." They continue not in mere suspense, but renouncing self-confidence, law-confidence, and creature confidence, have betaken themselves to him as their only refuge, casting anchor on the promise of the gospel.

MARK 3. If the condemning power of sin is removed, the reigning power of sin is removed too, and contrariwise: Rom. vi. 14, "For sin shall not have dominion over you: for ye are not under the law, but under grace." If the condemned man has got his remission, he is taken out of his irons, and his prison, and the power of the jailor. The chains of reigning lusts rattling about thee, declare thee a condemned man still; but it is otherwise with the pardoned, Rom. viii. 1, 2, "There is no condemnation to them which are in Christ Jesus, who walk not after the flesh, but after the Spirit. For the law of the Spirit of life, in Christ Jesus, hath made me free from the law of sin and death." If ye are justified, ye are washed, 1 Cor. vi. 9, 10, 11.

MARK 4. If the sentence be reversed, ye will be habitually tender in your conscience with respect to temptations, sin and duty, and appearances of evil. Hence Paul could say, Acts xxiv. 16, "Herein do I exercise myself, to have always a conscience void of offence toward God, and toward men." The man who under the sentence of death, has obtained a remission, will readily fear falling into the snare again. Hence we find this was Hezekiah's exercise, Is. xxxviii. 17, "Behold, for peace I had great bitterness; but thou hast in love to my soul delivered it from the pit of corruption: for thou hast cast all my sins behind thy back." Ver. 15, "What shall I say? he hath both spoken unto me, and himself hath done it: I shall go softly all my years in the bitterness of my soul." Absolved persons may be guilty of acts of untenderness; but habitual untenderness is a black mark of condemnation.

MARK ult. The fruits of faith in a holy life follow the reversing of the sentence. We are justified by faith without works; but the faith that justifies, produces good works. Hence we read, Acts xv. 2, of purifying the heart by faith. If the curse is removed, the fruits of the Spirit will spring up in the soul, Gal. v. 22, 23, "love, joy, peace, long-suffering, gentleness, goodness, faith, meekness, temperance." The apostle James shews that faith not to be true, that is not attended with the fruits of holiness."

Now, if the sentence once standing against you is reversed, then,

1. Love the Lord, who freely gave you your remission, instead of leading you forth to execution; as did the woman of whom our Lord says, Luke vii. 47, "Her sins, which are many, are forgiven; for she loved much." Remember the day when ye stood self-condemned and law-condemned before the Lord, and he said, Job xxxiii. 24, "Deliver him from going down to the pit, I have found a ransom."

2. Pity and be concerned for those that are as yet under the condemnation which ye are freed from, Tit. iii. 2, 3. Where people's contempt and disdain have the heels of their pity, compassion, and concern for the welfare and recovery of sinners, it is a sad sign; speaking forth more of pride and presumption, than of themselves being in a state of remission.

3. Walk humbly and tenderly. The remembrance of the sentence of death sometime lying on you, may humble you while ye live. It sets us ill to be proud and conceity, who owe our life to a remission. Stand aloof from the deadly snare; a pardoning God has said, "Go, and sin no more," John viii. 11.

4. Bear your troubles and trials in a world patiently. Your life was forfeited, and that is safe by grace. Why does a living man complain? This is a day wherein the Lord seems to be rising up to plead against the generation, bringing on common calamity. Take thankfully what falls to your share of it, in consideration that the sentence against your soul is reversed. If the seed should rot under the clod, and the beasts of the field perish under the stroke; kiss the rod, and be thankful, that the execution is not upon yourselves.

5. *Lastly*, Be of a forgiving disposition: Eph. iv. 32, "Be ye kind one to another, tender-hearted, forgiving one another, even as God for Christ's sake hath forgiven you." The Saviour that brought in remission of sins, binds us to love our enemies; and the bitter revengeful spirit against others speaks us unforgiven, Matth. vi. 15, "If ye forgive not men their trespasses, neither will your Father forgive your trespasses."

But if ye are of those against whom the sentence still stands in the court of heaven, lay the matter to heart, and consider it as a most heavy case, as it is indeed, deserving tears of blood. And so I proceed to

USE 3. Of Lamentation. We may here lament over the case of every ungodly one, and natural man. The state of one under sentence of death, is a lamentable case. O ungodly sinner, however easy thou art, God's law has condemned thee, and thou art under the sentence of eternal death, John iii. 36, "He that believeth not the Son, shall not see life; but the wrath of God abideth on him." See thy heavy case in this glass.

1. You are forfeited of your covenant-right to the creatures, as a condemned person. Whether thou hast little or much in the world, it is a sorry right you have to it; a mere providential right, such as a condemned man to his meat, till the day of execution come. Therefore "a little that a righteous man hath, is better than the riches of many wicked," Psal. xxxiv. 16. There is little satisfaction in that.

2. God is your enemy, befriend you who will, John iii. 36. forecited. He bears a legal enmity against thee, as a just judge against a condemned man. Ye can have no communion with him: Amos iii. 3, "Can two walk together, except they be agreed?" All comfortable intercourse betwixt God and thy soul, is drowned in the gulf of thy state of condemnation. There can be no peace between God and you. To allude to the conference between Joram and Jehu, 2 Kings ix. 22, "And it came to pass when Joram saw Jehu, that he said, Is it peace, Jehu? And he answered, What peace, so long as the whoredoms of thy mother Jezebel, and her witchcrafts are so many?" How can they have peace with God, whom his law condemns? What peace ye have in your consciences, God allows not, Is. lvii. 21.

3. Nothing you do can be acceptable to God; there is a lasting cloud over your heads that never clears: Psal. vii. 11, "God is angry with the wicked every day." While the condemning curse of the law lies on a man, it blasts all the good he does: Tit. i. 15, "Unto them that are defiled, and unbelieving, is nothing pure; but even their mind and conscience is defiled." Hag. ii. 12, 14, "If one bear holy flesh in the skirt of his garment, and with his skirt do touch bread, or pottage, or wine, or oil, or any meat, shall it be holy? And the priests answered and said, No. Then answered Haggai, and said, So is this people, and so is this nation before me, saith the Lord; and so is every work of their hands, and that which they offer there is unclean." It mars sanctifying influences,

without which there can be no fruit, John xv. 5, "for without me ye can do nothing." Hence all ye do is turned to sin.

4. The sentence against you is confirmed daily. The truth of God confirms it: Num. xxiii. 19, "God is not a man, that he should lie, neither the son of man, that he should repent: hath he said, and shall he not do it? or hath he spoken, and shall he not make it good? And the cords of thy guilt are growing stronger and stronger; for the grounds of condemnation against thee are multiplying; while none of the old debt is removed, but new is still contracted. And though one may think, that it is but dying for all; yet the punishment will be increased, as evil works are; for men will be rewarded according to their deeds.

5. Justice craves execution against thee. There was a cry to heaven against Cain, and against Sodom: and so there is against every ungodly sinner, Jer. ix. 9, "Shall I not visit them for these things? saith the Lord: shall not my soul be avenged on such a nation as this?" Mercy may suspend execution a while against the ungodly; but if they continue in that state, it cannot reverse it; since God cannot cease to be just.

6. All is ready for the execution. The bow is bent to let fly the arrows of wrath against thee, the arrows of death, Psal. vii. 12, 13. The pile of fire is set on, Is. xxx. 33, "For Tophet is ordained of old: yea, for the king it is prepared; he hath made it deep and large: the pile thereof is fire and much wood, the breath of the Lord, like a stream of brimstone, doth kindle it." When thou liest down, thou hast no security, that it shall not be executed ere thou arise, &c.

7. *Lastly,* Thy life depends, as to thee, only on God's long-tried patience and long-suffering, procuring thy reprieve from day to day, if so thou wilt sue out thy pardon. As secure as thou art, the sword of justice hangs over thy head, by the worn hair of long-tired patience; which if once broken, thou art gone for ever.

USE ult. Of Exhortation. Wherefore bestir yourselves to get out of the state of condemnation, to get the sentence reversed.

MOTIVE 1. It is a sad and miserable life to live in the state of condemnation. For in effect such a life is a continued death. (1.) It is a dishonourable life. Condemnation fixes a blot and stain on man, speaks him guilty of crimes for which he is not worthy to live. And surely the judgment of God is according to truth. (2.) It is an uncomfortable life: Is. lvii. 21, "There is no peace, saith my God, to the wicked." There is enough in it to squeeze the sap out of all created comforts; and for the con-

solations of God, they can have none of them, Amos iii. 3, " Can
two walk together, except they be agreed?" The joy and comfort of a natural man is but like that of a madman; and so when
he comes to himself, all is swallowed up in that, he is a condemned
man. This the prodigal found, Luke xv. 17, "And when he
came to himself, he said, How many hired servants of my father's
have bread enough and to spare, and I perish with hunger! (3.)
It is an unsafe life; John iii. 36, " He that believeth not the Son,
shall not see life; but the wrath of God abideth on him." Amidst
all thy mirth and jollity, the sword of justice is hanging over thy
head by a hair, and every moment, for all that thou knowest, it
may fall, and cleave thee asunder. This our Lord threatens in the
parable of the wicked servant, Matth. xxiv. 50, 51, " The Lord of
that servant shall come in a day when he looketh not for him, and
in an hour that he is not aware of; and shall cut him asunder, and
appoint him his portion with the hypocrites: there shall be weeping
and gnashing of teeth."

MOTIVE 2. The reversing of the sentence by a remission, is not so
easily obtained as men are apt to imagine. Many think there is no
more ado, but after a careless graceless life, when they come to die,
to commend their souls to God, with a " God have mercy on me;"
and all will be safe. But they that get out a remission, get it so
as they are taught other thoughts of it. Hence is that exclamation
of the church, Micah vii. 18, " Who is a God like unto thee, that
pardoneth iniquity, and passeth by the transgression of the remnant
of his heritage? he retaineth not his anger for ever, because he de-
lighteth in mercy." Consider,

1st, Sin is the greatest of evils, the deepest of all stains to wash
out. Fair words, nay tears, nay not the blood of bulls and goats,
not the blood of one's own body will wash it out; only the blood of
the Son of God: Heb. xi. 22, " Without shedding of blood is no remission." Compared with 1 John i. 7, "The blood of Jesus Christ
his Son cleanseth us from all sin." Sin is the most contrary to
God's nature: Hab. i. 13, " Thou art of purer eyes than to behold
evil, and canst not look on iniquity." And therefore it is the object
of his greatest loathing. Going on in sin, thou art engaged against
all the attributes of God. Sin has marred the whole frame of God's
workmanship, provoking him to break it in pieces. Can it be easy
to get all this buried in forgetfulness with a jealous God?

2dly, God's giving remissions, is one of his greatest works.
Hence is that prayer of Moses, Num. xiv. 17, 19, " And now, I beseech thee, let the power of my Lord be great, according as thou
hast spoken. Pardon, I beseech thee, the iniquity of this people,

according unto the greatness of thy mercy, and as thou hast forgiven this people, from Egypt even until now." This is a work greater than the making of a world. That was done by a word spoken But in this case, justice stands up for satisfaction, truth for the honour of a broken law, and wisdom finds a way for mercy only by the blood of Christ: John iii. 16, " God so loved the world, that he gave his only begotten Son, that whosoever believeth in him, should not perish, but have everlasting life."

3*dly*, Sad breakings of heart do sinners ordinarily endure, ere they being once touched with sense of sin, get the pardon of it. This was the case of Peter's hearers, Acts ii. 37, " They were pricked in their heart, and said unto Peter, and to the rest of the apostles, Men and brethren, what shall we do ?" Paul can tell you from his experience of the terror of the Lord ; David of broken bones. However lightly ye think now of the way of coming at it ; a medicine given you for sweating out the poison of sin, will readily make you sick at heart, and perhaps bring you to the last gasp, Is. xxxiii. 24.

MOTIVE 3. Howbeit, God is now on a throne of grace to grant remissions: 2 Cor. v. 19, " God is in Christ, reconciling the world unto himself, not imputing their trespasses unto them." Ye may get a pardon now in the Lord's own way : Is. lv. 7, " Let the wicked forsake his way, and the unrighteous man his thoughts : and let him return unto the Lord, and he will have mercy upon him ; and to our God, for he will abundantly pardon." Heaven's white flag of peace yet hangs out, the market of free grace stands open, an indemnity is proclaimed in the gospel : Acts xiii. 38, " Be it known unto you, men and brethren, that through this man is preached unto you the forgiveness of sins."

MOTIVE 4. *Lastly*, Access to remissions will not last: Is. lv. 6, " Seek ye the Lord while he may be found, call ye upon him while he is near." Abused patience will break out into fury : Luke xiii. 24, 25. " Strive to enter in at the strait gate : for many, I say unto you, will seek to enter in, and shall not be able. When once the master of the house is risen up, and hath shut to the door, and ye begin to stand without, and to knock at the door, saying, Lord, Lord, open unto us ; and he shall answer, and say unto you, I know you not whence you are." Beware ye sit not your day of grace, and delay not till ye will find no place for repentance : Luke xiv. 24, " For I say unto you, that none of those men which were bidden, shall taste of my supper."

OBJECTION. My sins are great. ANSWER. Neither the greatness multitude, nor backsliding into them will hinder . Is. i. 18. " Come

now and let us reason together, saith the Lord: though your sins
be as scarlet, they shall be as white as now; though they be red like
crimson, they shall be as wool." Is. lv. 7. "Let the wicked forsake his way, and the unrighteous man his thoughts: and let him
return unto the Lord, and he will have mercy upon him; and to
our God, for he will abundantly pardon." Jer. iii. 22. "Return,
ye backsliding children, and I will heal your backslidings." The
Lord has set up instances of pardoning mercy, that none may despair;
as Adam, Manasseh, Paul, and the Jews, crucifiers of Christ.

DIRECTION 1. Be sensible of your sin; of the evil of it; of the
mischief done to yourselves, and the injury and dishonour done to
God. Look to the law, the justice of God, &c.

DIRECTION 2. Go to God, and confess your sins fully and freely:
and condemn yourselves, acknowledging yourselves justly condemned
by the law, and God to be righteous if he should execute the sentence.

DIRECTION ult. Look to Jesus Christ the propitiation held forth
to you in the gospel, his unspotted righteousness offered to you, and
the covert of his blood, the retiring place for safety to guilty creatures. Believe the gospel, that these are made over to you therein,
and take possession thereof, by trusting wholly thereon to your remission, and the santification of your nature; John iii. 16. "God so
loved the world, that he gave his only begotten Son, that whosoever
believeth in him, should not perish but have everlasting life." So
shall ye be united to Christ by faith.

Take that advice, which the servants of Benhadad offered to their
master, 1 Kings xx. 31. Put on the sackcloth of deep humiliation,
ropes about your necks, acknowledging ye are worthy of death,
and go forth to Christ by faith; for the King of Zion is a merciful king, and will save your life.

DOCTRINE II. The Lord oftentimes does not soon come to the
execution of the sentence against ungodly men, evil-workers; but
delays it for a time.

In prosecuting this doctrine, we shall,

I. Take a view of the method of Providence in this matter.

II. Account for this slow method of Providence.

III. Make application of the subject.

I. We shall take a view of the method of Providence in this matter. There is a twofold method of Providence with the ungodly,
evil-workers, in respect of execution against them; namely, a swift
and a slow method.

First, There is a swift method the Lord sometimes takes with sinners: Mal. iii. 5. "I will come near to you to judgment, and I will be a swift witness against the sorcerers," &c. Sinners adventure on evil works; and God sentences them for them presently, and pursues them hard with execution, without delay. (1.) Sometimes the sinner has an ill work in design, and the Lord counts his will for the deed, and prevents by a speedy execution; as in Haman's case. He hatched the mischief, but he did not see it come forth. (2.) Sometimes the sinner is in actual motion to the ill work, and execution is done on him ere he get it performed. So it fared with the rebellious Israelites, in their attempting to go into the promised land, Num. xiv. 44, 45. And so it fared with Jereboam, putting forth his hand to lay hold on the prophet, 1 Kings xiii. 4; and with Uzziah having the censer in his hand, 2 Chron. xxvi. 19. (3.) Sometimes the execution trysts with the very doing of the ill work, so that the sinner is taken away with the stroke in his sin. Thus fared it with Nadab and Abihu offering strange fire, Lev. x. 1, 2; with Zimri and Cozbi cut off in the act of uncleanness, Num. xxv. 8; and with Herod, who was eaten up of worms for his Atheism and blasphemy, Acts xii. 23. (4.) Sometimes as the ill work is done out and ended, the execution begins. So it fared with Sennacherib's blasphemous letter. He had writ it, and it was read; so his sin was completed; and that very night the Lord smote his army, and soon after himself, 2 Kings xix. 14, 35. &c. (5.) Sometimes the execution keeps pace with the ill work, and the one goes on as the other does; judgment in the several degrees following hard at the heels of the sin. So it fared with Hiel, in his building of Jericho, 1 Kings xvi. ult. (6.) Sometimes execution begins with the sinner's beginning to reap the fruit of his sin when he leans upon his wall, a serpent bites him. So it fared with Ahab taking possession of Naboth's vineyard, 1 Kings xxi. 18, 19. And so it fared with the lusters in the wilderness, Psal. lxxviii. 30, 31. (7.) *Lastly,* Sometimes when one's sin begins to work, in its bitter fruits and effects on others, it recoils on the sinner himself. So it fared with Judas the traitor, Matt. xxvii. 3, 4, 5. It is a sport to some to do mischief to others; but ere all be done, it may, in the just judgment of God, come as heavy on themselves as on their neighbour.

Secondly, There is a slow method the Lord takes oftentimes with sinners, Neh. ix. 17. They commit their evil works; the sentence is presently passed for them: but then the execution is delayed, Psal. l. 21. And that is what is particularly noticed in our text. Concerning this method I offer these observes.

1. The sinner may get his evil work contrived and accomplished,

without any let in this way from Heaven, by any execution against him. There is a God in heaven who has his eye upon him all along; but that God keeps silence, and lets the sinner take his swing, Psal. l. 21. He could cut him off from the purposes of his heart, and break his arm, that he should not accomplish his work : but he does it not.

2. The ill work being done without let, the sinner may also for a time pass unpunished, and as little notice may seem to be taken of it, as if there were not a God to judge upon the earth, Ezek. ix. 9. There are times wherein holy Providence, as it were, winks at ungodly sinners, Acts xvii. 30. Hence God is said to awake to judgment, when that time is over, Psal. vii. 6.

3. Yea, ill works may not only for a time escape unpunished, but undiscovered too, Hos. xii. 7, 8; Prov. xxx. 20. There are many abominations that appear with open face in the world; but there are perhaps more that are not discovered, being reserved to the judgment of the great day, 1 Tim. v. 21; Rom. ii. 16. An omniscient God could pull the vail off them, but in the slow method it is long a-doing.

4. Sinners finding it go thus, encourage themselves in evil, repeat their evils works, add sin to sin, and give themselves the loose in their sinful courses. This is observed in our text. None go to the highest pitch of wickedness all of a sudden, but by degrees.* Ill works at first have a terror about them, and the sinner trembles under some fearful expectation at first: but a long-suffering God strikes not, thence the sinner gathers courage, Psal. lxiv. 5. and ventures again, and the terror wears off by degress.

5. Nay sinners may prosper in an ill course. So far may they be from execution done against them, that they may thrive in the world in it: Psal. xxxvii. 35, " I have seen the wicked in great power, and spreading himself like a green bay-tree." The sun of worldly prosperity may shine light and warm on men in a course of sin, gone away from God, and God from them. Yea, objects of God's indignation may in that respect be treated as if they were the darlings of Heaven ; and the objects of God's special love, as if they were the buts of his wrath : Eccl. viii. 14, " There is a vanity which is done upon the earth, that there be just men unto whom it happeneth according to the work of the wicked : again, there be wicked men to whom it happeneth according to the work of the righteous." This has been sometimes puzzling to the saints, as to Jeremiah, See chap. xii. 1, 2.

---

* *Nemo repente sit turpissimus.*

6. More than that, they may prosper by their ill works, they may enjoy the fruits of their sin, and thrive by their ill courses; as Ephraim did, Hos. xii. 7, 8. Riches are called the mammon of unrighteousness, because ofttimes they are got together by unrighteousness. Many a fair estate, and great worldly wealth has been got together by oppression; yea the foundation of some has been laid in blood, Hab. ii. 12. A plain evidence, that men may not only prosper in, but by sin.

7. Sinners may get a long time of it, wherein they sin, and God spares still. The old world got a long day of 120 years. Job observes, that the wicked may live, and become old, and continue prosperous too, Job xxi. 7, and Is. lxv. 20. Sometimes God quickly cuts off men in a course of sin: but it is not always so; but men may grow gray-headed in the way of wickedness.

8. The Lord may seem to be in his way to execute the sentence sometimes, and yet may give another delay; his hand stretched out, he may withdraw again, Psal. lxxviii. 38. Criminals may be set on the brow of the hill, and yet be returned safe, and make a very ill use of the deliverance, turning worse on the back of it. The 120 years being out, the old world got seven days more respite, and they gave themselves the loose. See Matt. xxiv. 38.

9. When execution is at length begun, it may be carried on very leisurely for a time: the drops may come very few and soft before the shower, Is. ix. 1. God may deal very gently with impenitent sinners, even when he is risen up against them, before he come to the full execution. God's judgments coming with iron hands, may yet proceed with leaden feet in slow pace.

10. *Lastly*, More than all that, the execution may be entirely put off during this life. Men may live wickedly and prosperously, die peaceably, and be buried honourably; and so would wholly escape with their ill works, were it not that there is another world and an after-reckoning, and that there is no delay of execution there. This is plain from Eccl. viii. 10, "I saw the wicked buried, who had come and gone from the place of the holy, and they were forgotten in the city where they had so done." Luke xvi. 19, 22, "There was a certain rich man, which was clothed in purple and fine linen, and fared sumptuously every day. The rich man also died, and was buried." Psal. lxxiii. 4, "There are no bands in death: but their strength is firm." Sometimes God makes the world witness to the execution of the sentence against an ill work: but oft-times men get out of the world without it, in this slow method of providence.

II. We shall account for this slow method of providence. And there is much need to do it, because there is a mystery of providence in it that is not easy to unriddle, and among men there are sad blunders about it. And,

1. It is wrested by many a sinner in his own case, to his own ruin, Prov. i. 32. We naturally have such high thoughts of the world's smiles, that we are apt to imagine God thinks highly of them too, and that he expresses his special love and kindness by them. But quite the contrary: Rev. iii. 19, "As many as I love, I rebuke and chasten." Hence a prosperous sinner can hardly imagine himself not to be a favourite of Heaven, at least cannot think God is so angry with his way as some would give out; and so he continues secure in his course, Psal. l. 21.

2. Being misunderstood, it is ruining to many spectators, and is in hazard of turning them atheistical, and contemners of religion: Mal. iii. 14, 15, " Ye have said, It is vain to serve God: and what profit is it, that we have kept his ordinance, and that we have walked mournfully before the Lord of hosts? And now we call the proud happy: yea, they that work wickedness are set up; yea, they that tempt God are even delivered." There are many who have no inward principle of religion. Now, when these see that there is worldly advantage to be got by it, they embrace it, like the mixed multitude from Egypt: but when they see the way of wickedness prosperous, and sinners to keep the road for all the threatenings against them, and the godly afflicted and bowed down for all the promises to them; they are ready to think, that the threatenings and promises of the word are both but empty sounds, and that they see so.

3. There is a difficulty in it, that has puzzled many a great saint, and made him to stagger. So ready are we to walk by sense, not by faith. This was a knotty piece of the book of providence to Jeremiah, though he resolved to believe over the belly of sense, Jer. xii. 1, 2; and to Habakkuk, chap. i. 2, 3, 4. It had almost carried Asaph quite off his feet, Psal. lxxiii. 2—13, 14.

4. There being a darkness on the minds of all men with respect to the methods of divine procedure, they are apt to imagine an inconsistency of this method of providence with the perfections attributed to God. And there are four divine perfections, that are apt to run a risk with poor sinners blind and rash in judging.

1st, His omniscience, whereby he seeth and noticeth all things done in the world, Prov. xv. 3, " The eyes of the Lord are in every place, beholding the evil and the good." But when men themselves are conscious of their own wickedness, and yet see that God does not proceed against them for it, they are apt to say, as Ezek. ix. 9,

" The 'Lord hath forsaken the earth, and the Lord seeth not."
So the Psalmist represents men going on in their wickedness, secure
as to any notice to be taken of it from heaven, Psal. xciv. 5, 6, 7,
" They break in pieces thy people, O Lord, and afflict thine heritage. They slay the widow and the stranger, and murder the
fatherless. Yet they say, The Lord shall not see: neither shall
the God of Jacob regard it." Therefore Job asserts it on that occasion, chap. xxiv. 1, " Why, seeing times are not hidden from the
Almighty, do they that know him, not see his days ?

2dly, His holiness, whereby he is pure in himself, and cannot
but hate all impurity and sin in his creatures. It is certain that it
is so. The angels proclaim it, Is. vi. 3, " Holy, holy, holy is the
Lord of hosts." The Psalmist pointedly declares it, Psal. v. 4, 5,
" Thou art not a God that hath pleasure in wickedness : neither shall
evil dwell with thee. The foolish shall not stand in thy sight : thou
hatest all workers of iniquity." But when men see this method of
providence with ungodly sinners, they can hardly believe it, Psal. l.
21, " These things hast thou done, and I kept silence : thou thoughtest that I was altogether such a one as thyself: but I will reprove
thee, and set them in order before thine eyes." For, think they, if
it were so, how could he bear with such unholiness in sinners affronting him, and trampling on his laws ? Therefore the Prophet asserts
it on that very occasion, but withal owns a difficulty of reconciling
this method of providence with it, Hab. i. 13. " Thou art of purer
eyes than to behold evil, and canst not look on iniquity : wherefore
lookest thou upon them that deal treacherously, and holdest thy
tongue when the wicked devoureth the man that is more righteous
than he ?"

3dly, His justice or righteousness, whereby he so hates sin that he
cannot but punish it. It is certain it is so, Gen. xviii. 25. " Shall
not the judge of all the earth do right?" He has demonstrated it
in the death of his own Son. But when men see ungodly sinners
going on in their sin unpunished, they are apt to think, that God is
not so very just in that matter, as some give him out to be ; for they
cannot see sin get a just recompense. Therefore Jeremiah asserts
it on that occasion, Jer. xii. 1. " Righteous art thou, O Lord."

4thly, His goodness to his own people, whereby being good in
himself, he does good to them that are good. It is certain it is so,
Psal. xxxiv. 8, 9, 10. " O taste and see that the Lord is good :
blessed is the man that trusteth in him. O fear the Lord, ye his
saints : for their is no want to them that fear him. The young lions
do lack and suffer hunger : but they that seek the Lord shall not
want any good thing." The prophet got it in commission, Is. iii. 10.

" Say ye to the righteous, that it shall be well with him : for they shall eat the fruit of their doings." But when men see this method of providence dangling ungodly sinners, and smiting the godly, they are apt to think it is not so. And therefore Asaph asserts it on that occasion, Psal. lxxiii. 1. " Truly God is good to Israel, even to such as are of a clean heart."

Now, to remove these misconstructions, and account for the slow method of providence, I offer these considerations.

First, This method is taken to bring sinners to repentance, and prevent their ruin, 2 Pet. iii. 9. ; and it is becoming the perfections of a merciful God, therefore to use it. By this means sinners,

1. Have time and space to repent given them, Rev. ii. 21. Were they always taken away just in the heat of their unmortified lusts, we would be ready to cry out of severity, Num. xvii. 12. But God gives them leave to cool ordinarily, if so they will bethink themselves, and turn to the Lord, and so prevent their own ruin.

2. They are invited to repentance, and drawn towards it with the softest methods. Rom. ii. 2. Every sparing preventing, bounteous mercy the impenitent meets with, calls aloud to him to repent. It says to him, " Do thyself no harm :" it upbraids him with wilfulness for his own ruin, why will ye die ? with ingratitude, Is this thy kindness to thy friend ? And so hereby,

1st, God has the glory of some perfections, which otherwise would not shine forth so illustriously.

(1.) He has the glory of his long-suffering and patience : 2 Pet. iii. 9. " The Lord is long-suffering to us-ward, not willing that any should perish, but that all should come to repentance." Grave observers of the method of providence must cry out, O wonderful long-suffering of a God ! The patience of the meekest man on earth, would be quite worn out with less than the half of what a God bears with.

(2.) He has the glory of his universal good-will to poor sinners of mankind, 2 Pet. iii. 9. forecited. 1 Tim. ii. 4. " Who will have all men to be saved, and to come unto the knowledge of the truth." Justice is his act, his strange act ; but mercy is what he has a peculiar delight in. He is slow to anger, but ready to forgive. This is written in very legible characters in this method.

(3.) He has the glory of his overcoming goodness. To do evil for good, is devilish ; to do good for good, is human : but to do good for ill is divine. Here shines forth the glory of the divine goodness, overcoming evil with good, Luke vi. 35. This is goodness becoming a God !

2dly, As to the sinner, it issues always in one of two things.

(1.) His recovery, to the saving of his soul from sin, and perishing eternally. And God, who has a due value for immortal souls, sees that a great thing; and treats it as worth the waiting on, Luke xv. 7. The Scripture holds out this as a noble attainment, Jam. v. 20. " Let him know, that he which converteth the sinner from the error of his way, shall save a soul from death, and hide a multitude of sins." How many are there singing Hallelujahs in heaven this day, by means of the slow method, that by the swift method had been roaring with the damned? " Had I died before threescore and sixteen, I had perished, for I knew not Christ." Turk. hist. pag. 96.

(2.) Or else his being left inexcusable, Rom. i. 20. The longer God has borne with, and the more kind he has been to impenitent sinners, the more inexcuseable they will be; and the more will God's severity against them be justified. And so this method tends to the clearing of God's justice.

Secondly, In the slow method God takes with sinners, he often has an eye to posterity; and that,

1. To posterity in general. And it is of use to them, whether the sinner so spared repent or not. If he repent, it is of noble use to encourage them that come after, to turn to God. How useful to many one has been the slow method which God took with Manasseh and Paul! 1 Tim. i. 16. If he repent not, and vengeance seize him at length in sight of the world, he becomes a warning piece to others that come after, Psal. xxxvii. 35—37. Though it do not, his memory rots; and the conscience of every one that notices his wickedness silent and at an end in the grave, judges him to have spent his life foolishly, Job xxiv. 19, 20. Thus many who are of no use in the world to others but for mischief, God in his providence makes good use of them.

2. To the sinners' own posterity; and that,

1st, To their posterity yet unborn. There may be vessels of mercy in the loins of vessels of wrath. Many graceless parents have been fathers and mothers of gracious children. It is for the elect's sake that the world is kept up; and if the last elect were born and brought in, the world will quickly be at an end. The law spares a condemned woman, if she is with child, till she has brought it forth: and God often spares long, condemned sinners, for the elect that may be in their loins, Matth. xxiv. 22. There was a sentence passed against the generation which came out of Egypt, which for this very reason was about thirty-eight years ere it was executed on some.

2dly, To their posterity already born; and that two ways.

(1.) As Satan gives some a surfeit of religion and sobriety in their parents; so God makes reprisals on him, by giving others a horror of sin and wickedness in theirs, Ezek. viii. 14. And God spares them, that they may be a glass wherein their posterity may have a view of the hatefulness of sin. A wretched office, but it justifies the slow method of a holy God.

(2.) Men are often punished in their posterity. Many a poor child has smarted upon the occasion of the parent, and many a fair and flourishing family has wickedness raised. A holy just God sometimes pursues quarrels against some evil-workers through several generations, as is threatened in the second command. The third and fourth generation are mentioned, because men may live to see themselves punished in their children, grandchildren, and great-grandchildren. And they may be spared in this slow method for that very end. Witness Zedekiah.

Thirdly, In the slow method God takes with sinners, he has an eye to his own people : 2 Cor. iv. 15, " For all things are for your sakes, that the abundant grace might, through the thanksgiving of many, redound to the glory of God." As the world is kept up for the sake of God's people, so it is guided as it is by providence for their sakes. And it is their good that is designed by it: Rom. viii. 28, " And we know that all things work together for good, to to them that love God, to them who are the called according to his purpose." The way that it comes to be for their good, is by means of the sharp trial they have by it. So God takes the slow method with ungodly sinners for the trial of his own children. And it is a sharp trial to them two ways.

1. They smart sore under their wickedness. Ungodly men are God's rod, as the Assyrians was God's hand against his people, Psal. xvii. 14. Oft-times they feel as much at their hand, as makes them smart by the rod : Hab. i. 12, " O Lord, thou hast ordained them for judgment, and O mighty God, thou hast established them for correction." They always see as much of them, as occasions to them many a heavy heart, ver. 3, " Why dost thou shew me iniquity, and cause me to behold grievance ? for spoiling and violence are before me : and there are that raise up strife and contention." Wherefore since God's people need the rod, it is preserved, and not flung into the fire.

Meanwhile this tends to their good. The ungodly oblige them to pray, watch, live in the exercise of faith, more than otherwise they would do. Hence many times the most tender Christians are found among the most notoriously profane neighbours, like Lot in Sodom, who carried not so well in the cave. For as the godly are eyesores to the wicked, so the wicked are often as whetstones and files to the godly.

2. They smart the sorer under their own afflictions : Psal. lxxiii. 10, " Therefore his people return hither : and waters of a full cup wrung out to them." The prosperity of the wicked carries the afflictions of the godly to a pitch ; and sometimes to a dangerous pitch, through the sleight of Satan improving it against them. This was the case of Asaph, Psal. lxxiii. 12—14, " Behold, these are the ungodly, who prosper in the world, they increase in riches. Verily, I have cleansed my heart in vain, and washed my hands in innocency. For all the day long have I been plagued, and chastened every morning." Job's friend's acted Satan's part on that bottom, endeavouring to prove him an unsound man, because he was a man so afflicted.

But this also tends to their good. It makes them look more concernedly into their Bible, and find sweet and relief where otherwise they would find no more than others do ; as we see in Asaph's case, Psal. lxxiii. 16, 17, " When I thought to know this, it was too painful for me : until I went into the sanctuary of God ; then understood I their end." And it makes them to look more narrowly into their own hearts, and to their sincerity, Job x. 7. It obliges them to live more by faith, and not by sight ; to the exercise of hope, patience, &c.

Fourthly, In this slow method, God often carries on his awful yet holy work of hardening sinners. There is such a work : Rom. ix. 18, " Therefore hath he mercy on whom he will have mercy ; and whom he will, he hardeneth." And it is a most dreadful plague and judgment, whereby God ceasing to punish men for their sins one way, punishes them another way in a dreadful manner. This appears, if ye consider,

1. It is a spiritual stroke, lighting on the soul, and therefore, more terrible than external strokes on people's bodies or substance, Rom. i. 28. Hereby the mind is blinded, the will doubly enslaved to lust, and the conscience seared : a kind of stroke rife this day.

2. It is a stroke, whereby the disease of sin is increased, and the gospel-remedy is rendered ineffectual. The heart being hardened, the loose is given to lusts that before were under some restraint, Eph. iv. 19 ; and the means of grace become useless, if not noxious : the hardened heart turning the food of the soul, as it were, to poison in effect, Is. vi. 10 ; 2 Cor. ii. 16.

3. It is a fearful preparative to utter destruction, Rom. ix. 22. A nasty earthen vessel, that gets leave to contract more and more nastiness, and is not purged and cleansed, is, designed to be broken

in pieces, and thrown away: Ezek. xxiv. 13, "In thy filthiness is lewdness: because I have purged thee, and thou wast not purged, thou shalt not be purged from thy filthiness any more, till I have caused my fury to rest upon thee." So it is awful.

Yet it is a holy work in the hand of the Lord. God is holy in his hardening, as well as in his softening-work, Is. vi. 3, compared with ver. 10. For,

1. God hardens no soft hearts, hardens none but those who first harden themselves, Rom. i. 28. Men first shut their own eyes to the light, and then a just God blinds their eyes: they are wilful in their sin, and God gives them their will, Hos. iv. 17. For who can say he is obliged to strive on with them still?

2. Sin is a meet punishment of sin, Rom. i. 27. And therefore it is just with God to punish sin by sin, to take off the restraint from those who cannot endure it; to let them fall into the mire, and lie in it, that will needs be in it.

Now, God in this slow method often carries on this hardening work; and that both on the sinner himself and others.

1. In this method oft-times the sinner himself is hardened judicially. God is at much pains with sinners to bring them back from their sinful courses; he trysts them with rebukes from his word, convictions, terrors, and anxieties, and adds to these sharp crosses and afflictions. But they struggle against all these, and over the belly of them pursue their sins: so God judicially hardens them, and carries on that fearful work in the slow method.

1st, Denying or withdrawing his grace, and giving them up to their own lusts, Psal lxxxi. 12. There is restraining grace given to many, who never get sanctifying grace; good motions, thoughts, and convictions are put into their hearts: these the Lord withdraws, and leaves men to the swing of their corruptions; as he did Ephraim, Hos. iv. 17, "Ephraim is joined to idols: let him alone." They rebel against the light, and the Lord lets it die out. They are impatient of restraint, and the Lord takes it off. They like the government of their lusts, and the Lord gives them up to them.

2dly, Giving them up to Satan to be hardened by him, as the executioner of God's just vengeance, 2 Cor. iv. 3, 4. Men resisting, grieving, and vexing the Holy Spirit of God, provoke him to depart, and to leave them in the hand of the evil spirit, who then finds easy work with them; as in Saul's case. Hereby Satan's power over them is confirmed, the opposition to his interest in them is much removed, and so his influence over them is increased.

God proceeding in the slow method with the sinner in this case, doth awfully carry on the hardening work upon him. In which we may observe,

(1.) Their impunity hardens them. They venture on sin, God in anger lets them go on unpunished, Hos. iv. 14. And Satan and their own corrupt hearts improve that to the encouraging and strengthening them in their sins. Thence a wind from hell rises that fills their sails. Hence in the text, Because sentence against an evil work is not executed speedily; therefore the heart of the sons of men is fully set in them to do evil.

(2.) Their prosperity in the world hardens them: Psal. lxxiii. 5, 6, "They are not in trouble as other men: neither are they plagued like other men. Therefore pride compasseth them about as a chain: violence covereth them as a garment." The hotter the sun shines, the clay becomes the harder: and the warmer the sun of worldly prosperity shines on the sinner given up to his own lusts and the power of Satan, he, like a dunghill, becomes the harder, and sends forth the more rank savour.

(3.) In the soft dealings of Providence with them, objects, occasions, and means to do their ill works, are justly laid before them: they are tempted, flattered, and encouraged by others. And thus the warm influence of providence on them in external things, which should lead them to repentance, is, by means of their own lusts to which they are left, turned hardening and ruining to them: Prov. i. 32, "For the turning away of the simple shall slay them, and the prosperity of fools shall destroy them." These are to them like a full wind to a ship without ballast, in a storm.

(4.) Proper means for checking them are in the just judgment of God rendered ineffectual, and that hardens them. Thus it was with Pharaoh: the miracle of the rod turned into a serpent, waters into blood, bringing in the frogs, seemed to Pharaoh's eye-sight done by the magicians too. And thus were they rendered ineffectual to him.

(5.) *Lastly*, The adversity and frowns of Providence on the serious godly, harden them, Job xii. 4, 5, 6. These are improved, by the sleight of Satan, to the contempt of both the religious and religion.

2. In this method God carries on a hardening work upon ungodly spectators of it. Hence there is a woe to the world, because of offences, Matth. xviii. 7. The generality of men have so little sense of religion, and insight into the mysteries of Providence, that they are apt to think that that is the best way which is the most prosperous, Prov. xix. 4. Hence there was a generation that would needs make that the standard of religion; Jer. xliv. 17, 18, "But we will certainly do whatsoever thing goeth forth out of our own mouth, to burn incense unto the queen of heaven, and to pour out

drink-offerings unto her, as we have done, we and our fathers, our kings and our princes, in the cities of Judah, and in the streets of Jerusalem : for then had we plenty of victuals, and were well, and saw no evil. But since we left off to burn incense to the queen of heaven, and to pour out drink-offerings unto her, we have wanted all things, and have been consumed by the sword, and by the famine." And so the Lord doth in his holy providence lay that method of it before worldly and carnal men, at which they, by reason of their own wilful blindness, do stumble, to their own ruin, Mal. iii. 14, 15, forecited.

Fifthly, The general method of Providence in managing the world, is soft to his adversaries, and sharp to his own children in this life : 1 Cor. xv. 19, " If in this life only we have hope in Christ, we are of all men most miserable." Rev. iii. 19, " As many as I love, I rebuke and chasten." This is the general rule, thought it admits of exceptions, both in the case of the one and the other. God's adversaries sometimes meet with sharp things, his children with soft. But the general and ordinary course of providence is soft to the former, and sharp to the latter.

This appears particularly in two things.

1. God's children are held shorter by the head, in point of particular rebukes of Providence, than his adversaries are.

1*st,* God sharply noticeth many things in his own, that he will pass in others, and greater too. Hence said Job, " If I sin, then thou markest me, and thou wilt not acquit me from mine iniquity," chap. x. 14. The common proverb holds here, One man had better steal a horse, than another look over the hedge. A child of God many times pays dearer for a vain thought, than others for a vile action; for a rash word, than others for blasphemy and contrived wickedness. How did Moses smart for an unadvised word ? Psal. cvi. 32, 33, " They angered him also at the waters of strife, so that it went ill with Moses for their sakes : because they provoked his spirit, so that he spake unadvisedly with his lips." Compare Num. xx. 10, 12, " And Moses and Aaron gathered the congregation together before the rock, and he said unto them, Hear now, ye rebels; must we fetch you water out of this rock ? And the Lord spake unto Moses and Aaron, Because ye believed me not, to sanctify me in the eyes of the children of Israel ; therefore ye shall not bring this congregation into the land which I have given them." But see Psal. lxxiii. 9, 10. " They set their mouth against the heavens; and their tongue walketh through the earth. Therefore his people return hither; and waters of a full cup are wrung out to them."

2dly, When both meet with rebukes for an ill thing, his own oft-times get the sharpest. Hence the lamenting church says, Lam. i. 12. "Is it nothing to you, all ye that pass by? behold and see, if there be any sorrow like unto my sorrow, which is done unto me, wherewith the Lord hath afflicted me, in the day of his fierce anger." The controversy for unworthy communicating was pleaded with some godly Corinthians, to the sickening of their bodies, yea even to death, 1 Cor. xi. 30. "For this cause many are weak and sickly among you and many sleep.

2. A lot of adversity is in a peculiar manner the lot of God's people in this life, and the world smiles most on its own friends: John xvi. 33. "These things have I spoken unto you, that in me ye might have peace. In the world ye shall have tribulation: but be of good cheer, I have overcome the world." Psal. lxxiii. 10. "Therefore his people return hither; and waters of a full cup are wrung out to them." In the case of the church and people of God in this life, adversity seems to be the rule and ordinary course, prosperity the exception: but in the case of the men of the world, prosperity the rule, and adversity the exception. This appears,

1st, From the Scripture, wherein we find the rod of adversity the beaten path in which the saints under the Old and New Testament have walked: the godly often groaning under the weight of their own afflictions, and the weight of prosperous wickedness in their enemies. The Cainites build cities, and have the harp and organ among them; while the church dwell still in tents: Abraham a stranger in the land of promise, while the cursed Cannanites enjoy it: Jacob's posterity in slavery in Egypt, while the Edomites were settled in their own land, having a king of their own. Perhaps among the Jews in Canaan worldly prosperity was more annexed to piety, agreeable to the dispensation they were under, wherein temporal promises bear great bulk. But consider that people in comparison with other nations, and ye will find their prosperity very short, in comparison of their neighbours, and their adversity very long: Zech. i. 11, 12. "And they answered the angel of the Lord that stood among the myrtle trees, and said, We have walked to and fro through the earth, and behold, all the earth sitteth still, and is at rest. Then the angel of the Lord answered and said, O Lord of hosts, how long wilt thou not have mercy on Jerusalem, and on the cities of Judah, against which thou hast had indignation these threescore and ten years?" But under the New Testament the thing is most clear. Our Saviour points out this as the stated method of Providence; Luke vi. 20—26. "And Jesus lifted up his eyes on his disciples, and said, Blessed be ye poor: for yours is the kingdom of God. Blessed are ye that hunger now: for ye shall be filled. Blessed are ye that weep now: for ye shall laugh. Blessed are ye that when men shall hate you, and when they shall separate you from their company, and shall reproach you, and cast out your name as evil, for the son of man's sake. Rejoice ye in that day, and leap for joy: for behold your reward is great in heaven: for in the like manner did their fathers unto the prophets. But woe unto you that are rich: for ye have received your consolation. Woe unto you that are full: for ye shall hunger. Woe unto you that laugh now: for ye shall mourn and weep. Woe unto you when all men shall speak well of you: for so did their fathers to the false prophets." Chap. xvi. 25. "But Abraham said, Son, remember that thou in thy lifetime receivedst thy good things, and likewise Lazarus evil things: but now he is comforted. and thou art tormented."

2dly, From experience and observation. One needs but to open his eyes, and look about through the world, and he cannot miss to see the world's greatest favours bestowed on them who have least sense of God and religion; wickedness triumphant, while serious godliness is pressed down; sinners often laughing while saints weep.

Now, this method becomes the divine wisdom. For,

(1.) At this rate the evil have a taste of good, and the good a taste of evil, Luke xvi. 25. forecited. The former, who will at length drink deep of endless sorrow, are patiently borne with, to bring them to repentance: the latter, who shall rejoice for evermore, have now the trial of a weeping time.

(2.) As a father is more concerned for, and exact in the correcting of the faults of his own children, than of his servants; so is our Father in heaven with respect to his family. The more he loves, the more he corrects with his rod: Amos iii. 2, "You only have I known of all the families of the earth: therefore I will punish you for all your inquities." There are some who are to dwell with him for ever: there are others who are to depart from him for ever. What wonder, that he is at more pains to purify the former than the latter !

(3.) This is most agreeable to the way he took with his own Son and his enemies. While Christ was in the world, he was a man of sorrows, and acquainted with grief; the wind blew in his face continually, till he was cruelly put to death on the cross. The axe lay at the root of the Jewish church and state, his enemies; yet was it not wielded against them all the time he was among them, nor till about forty years after. This was the pattern that is copied after in this method: Rom. viii. 29, "For whom he did foreknow, he also did predestinate to be conformed to the image of his Son, that he might be the first-born among many brethren."

Sixthly, Though the slow method seems strange to us short-sighted creatures, it is not at all strange being viewed in the glass of the infinite perfections of the divine nature. A thing will appear in a shallow river, that being cast into the sea will appear no more. We wonder at the slow method of providence, while we look to men ; but we will cease to wonder if we look to God, and observe, that,

1. God is eternal, from everlasting to everlasting, Psal. xc. 2. If men do not soon pursue their quarrels, death may snatch them away, and they can have no access more to do it : but however long the Lord delays pleading his quarrel, he can lose no time, for he is eternal.

2. In God's eternal duration there are no differences of time; all is present to him. Time is for measuring created beings, but not the infinite being. So a thousand years and one day are alike unto him, whatever odds there is betwixt them to us : Psal. xc. 4, " For a thousand years in thy sight are but as yesterday when it is past, and as a watch in the night." This consideration the apostle suggests, 2 Pet. iii. 8, " One day is with the Lord as a thousand years, and a thousand years as one day."

3. He sees exactly the time appointed for execution against every impenitent sinner, and will not let it pass beyond that, one moment : Hab. ii. 3, " For the vision is yet for an appointed time, but at the end it shall speak, and not lie : though it tarry, wait for it ; because it will surely come, it will not tarry." We see the beginning and middle of things, but cannot forsee the end. God sees all at once. Well can he bear with ungodly sinners, for he sees their day coming with speed, Psal. xxxvii. 13. What needs haste in respect of God? for he sees the sinful creature is fading, and will drop down into a grave ere long, Psal. lxxviii. 38, 39.

4. He knows what he intends to do, and none can hinder : Dan. iv. 37, " All the King of heaven's works are truth, and his ways judgment, and those that walk in pride he is able to abase. The prince that is afraid of the rebels, will strive to crush them ere they gather to a head ; but he that knows he can crush them when he will, may let them gather all their strength together. God can carry on the designs of his glory, by bearing long with impenitent sinners : Rom. ix. 17, " For the scripture saith unto Pharaoh, Even for this same purpose have I raised thee up, that I might shew my power in thee, and that my name might be declared throughout all the earth." Thus also he can laugh at the trial of the innocent :

Job ix. 23, " If the scourge slay suddenly, he will laugh at the trial of the innocent." Like a father holding his child in his hands over a deep pool ; the child cries, and the father smiles.

5. *Lastly,* He is infinitely blessed in himself ; and nothing the creature can do against him can hurt him ; nor in the least disturb his repose in himself : Job xxxv. 6, 8, " If thou sinnest, what dost thou against him ? or if thy transgressions be multiplied, what dost thou unto him ? Thy wickedness may hurt a man as thou art, and thy righteousness may profit the son of man." If the whole creation should conspire against him, opening their mouths against the heavens, and doing to the utmost of their power against him ; he might contemn their impotent malice, they would be but like men running their heads against a rock. The longest interval of time cannot make him weary : Is. xl. 28, " Hast thou not known ? hast thou not heard, that the everlasting God, the Lord, the creator of the ends of the earth, fainteth not, neither is weary ?

Seventhly, There is a necessity for both the swift and slow methods being used by Providence in the government of the world ; it is so corrupt and atheistical. And,

1. The swift method is necessary to shew, that there is a God to judge upon the earth : Psal. lviii. 10, 11, " The righteous shall rejoice when he seeth the vengeance : he shall wash his feet in the blood of the wicked. So that a man shall say, Verily there is a reward for the righteous : verily he is a God that judgeth in the earth." For as ordinary as the slow method is, there are never wanting instances now and then of swift process against ungodly sinners : which is necessary to bear testimony to the being of a God, and of a providence concerned in human affairs. And there are as many of these, as may give sufficient warning to all.

2. The slow method is necessary, to shew there is a judgment to come : 2 Thess. i. 4—7, " We ourselves glory in you in the churches of God, for your patience and faith in all your persecutions and tribulations that ye endure. Which is a manifest token of the righteous judgment of God, that ye may be counted worthy of the kingdom of God, for which ye also suffer : seeing it is a righteous thing with God to recompense tribulation to them that trouble you ; and to you who are troubled, rest with us : when the Lord Jesus shall be revealed from heaven, with his mighty angels," &c. What the carnal world improves in behalf of Atheism, is necessary to prevent Sadduceism : for if all men's wickedness were punished in this life, it would thence be concluded, that there were no after-reckoning : but there is never a sentence passed against an evil work, that is missed to be executed now, but is a pledge of the judgment to come.

Lastly, The slowest vengeance against impenitent sinners will be sure vengeance; and the slower it is in coming, it will be the sorer when it comes: Deut. xxxii. 35, "To me belongeth vengeance, and recompense; their foot shall slide in due time : for the day of their calamity is at hand, and the things that shall come upon them make haste." The old world was spared a hundred and twenty years, but was swept away at length.

1. Let sinners be spared never so long, not one of all their ill works will, or can be forgotten. They may have forgot them themselves, but God never will. There is a book of remembrance of their ill, as well as of the saint's good words and works: Amos viii. 7, "The Lord hath sworn by the excellency of Jacob, Surely I will never forget any of their works." Psal. l. 21, "These things hast thou done, and I kept silence : thou thoughtest that I was altogether such a one as thyself : but I will reprove thee, and set them in order before thine eyes."

2. The longer sinners are spared, their counts will be the greater, and all will come on at once, Luke xi. 50, 51; 1 Sam. iii. 12. It is people's mercy, that God ceaseth not to be a reprover to them; as it is the mercy of weak people to pay their debt by littles, whereas they are broken if it get leave to run on.

3. When it comes on the impenitent sinner, God will charge both the interest and the principal sum together. They shall not only pay for their ill works, but for their mercies, and the sparing they have gotten: Rom. ii. 4, 5, "Or despisest thou the riches of his goodness, and forbearance, and long-suffering; not knowing that the goodness of God leadeth thee to repentance? But after thy hardness and impenitent heart, treasurest up unto thyself wrath against the day of wrath, and revelation of the righteous judgment of God." What aggravated their sin, will aggravate their condemnation and punishment.

And how long soever the execution of the sentence against ungodly sinners, evil-workers, may be delayed, and how many external favours of providence be heaped on them; all will appear but small and short, when one considers,

1st, The severity of the execution when it comes. They will at length be cut asunder, Matt. xxiv. 51. In flaming fire he will take vengeance on them, 2 Thess. i. 8. They will fall into the hands of the living God.

2dly, The eternity of it. That is a killing aggravation in the sentence, Depart into everlasting fire. If the worm were once awakened, and set on them, it dieth not; the fire once kindled, will not be quenched.

Use 1. Of Information. What is said may inform us,

1. That present ease and prosperity in the world is not a sure sign of God's special favour, Eccl. ix. 1, 2. Indeed men are apt to construe it so; and Satan and the deceitful heart help them to draw such a conclusion. But so far is it from being such a sign, that it may very well consist with their being in a state of wrath, under a sentence of condemnation; and is so with many.

2. That present ease, impunity, and prosperity, is no security against the time to come. Men are ready to be secure upon it, and to dream that to-morrow will be as this day: Psal. x. 6, " He hath said in his heart, I shall not be moved: for I shall never be in adversity." But the mountain may be standing sure now, that ere long may be overturned. The sun shined fair on Sodom, the morning of that day in which God rained fire and brimstone on it. The rich man was full of thoughts of ease in that day, in the night whereof he was struck, Luke xii. 18, 19, 20.

3. There cannot be such worth in outward prosperity, nor such evil in affliction, as we generally imagine. For a holy, wise God would never heap what is really best on the objects of his wrath, and what is really worst on the objects of his love. Were there as much real value in the world's wealth, ease, and honour, health, strength, silver, gold, &c. as we imagine; or were there as much evil in trouble, adversity, &c. as we think, would they be so dealt, as that the greatest share of the former should be given to the condemned, and of the latter to the justified? It is owing to the weakness of human sight, that so much beauty appears in some human faces, and in some victuals we feed on. If they were looked to with a microscope, the beauty would disappear. Faith is the microscope here, Eccl. i. 2 ; 2 Cor. iv. 17, 18.

4. God is a patient and long-suffering God, not subject to passions as we are, 2 Pet. iii. 9. If he were liable to the transports of passion as we are, the world would have been many times burnt to ashes ere now; considering the provocations given to the eyes of his glory. But the infinite mind enjoys the profoundest serenity and calm, beholding all the confusions of evil-workers in the world.

5. *Lastly*, Sad and heavy strokes may be abiding a land and generation, though long warded off. Long has the Lord borne with this apostatising generation in principle and practice ; and long have we been threatened: and through the delay, we have been brought to say, " The days are prolonged, and every vision faileth," Ezek. xii. 22. But a reprieve is no pardon ; the cloud is still hanging over our heads, and it is to be feared, that some will live to see a fearful breaking of it.

USE 2. Of Exhortation. And,

1. Let ungodly sinners be exhorted to repent of their evil works, and beware of abusing the divine patience with them. Ye have heard the slow method rationally accounted for : If hereafter ye will deceive yourselves, and turn the grace of God into wantonness, encouraging yourselves in sin from your impunity and prosperity ; know, that ye are wilfully blind, that ye shall be inexcusable, and your blood will be on your heads. But,

1st, Let the sense of gratitude move you to repentance, Rom. ii. 4. Think with yourselves, what case ye had been in, if God had struck you down, as he could, in the very act of your evil work ; how you might have been beyond all hope and possibility of recovery. You owe your life to the slow method of providence ; his patience exercised towards you has kept your soul back from the pit. Therefore repent, and go no farther on.

2dly, Let the account ye have heard of the slow method, frighten you from abusing it. I am sure, ye cannot but see now, that there is no ground to take encouragement to sin from it. Consider what has been said, and shew yourselves men. If ye go on to abuse it so, ye make a jest of a most serious and wise dispensation of providence. Ye turn your food into poision, and stumble at noon-day. And it will be a sure presage of everlasting ruin to you : Hos. xiv. 9, " Who is wise, and he shall understand these things ? prudent, and he shall know them ? for the ways of the Lord are right, and the just shall walk in them : but the transgressors shall fall therein."

2. Let all beware of censuring the slow method of providence with ungodly sinners, evil workers. Take heed how ye speak on that head ; beware of risings of the corrupt heart upon it. For however rationally ye think ye pronounce upon the matter, sooner or later ye shall be made to recant that sentence, either in mercy, as Job did, chap. xlii. 3, and as Asaph did, Psal. lxxiii. 22, or in wrath, Mal. iii. 14, 15, with 18. Consider,

1st, There may be a mystery in the dispensations of providence ; but there can be no iniquity, error, or mistake : Deut. xxxii. 4, " He is the rock, his work is perfect : for all his ways are judgment : a God of truth, and without iniquity, just and right is he." Silently adore that wisdom and the deep design of providence which ye cannot see through, that certainly are in the slow method God uses with some ungodly sinners, evil-workers. Though ye cannot see how God's glory can miss to suffer by it, believe that God will doubtless get glory by it.

2dly, The mystery of that dispensation in the case of every ungodly sinner, will be opened out before the world at length, to the satisfaction of all humble waiters; and the confusion of the impenitent evil-workers, scoffers, and murmurers: 1 Cor. iv. 5, " Judge nothing before the time, until the Lord come, who both will bring to light the hidden things of darkness, and will make manifest the counsels of the hearts: and then shall every man have praise of God. Be not rash, wait the end, and then ye shall be allowed to judge: Prov. xviii. 13, "He that answereth a matter before he heareth it, it is folly and shame unto him." But why should ye judge of the web of providence ere it be wrought out?

3. Fret not at, neither envy prosperous wickedness: Prov. xxiii. 17, "Let not thine heart envy sinners: but be thou in the fear of the Lord all the day long," Psal. xxxvii. 1, "Fret not thyself because of evil-doers, neither be thou envious against the workers of iniquity." Who would envy the state of a condemned man, though he have a long reprieve, and enjoy many comforts in the iron house? Such is the case of the ungodly, whatever world's ease they have. And therefore they are just objects of pity and compassion, but not of envy. One had better be a pardoned one in the depth of worldly misery, than in a state of wrath and condemnation in the top of worldly felicity, "For what is a man profited, if he shall gain the whole world, and lose his own soul? or what shall a man give in exchange for his soul? Matth. xvi. 26. Consider,

1st, Such fretting and envy proceeds from a distempered heart: Psal. lxxiii. 22, "So foolish was I, and ignorant: I was as a beast before thee." See Mal. iii. 15. It is the produce of a mixture of ignorance, rashness and inconsideration, unbelief and worldly-mindedness. And there needs only to cure it, to have our eyes opened, to see things in their true state; the laying aside of unruly passions; faith and due weanedness from the world: Psal. xxxvii. 1. 2, "Fret not thyself because of evil-doers, neither be thou envious against the workers of iniquity. For they shall soon be cut down like the grass, and wither as the green herb."

2dly, Every one's state is to be rated, according as it is before God. If God be one's friend, he is a happy man, though the world should never give him its word nor kind look. If God is one's enemy, he is a miserable man, though all the men and things of the world should favour him to his wish. For as is one's state with God, so is his present safety; and so will be his well or woe through eternity.

4. Let all learn to regulate their conduct by the example of God in this his government of the world, so far as it is proposed for our imitation: Eph. v. 1. "Be ye therefore followers of God as dear children." And we may learn from it,

1st, To be patient and slow to anger. How ill does it become us to be so ready to fire at every provocation, against our fellow-creatures; when the highest One uses so much patience towards us? Matth. xviii. 23, &c. The more meekly and patiently one carries himself, he is the more like unto God, who hath set us an example.

2dly, To learn to bear with sinners, in order to the seeking of their recovery: Gal. vi. 1. "Brethren, if a man be overtaken in a fault, ye which are spiritual, restore such an one in the Spirit of meekness; considering thyself, lest thou also be tempted." Not that we are to suffer sin upon him, so far as it is in our power to remove it. God can bring good out of evil, but we cannot do that: therefore that part of the conduct of Providence towards the ungodly, we are not called to imitate. But let us be followers of God, in dealing still with the worst of sinners to recover them, and not give them over for hopeless.

3dly, To do good to the worthless, unthankful, and evil: Luke vi. 35. "Love ye your enemies, and do good, and lend, hoping for nothing again: and your reward shall be great, and ye shall be the children of the Highest: for he is kind unto the unthankful, and to the evil." It is a naughty world, that people had need of such a principle to prompt them to do good to others. If we confine our good to those that do good to us, what do we more than others? If we confine it to those worthy of it, we do it only for the creature's sake. But if we propose to follow the example of God, we will do good to all as we have access, and act from a Christian principle in it.

5. *Lastly,* Let us not be secure with respect to the case of the land and generation we live in. Let us not think that God has forgotten the iniquity of our fathers in their perfidy and cruelty against the godly for his cause; or that he approves of the course of apostacy from the truth and holiness of the gospel this day, whereby the present generation has entered itself heir to the apostatising, persecuting generation that went before. The sentence is not executed, yet it is but delayed; therefore we may look for it, if repentance prevent it not.

DOCTRINE III. God's delay of execution is often miserably abused by sinners, to the filling of their hearts to do evil, and sinning more and more.

In discoursing this doctrine, I shall,

I. Point out the abuse of God's patience in the delay of execution, that ungodly sinners make, to the filling of their hearts to do evil.

II. Shew how it comes to pass, that sinners so abuse God's patience with them.

III. Make application of the doctrine.

I. I shall point out the abuse of God's patience in the delay of execution, that ungodly sinners make, to the filling of their hearts to do evil.

1. They abuse it to carnal security: Psal. x. 6, " He hath said in his heart, I shall not be moved : for I shall never be in adversity." Finding that God does not execute his threatenings against them, they conclude they are in no hazard : and they begin to look on them as mere scarecrows, ver. 5, " His ways are always grievous ; thy judgments are far above out of his sight." And so they go on securely in their ungodly courses. Hence it is that the execution overtakes them quite unexpectedly : 1 Thess. v. 2, 3, " The day of the Lord so cometh as a thief in the night. For when they shall say, Peace and safety ; then sudden destruction cometh upon them, as travail upon a woman with child ; and they shall not escape."

2. They abuse it to a sensual life, wherein their aim is not to keep a clean conscience, but to gratify their senses, as their circumstances in the world will permit ; as the rich man did, Luke xii. 19, " I will say to my soul, Soul, thou hast much goods laid up for many years ; take thine ease, eat, drink and be merry." So the more that Providence favours them in external things, the more sensual they are, fulfilling the desires of the flesh and of the mind : Hos. xiii. 6, " According to their pasture, so were they filled : they were filled, and their heart was exalted ; therefore have they forgotten me." Hence the lives of many are trifled away, and wholly spent in making provision for the flesh, " the lust of the flesh, the lust of the eyes, and the pride of life." And that is endless business : Eccl. i. 8, " All things are full of labour, man cannot utter it : the eye is not satisfied with seeing, nor the ear filled with hearing."

3. They abuse it to impudence in sin, Jer. vi. 14, 15. When God strikes men in a sinful course, they are ashamed readily as pointed at by the hand of heaven, as transgressors : but when men prosper in a sinful course, they put on a brow of brass, they gather a stock of impudence in sin, as if Providence had given them a patent for wickedness : Psal. lxxiii. 5, 6, " They are not in trouble as other men : neither are they plagued like other men. Therefore pride compasseth them about as a chain : violence covereth them as a garment."

4. They abuse it to contempt of God, and all that is sacred : Psal. lxxiii. 9, " They set their mouth against the heavens ; and their tongue walketh through the earth." Agur saw the danger of this snare, and therefore prayed thus, Prov. xxx. 8, 9, " Remove far from me vanity and lies ; give me neither poverty, nor riches,

feed me with food convenient for me : lest I be full, and deny thee, and say, Who is the Lord ? or lest I be poor, and steal, and take the name of my God in vain." Israel fell into it : Deut. xxxii. 15, " Jeshurun waxed fat, and kicked : thou art waxen fat, thou art grown thick, thou art covered with fatness ; then he forsook God which made him, and lightly esteemed the Rock of his salvation." The ungodly have not love to God : if they have any thing that way of such affections, it is fear of him, a slavish fear of his wrath, springing from the love of themselves : this fear they lose also, when God delays to strike. And so it issues in contempt, as is natural in the case of one we neither love nor fear. And then all that is sacred is despised.

5. They abuse it to sinning more diffusely, giving loose reins to their several lusts, Jer. vii. 9, 10. One sin makes way for another, and prosperity in a sinful course gives many occasions of sin : and as the vicious stomach, the more it receives, breeds the more ill humours ; so the more one prospers in a sinful course, the more vile does he grow.

6. They abuse it to sinning more eagerly ; Eph. iv. 19, " Being past feeling, they have given themselves over unto lasciviousness, to work all uncleanness with greediness." The more that lusts are fed, the more strong they grow, and carry out the man more violently to satisfy them. So that the heart in t hat case is like a ship having a full gale of wind, and is eagerly set to do evil.

7. *Lastly,* They abuse it to incorrigibleness and obstinacy in sin, Jer. xxii. 21. A prosperous sinner quickly gets above reproofs, Hos. iv. 4. As affliction tends to humble, prosperity puffs up an ungracious heart : and the heart swelled with pride scorns to stoop, till God by his grace or judgments do lay it.

II. How comes it to pass that sinners so abuse God's patience with them ?

1. Sin reigning in the ungodly, fear of wrath is their highest motive to good, and most forcible restraint from evil : and so when that restraint is taken off by the delay of execution again and again ; the heart naturally goes to its own bias, and is like the wild ass's colt snuffing up the wind at her pleasure. The love of holiness for itself, and likeness to God, would prevent it.

2. They mistake the design of providence. They misinterpret the slow method of procedure with them, Psal. l. 21. The design of it is to lead them to repentance ; but that they notice not. But they construe it, as if God approved of their ways, or had such a regard for them, that he will not be so angry with them, as one would make them believe : they cannot think that he is so very

angry at their sin, while they prosper in it by his providence.

3. There is a root of Atheism in the hearts of all men naturally, and it reigns in the ungodly: Psal. xiv. 1, "The fool hath said in his heart, There is no God." Unless God be every now and then proving his being, providence, and justice to them, by his works of judgment on themselves; they are apt to forget him, and deny him. It is the interest of men wedded to their lusts, that there were not a God; or, if there be, that he were not such as the scripture represents him. So they are ready to entertain every thing that may favour it.

4. *Lastly*, The Lord often in that way carries on a holy hardening work. In which case, Satan and the evil heart conspire to this abuse.

USE 1. Of Information. This lets us see,

1. That we need not be surprised to see sinners escaping with one evil work fall into another, and so on; growing still more vile, the more outward favours are heaped on them. It is but a fulfilling of this scripture. Providence often has an odd aspect in our view, till we carry the matter to the Bible; and there we see it exactly answering the word.

2. It is good for men to be under frequent rebukes of Providence. Affliction is sore, but it is the more safe lot, Psal. cxix. 71. In the one men are put in mind of their sins, in the other they are apt to forget both their God and themselves. It would be profitable for the afflicted to consider the wretched abuse the heart is ready to make of ease and prosperity.

3. Slow vengeance will be sore vengeance, when it comes. For the longer it is a-coming, sin goes the deeper: the more God spares impenitents, the more they treasure up wrath against the day of wrath; the counts run on, and swell the more. So whether we consider it coming on in time or in eternity, the heavier will it be.

4. *Lastly*, Great is the corruption of human nature. See it here as in a glass, how the mercy and goodness of God is despised by the corrupt heart, that will not be drawn by such cords of love. See how it turns our food into poison, and that which should be for our welfare into a snare and trap. See it an ungrateful nature, apt to be insensible of the ties of gratitude to our best benefactor.

USE 2. Of Exhortation. Take heed of abusing the patience of a long-suffering God, of turning his grace, goodness, and forbearance into wantonness, of your heart filling to do evil while God spares.

1. Consider the evil of it. There is in it,

1st, An over-valuing of ourselves, as if we deserved not to be worse treated, and therefore were nothing obliged to our benefactor: Hab. i. 16, " They sacrifice unto their net, and burn incense unto their drag: because by them their portion is fat, and their meat plenteous." Men, who are not bettered by God's goodness, their hearts swell in pride, as patience is used towards them: Psal. lxxiii. 5, 6, " They are not in trouble as other men : neither are they plagued like other men. Therefore pride compasseth them about as a chain : violence covereth them as a garment."

2dly, An undervaluing of others whom providence doth not treat so softly. Hence Job said, chap. xii. 5, " He that is ready to slip with his feet, is as a lamp despised in the thought of him that is at ease." How lightly do many that are at ease, look on the heavy things others suffer? They are as unconcerned with them, as if they were creatures of an inferior rank. Were men sensible of God's goodness, in his patience towards them, it would make them sympathize with others, wondering that it is not worse with themselves, 2 Chron. xxviii. 10.

3dly, A monstrous abuse of the creature, and comforts of life, Hos. ii. 8. The use of the creature was given to man, for his comfort indeed; but always in subserviency to the glory of God. But abusers of divine patience turn the weapons against God, which he has armed them with for his service: Deut. xxxii. 15, " But Jeshurun waxed fat, and kicked: thou art waxen fat, thou art grown thick, thou art covered with fatness; then he forsook God which made him, and lightly esteemed the Rock of his salvation." They are called adulterers 'and adulteresses, James iv. 4, because they bestow God's good gifts on their lusts, ver. 3. Hence the creation groans under the burden of the ungodly, evil-workers, Rom. viii. 22.

4thly, A denying the due tribute to our Sovereign Lord and King. All that we have we hold of him, in the way of free mercy, Lam. iii. 22. The king in his palace, and the beggar in his cottage, is God's tenant: our food and raiment, coarse or fine, with conveniencies of life, are given us of God. We can pay him nothing, but the tribute of praise in our lips and lives: and that is denied. Hence,

5thly, Monstrous ingratitude, a sin of a deep dye: Deut. xxxii. 6, " Do ye thus requite the Lord, O foolish people and unwise? is not he thy father that hath bought thee? hath he not made thee, and established thee?" It is a devilish disposition of heart, that cannot be won with benefits; a base spirit, which good done them cannot engage. But abusers of mercies, the more God loads them with benefits, the more they load him with their provocations.   Ah! shall men sin, because grace abounds? shall their hearts be filled in them to do evil, because sentence against an evil work is not speedily executed?

6*thly*, Practical blasphemy, as if men should say, they are hired to be vile, Jer. vii. 9, 10.   Abusers of the doctrine of the gospel, to licentiousness, make Christ the minister of sin : therefore abusers of the kind providence of God to that end, make God in his government of the world so.   While Heaven smiles in outward favours on men, and they use them so, the language of that practice is blasphemous.

7*thly*, Much Atheism and contempt of God.   It is a denial of his providence, as if he had no concern about human affairs, Ezek. ix. 9. It makes a jest of his threatenings in his word, 2 Pet. iii. 3, 4.   It misrepresents his holy nature, Psal. l. 21, or bids him defiance, Is. v. 19, and throws off his yoke, Psal. xii. 4.

2 Consider the danger of it.   If ye go on so,

1*st*, Ye will make your recovery aye more and more hopeless, Jer. vi. 29, 30.   Sin is a current, the farther it runs, the deeper it grows : and the more goodness men sin against, the more is their heart hardened, and their consciences seared.   Withal it provokes God to give up with men, leave striving with them, and give them up to their lusts, and to the devil, to be hardened more.

2*dly*, If God have any thoughts of good towards you, it will make your recovery more difficult.   Strong diseases must have strong remedies : and long abused patience will make broken bones, at best; if ye be saved, it will be so as by fire.   At best ye are but laying up for bitter repentance : the more loose and licentious one is in an unconverted state, the more severe pangs and throes he will readily find in the new birth.   Witness Manasseh, Paul, &c.

3*dly*, Be it as it will, that patience will have an end; ye shall not sin on and God spare on very long.   The coupling of these two will be broken, and God will shew you that he will bear no longer with your abuse : Eccl. vii. 6, " For as the crackling of thorns under a pot, so is the laughter of the fool."   Ye will find God will awake to judgment, and wake you out of your dream ; and ye will either be his converts, or broken to pieces by him.

4*thly*, The breaking up of patience with you is likely to be very sudden and surprising, 1 Thess. v. 2, 3.   So was it with the rich man, Luke xii. 19, 20.   God bore long with the old world, but at length the deluge came on like a thunderclap, in the midst of their carnal mirth and jollity.   God does it in just recompense of long abused patience.

Lastly, Abused patience, when it breaks off, will turn to fury;* and the longer God has delayed execution, the more severe will it be when it comes on, Lev. xxvi. 28. The more a man has had in trust, his accounts will be found the greater and the harder to clear off, when once the creditors fall on him. It is most pleasing to the flesh, to live in ease and fulness; but the abuse of these will make a more fearful reckoning, than otherwise.

DOCTRINE IV. Though the execution be never so slow, it will be sure, against impenitent sinners, evil-workers,

In handling this doctrine it is proposed to shew,

I. In what respects the execution against impenitent sinners, evil-workers, will be sure.

II. That the execution against them will be sure.

III Apply the doctrine.

I. In what respects will the execution against impenitent sinners. evil-workers, be sure? It will be sure, in respect of,

1. The full tale of their evil works: Eccl. xii. 14, "For God shall bring every work into judgment, with every secret thing, whether it be good, or whether it be evil." Neither the multitude of them, nor the long time they lie over unreckoned for, will cause any of them to be forgotten. But the ill works of the several periods of the sinner's life, will be charged home upon him exactly. For God keeps a register of all their evil works, a book that will be opened at the last day, Rev. xx. 12; and has sworn that none of them shall be forgotten, Amos viii. 7.

2. The whole aggravations of their evil works, Jude ver. 15. A just God will remember against impenitent sinners, the manner as well as the matter of their sins; the time, place, and other circumstances of their evil works, will be remembered against them. Their abused mercies, the light they rebelled against, the warnings from the word and providence they slighted, the effects their ill example had on others, the snares others were entangled therein by their means, &c. will all be charged on them.

3. The conviction of their own consciences, Jude ver. 15. Sinners now find ways to cloak and cover their evil works, to deny or mince them: and few will now suffer themselves to be admonished or reproved, but they have a great deal to say in their own defence; but the lying lips, and tongues that speak proudly, will then be put to silence, Matt. xxii. 12. The light of conscience will then be like broad day-light, that is now as the darkness of the night. It will convince them clearly of what shall be laid to their charge, that

* *Patientia saepe læsa sit furor.*

they can no more deny it, John viii. 9; and of the justice of God in proceeding against them, Psal. l. 6.

4. Just punishment brought on them for their evil works, 1 Thess. v. 3. While God delays, men dream with Agag, that the bitterness of death is past: but they will find themselves deceived, as he when Samuel took the sword and hewed him in pieces before the Lord. They cannot escape the due demerit of their sin at length; but as the needle draws the thread after it, sin will draw wrath. Judgment is sin's shadow.

5. The correspondence there will be between their sin and punishment. God will write every ungodly sinner's sin in his punishment. Oft-times it is so here with them, as in the case of Adonibezek, Judg. i. 7; but always so hereafter, as in the case of the rich man, Luke xvi. 19, with 24. Hence the worm is said never to die; signifying the eternal remorse they shall have for their evil works. And the degrees of punishment will be suited to the degrees of their sin. They that have committed many sins, shall have many stripes.

6. Its inevitableness, when once patience is come to an end: Luke xiii. 24, 25, "Strive to enter in at the strait gate: for many, I say unto you, will seek to enter in, and shall not be able. When once the Master of the house is risen up, and hath shut to the door, and ye begin to stand without, and to knock at the door, saying, Lord, Lord, open unto us; and he shall answer and say unto you, I know you not whence you are." The door of mercy may stand open long, but it will be shut at length. And then there is no more escaping. For,

1st, Omniscience will find out the flier, and discover his most secret crimes, and overthrow all his defences: Heb. iv. 13, "Neither is there any creature that is not manifest in his sight: but all things are naked, and opened unto the eyes of him with whom we have to do." Psal. cxxxix. 7, "Whither shall I go from thy Spirit? or whither shall I flee from thy presence?" There is no blinding of the eye of an omniscient judge.

2dly, Divine power will bring him under, and cause him to stand and receive the just reward of his deeds: Job ix. 4, "He is wise in heart, and mighty in strength: who hath hardened himself against him, and hath prospered? There will be no resisting of omnipotence: the stoutest sinner will be poured out like water before an angry God.

3dly, The divine severity will proceed over the belly of all entreaties, made out of time: Luke xiii. 24, 25. forecited. They that slight mercy while God's time for it lasts, will get no mercy when God's time is out, and theirs is come.

7. *Lastly*, Its eternity. The execution once on, will never be off; once begun, will never end: Mark ix. 44. In hell the worm dieth not, and the fire is not quenched. While God is, he will pursue the quarrel. The ungodly sin on as long as they are in the world, and live on as long as they will, they will not alter their course: and God will pursue them for ever, when once he has broke off.

II. That the execution against them will be sure, appears,

1. From the inviolable regard God has to the honour of his holy law, Is. xlii. 21. Sinners trample on it, slight its commands, and despise its threatenings; but God highly regards it, as that wherein he has eminently expressed the holiness of his nature. If sinners then honour it not in the way of duty, it will be honoured upon them in a way of judgment. God's regard to his law may be seen clearly,

1*st*, In the works of providence. As soon as sin entered into the world, and the law was broken, the face of providence on the world was quite changed. And it has blown continually since in the face of the creation less or more, Rom. viii. 22. Oft-times it has risen to violent storms, to avenge the quarrel of the dishonour of the holy law by sinners. Remember how, in that quarrel, Adam was driven out of Paradise, the world drowned by the flood, Sodom burnt, Jerusalem destroyed, with the many awful strokes brought on impenitent sinners in latter times.

2*dly*, In the work of redemption. God chose some from eternity unto salvation: but being breakers of the law, they behoved to be redeemed, and the price paid to the full reparation of the honour of the law. Christ the Son of God was their Redeemer; but that the law's honour might be seen to, he met with no sparing: Rom. viii. 32, "He spared not his own Son, but delivered him up for us all." So God wrote his regard to the law in the salvation of his elect, and blood of his Son.

2. The truth and veracity of God insures the execution. He has said, he will do it: Gen. ii. 17, "In the day that thou eatest thereof, thou shalt surely die." His Son has intimated to us from heaven, that impenitent sinners shall not escape: Luke xiii. 3, " I tell you, Nay, but except ye repent, ye shall all likewise perish." Every leaf of the scripture almost, has something to this purpose: "and hath he said, and shall he not do it? or hath he spoken, and shall he not make it good?" Num. xxiii. 19. God's truth must either fail, or ungodly sinners be reckoned with at length.

3. The justice of God requires it: Gen. xviii. 25, " Shall not the Judge of all the earth do right?" Men may be unjust judges, but God cannot. He will give every transgression a just recompense of

reward: for it is in his power to do it, and his nature requires it. He hates sin, and cannot but hate it; and therefore though he delay for a time, he will punish.

4. The constant conduct of providence hitherto confirms it. There have been multitudes of ungodly in the world; but may we not put the question, Job ix. 4, "Who hath hardened himself against him, and hath prospered?" Some have indeed been long spared, but did they not at length either bow or break before him? What came of the giants in the old world, of Pharaoh, of Korah, Dathan, and Abiram? These things happened for warnings to us. And if any have escaped during life, is there not sufficient evidence of execution on them in another world? as is evident from the case of the rich man, Luke xvi.

5. *Lastly*, The peremptory appointment of the day of general judgment, puts it out of question: Acts xvii. 30, 31, " And the times of this ignorance God winked at; but now commandeth all men every where to repent: because he hath appointed a day in the which he will judge the world in righteousness, by that man whom he hath ordained; whereof he hath given assurance unto all men, in that he hath raised him from the dead." The Judge is named for that effect already, the commission to him for that end has passed the seals in his resurrection; it is to be general, all must be judged by him; yea the sentence against the ungodly is conceived already, " Depart from me, ye cursed, into everlasting fire, prepared for the devil and his angels."

For USE I shall drop a word to,

1. The ungodly, evil-workers. And to you I would say,

1*st*, Let not your impunity for the present, make you secure for the time to come; as is the case of the wicked man, Psal. x. 6, " He hath said in his heart, I shall not be moved: for I shall never be in adversity." As sure as ye think your mountain now stands, it may suddenly be overturned; yea it shall assuredly, if ye repent not. God is giving you space to repent: do not trifle and dream it away, lest ye repent when it is too late.

2*dly*, Let not your observation of the prosperity of other sinners, encourage and harden you in your sinful course: as it did those, Mal. iii. 15, " And now we call the proud happy: yea, they that work wickedness are set up; yea, they that tempt God are even delivered." Ye have seen much of their sinful course, and of God's patience. But ye have not seen the end of it yet: Is. xvii. 11, "In the day shalt thou make thy plant to grow, and in the morning shalt thou make thy seed to flourish: but the harvest shall be a heap in the day of grief, and of desperate sorrow." Many a day has begun fair, and held on long so, that has had a foul evening. And whatever ye have observed of them, their prosperity in their ill course shall be their end in bitter repentance, or in their destruction, or else the word of truth fails.

3dly, Take the alarm in time, and flee from the wrath to come: Is. lv. 6, 7, " Seek ye the Lord while he may be found, call ye upon him while he is near. Let the wicked forsake his way, and the unrighteous man his thoughts: and let him return unto the Lord, and he will have mercy upon him; and to our God, for he will abundantly pardon." Know ye cannot prosper to the end, in your loose and licentious ways. Ye must come to Christ by faith, and leave the world lying in wickedness; must break off your sins by repentance; or else ye will perish. If ye do it not, ye will mind that ye have been fairly warned, and lament for ever your slighting it.

2. To the godly I would say,

1st, Beware of entertaining any idol of jealousy in your heart, wherewith the Lord may be provoked against you. He is impartial in his judgments, and even his own shall not escape: Is. xlii. 24, " Who gave Jacob for a spoil, and Israel to the robbers ? did not the Lord, he, against whom we have sinned ? for they would not walk in his ways, neither were they obedient unto his laws." Though being in Christ ye have shut the gulf as to condemnation, ye may be severely chastised; and ye may get broken bones for your transgressions, though ye cannot lose your souls.

2dly, Be not discouraged in the Lord's way, because in it ye meet with many sore trials, while others that are far from it go at ease. The work-ox goes with the yoke on his neck, while the slaughter-ox is full fed. But the former is preserved, while the latter is slain and hewed in pieces.

3 Lastly, To all I would say,

1st, Know that God is a holy jealous God. The way of sin is dangerous, and there will be no peace in the end of it.

2dly, Let us prepare to meet our God in the way of his judgments. God's proceedings against the land are slow, but they are like to be sure and sore. He has made the earth to quake beneath us, shown his anger from the face of the heavens above us.

REPENTANCE

Thomas Goodwin

ON REPENTANCE.

CHAPTER 1

Gather yourselves together, yea, gather together, O nation not desired; before the decree bring forth, before the day pass as the chaff, before the fierce anger of the Lord come upon you, before the day of the Lord's anger come upon you. Seek ye the Lord, all the meek of the earth, which have wrought his judgment; seek righteousness, seek meekness: it may be ye shall be hid in the day of the Lord's anger.—Zeph. II. 1–3.

The first chapter is throughout spent in a most fearful denunciation and description of a speedy and universal consumption decreed against the land of Judah, with the causes of it, which the prophet yet winds up in the words I have read unto you, with a gracious exhortation to repentance, to prevent the execution of that decree.

Wherein consider, first, the persons to whom this exhortation is made. First of all, he speaks collectively as to the whole nation: 'Gather together, &c., O nation,' calling them to a solemn and public repentance; which, secondly, is also to be understood as spoken particularly and distributively to every person in the nation, especially the impenitent: 'Search yourselves, O you not to be desired.' If, thirdly, he can prevail with none of them, he then more especially turns his speech to all the godly in the land, who had repented already, 'which have wrought his judgments;' however, 'seek ye the Lord,' &c.

Secondly, Consider the duties he exhorts them all unto, whereof, though some are more particularly spoken to the bad, some to the good, yet all concern all alike, which as they are laid down in the text, express the parts and ingredients into repentance, and order of them.

1. All collectively are to gather solemnly together; and, 2, being gathered, to search (for so as here anon the word is also to be understood) into the sins of the nation; so also collectively taken, which bring the judgment threatened.

And 2. Every particular person is particularly exhorted: 1, to search himself: 'Search yourselves into your own sins and estate before God;' 2, to judge of yourselves as men not to be desired, that is, out of the favour of God, and to whom his wrath was due, for so God judged of you, O nation not to be desired, and he speaks it to that end that they might judge so of themselves; 3, out of the sense of this to seek the Lord, to

158

seek his favour, and to pacify his wrath ; and, 4, that they might be sure to find him, to 'seek righteousness' also, grace as well as mercy, else they seek him in hypocrisy ; and, 5, more especially, to seek him in humility and meekness of spirit, seek meekness above all graces else; and, 6, do all this speedily, ' before the decree come forth.'

And in the third and last place, to stir up all to this, both good and bad, he adds motives.

First, Such as might quicken the bad : as, 1, God's patience was big with a decree, and that decree of wrath ; 2, a set day was appointed for the birth, when it would bring forth ; 3, the child would prove ' the fierce anger of the Lord ;' which, 4, would ' consume them as chaff,' and they not able to resist it.

Secondly, He adds a particular motive to the godly, that in case the day of the Lord's anger come upon the impenitent, yet if they would seek God now they should be hid in it.

In handling of which particulars I have rather chosen to give you the juice and strength of them as strained and concocted into application, and an use of exhortation, as here the prophet doth, than to spend this precious time afforded us in doctrinal discourses.

In which, if I shall be coarse and plain, and not prophesy smooth things to you, consider sackcloth becomes this day, as to pray in, so to prophesy in, as the two witnesses are said to do, Rev. xi. 3.

Speak first, you see here, the prophet doth of, and to the whole nation in the general; and so I have more especial commission to do this day, wherein every particular congregation assembled is to represent and personate the whole, and take upon them the sins of the whole nation, to confess them as their own, as the saints of old, Ezra and Daniel, did in all their fasts. But more especially we, who are a nation of ourselves (*gens togata*), and as a colony select and culled out of all the corners of it ; and so our sins are as the index of all the sins of the nation, and not only so, but as the original fountain of all the distempers through the whole.

The first thing he exhorts this nation to, is to ' gather together ;' that is (as I have it expounded, Joel ii. 15, 16), ' Sanctify a fast, call a solemn assembly, gather the people,' &c. God will have public penance ere he grants out a general pardon. And gathered together we are this day to this very purpose, so as that exhortation would be out of date, only let us bless the zeal and wisdom of authority, that hath thus gathered us together before the decree bring forth ; for that is the right season of this great ordinance. Preventing physic is best, and so this is here prescribed, and so hath been taken by the saints of old. In the 9th of Ezra, when the people had married the daughters of the nations, and the princes had been chief in this trespass, as soon as Ezra did but hear of this sin he rent his garment, sat down astonied, and fasted and prayed, as foreseeing a storm when such gross vapours ascended : ' For though yet,' says he, ' we remain escaped, yet wouldst thou not be angry till thou hadst consumed us ?' &c. ver. 14, 15.

But to gather together, and to call a general congregation, that is not all the prophet exhorts here the nation unto ; he calls them to a scrutiny also : ' Search yourselves.' The original word, say all interpreters, signifies *searching* as well as *gathering* ; and, say some, these two being conjugate duties, the Holy Ghost therefore concludes both in a word indifferently signifying both ; so as the word being twice repeated, they translate the first *gather*, the second *search*. Searching, which is the beginning of wisdom and repentance, being the end of fasting. And besides, that the plain and proper signification of the word bears both, so by way of metaphor it bears both also; for repentance, whereof searching ourselves is the beginning, is in Scripture phrase expressed by gathering a man's mind or wits together (that all our life perhaps before have been gadding a preferment-gathering, learning-gathering, credit-gathering, and the like things without us), but then to recollect and call in our thoughts, to 'come to ourselves,' as the prodigal's repentance is expressed, Luke xv. 17. 'To bethink ourselves,' or 'bring back to our hearts,' as the margin varies it in 1 Kings viii. 47, speaking there, as here, of true repentance. So as you see every way they agree both *re et nomine*.

And besides, the motive the prophet useth before and after, makes for this interpretation, which is the only motive I will use to quicken you to this duty at this time, ver. 12 of this former, the first chapter, 'I will search Jerusalem with candles;' and how is that? I will punish, &c.; for judgments are God's bloodhounds, which in the end find sin and sinners out; as in Ps. cx. 15, 'Break thou the arm of the wicked: seek for his iniquity till thou find none;' that is, till there be none of sins left unpunished; and therefore, says the prophet, to prevent God's search, 'Search yourselves;' as 'judge yourselves,' &c.

First, Into national sins; for he speaks to them as a nation: 'O nation not to be desired;' let us search, I say, for if we leave any of Rachel's idols hid in the straw, any of Achan's garments in the stuff, which we would conceal, God will come and search with candles but he will find them out. David inquired of God what national sin brought the famine, and it was found Saul's oppressing the Gibeonites, 2 Sam. xxi. 1; and desperate must the condition of that nation and people be, which, though they themselves 'declare their sins as Sodom,' and their plague-sores run and fester and stink in the nostrils of God and good men, yet, as those that have the plague, they cannot endure a scourge, no, not to have them touched with the tenderest and discreetest hand. And he that would make too diligent an inquisition may fear to be brought into one himself, much more must that nation be near destruction and drawing home when the fatal and deadly sins of it are skinned and healed slightly, as by the flattering prophets of old, till there be no healing, as the Spirit elsewhere speaks.

For this of ours, to search into whose sores and confess them it is that we are gathered together this day; though it be true of us as well in regard of sins as punishments, what Isaiah spake of his in the days of Hezekiah, 'From the sole of the foot to the crown of the head, it is full of wounds and bruises, and putrefying sores; the whole head is sick, and the heart is faint.'

Yet search I intend not into the distempers of the head and nerves, of the rulers and magistrates that give motion to the whole body; it is not for this assembly.

And, secondly, indeed search I need not into the outward sores of grosser sins which break out in the body of the people; they are all visible enough to every man's view and conscience.

But the inward corruptions of the blood and spirits; that is, of religion and worship of God, which is the cause of all those other distempers; these I rather desire you to make inquiry of.

First, Because it more properly belongs to this auditory to search into it, who are as the liver and heart, the fountain and cistern of both (for 'the priest's lips are to preserve knowledge, and the people to take the law at their mouths, Mal. ii. 7) ; and from us especially have all those veins and arteries their original, which carry and disperse all the corrupt blood and spirits through the whole body of the nation.

And secondly, also because it is the corruption therein which our prophet doth first and principally and in a manner point out in this chapter the first, from the 4th verse to the 7th, and so warrants me to apply what is found like to it to this nation as the object of their search, as the cause why God did not desire them, and the cause of ruin threatened.

For indeed, thirdly, nothing makes Christ to loathe a church that once received pure religion and undefiled from him (as Jesus speaks) as pure blood and spirits, than corruption herein, as you may see by those seven epistles of his writ since he went to heaven, Rev. 2d and 3d chapters, for this is the corruption of the vitals ; for the life lies in the blood, and if it be restored and then kept pure, outward blains will soon shale off.

Let us then view the state of religion and God's worship which this our prophet found in Judah, and take we this discovery or direction for us to search ours.

First, Flat and plain idolaters, *ex professo*, we find unpurged out of that state ; for which God will ' stretch his hand at the inhabitants, to cut off them who before were not cut short,' ver. 4.

Which idolatry is laid open in three things.

First, In having relics of Baal, idolatrous images, altars and rites for his worship.

Secondly, In having priests also the instruments of it, both *chemarim* (so called from their heat, as *kamar* signifies), their zeal to seduce others, and their activeness to propagate idolatry, as expositors note.   And, 2, priests, that is, ordinary chaplains in their houses.

Thirdly, Their idolatry practised in worshipping the host of heaven, and in the night, and so in secret (for the time of it) though on tops of houses. I shall not need bid you go search for these corruptions ; your consciences, I dare say, have had an eye upon popish altars, crucifixes, indulgences (called by some, as here, relics too, but of Baal) ; upon the Jesuits also more hot than ere the *chemarims ;* not seducers only, but incendiaries of the state, such spirits as inflame and make everywhere the blood so hot, as they cast nations into burning fevers, civil dissensions, and the secular priests with them ; for the purging of both which, our state wisely hath prescribed bleeding.   And their worshipping the host of heaven, the army of glorious martyrs, and saints, and angels, and a breaden host also, no man can be ignorant of ; for it is practised not as in the night, as with them, but as in the day.

The second sort he instanceth in are not idolaters *ex professo,* but they pretended the same ' reformed religion,' established, they swore, by God ; that is, worshipped him (for so you all know swearing by God is put to signify), and yet swore by Malchan also, retaining correspondency with both, and happily endeavouring to reconcile both.   Search if you find not those that do so with us, that would jumble light and darkness, by little and little bring in a twilight in opinions first, which the midnight will certainly follow ; who to that end revive things left out by our reformers as superstitious, and which ushered in popery at first, and who do it perhaps to symbolise and comply with popery, to make the transmutation the more easy.

The third sort are those that were turned back from the Lord, apostates either in opinion or practice, or truth professed once and acknowledged, and if in opinion, then in practice; for no man is better than his judgment, many are worse; and opinions that overthrow the practice of religion are worse than the grossest actual sins, by how much an act of treason is less than a law permitting it, or an opinion that it might be lawful. And when men are reduced to prove the first principles laid by glorious martyrs and apostles, it is a sign of great, and high, and irrecoverable fall in some, Heb. vi. 1, 2, ver. 4 compared.

However, if we retain the opinions, yet for the practice of godliness, and as to the approbation of it, 'Evil men wax worse and worse.' Compare but these times with the infant times of our first Reformation; Queen Mary's fires did heat England, and the examples of the blessed men then sealing the truth with their bloods, left behind it a general approbation of their ways, and those duties of godliness which they did profess and practise. Spiritual preaching was then prized; men might go far to hear sermons, and repeat them to their families and be reverenced. Men might have professed the fear of God in the utmost strictness of it, and have made conscience of their ways and not have been nicknamed; might have pleaded for the Sabbath, and sanctified it in the utmost strictness, spent it wholly in heavenly exercises (as our homilies' words are), and not have been accused of Judaism. But the memory of those godly men and their ways is now worn out, and a generation is come on that know not those Josephs; and now their brethren that worship God after the same way that they did are cried down.

If gross sins be to be spoken against, and sinners punished, men indeed seem to strike, but it is but with a dull and a faint blow with the back of the sword; but if but a hair be to be pared off a godly man's hand, men turn the edge and strike with all their might.

And whereas drunkenness and profaneness, contempt of God 'and good- ness, may pass and travel through the world, having neither passport of law or conscience to secure or countenance it, godliness, under the sus- picion of being a factious spy, is everywhere stopped, examined (though it have a passport of conformity to shew for itself), yea, and is sometimes whipped out of town for a renegade.

Nay, is it not, like Samson, brought up upon stages, which are often the devil's pulpits, though under another visor, to make the Philistines sport; yea, set up as a mark to be shot at out of God's place, the pulpit, and puritanism set up as the stalking-horse to stand behind, while they shoot through the loins of it?

᾿ Men are not only 'turned *from* the Lord' (as in the prophet here), but turned *against* him.

The fourth and last sort that Zephaniah speaks of are those who were never of any religion, that have not sought God, nor inquired for him, but live in this world without God, as atheists and ignorant persons, that have no knowledge, nor inquire they after any; and civil persons, that neglect calling upon God, and regard not the holy duties wherein he is to be sought; Gallios that 'care for none of these things;' and to search for such in the kingdom were to search out trees in the wood. The whole world is full of them. Nay, rather go and 'run through the streets,' as God bade Jeremiah, Jer. v. 1, 2, and see if you can 'find a man that seeks after God,' in comparison of multitudes do not, or a man who is inquisitive after him in his ordinances, as the church was in the Canticles, chap. v. ver. 6. Nay, run through the corners of the kingdom, you may see thou- sands of villages where people 'sit still in darkness and the shadow of death,' and if, happily, they should seek after God, it must be by 'groping,' as Paul says of the heathen, Acts xvii. 27 ; and indeed how should they! for, as Paul says, Rom. x. 14, ' How shall they call on him of whom they have not believed or known ? And how should they know and believe in him unless they have heard ? And how shall they hear without a preacher ? But have they not all heard ? Yes, the sound,' as the apostle says. But to ask one question more, ' How should they preach unless they be sent ?' I mean to their livings, and reside upon them over the souls of men, in which not men, but God, hath made them overseers. No wonder if Israel be said to be without God, if without ' a teaching priest,' 2 Chron. xv. 2, 3 ; not a *reading* priest only, but a *teaching*, who may explain the word of life ; as a schoolmaster doth not teach a scholar that only reads his lesson to him, but that also opens it. Why, then, is there a want of such ministers to instruct the people ? Is it that Christ, who, ' when he ascended, gave gifts unto men, for the work of the ministry,' and not only to convert, and to set in at first, but to build up his saints, Eph. iv. 8–12, hath yet been strait-handed towards this church of ours in dealing out gifts to men, or not to men enough, as labourers to be thrust forth into his vineyard ? Or is it that the chiefest fruit of Christ's ascension and main legacies left behind him was bare reading ? None of these things can be affirmed without undervaluing both his goodness and the power and efficacy of his ascension. Why, then, it lies on us, that the lights God hath set up, and are full of fuel, oil, and lightsome matter, as learning, gifts, &c., remain *cæca lumina*, or not dispersed, as your lights in your streets are in a dark night fixed in their proper candlesticks. It was one of the first works good Jehoshaphat did, 2 Chron. xvii., first, as to plant forces in all the cities of Judah, and set garrisons in the land of Judah and Ephraim, which Asa his father had taken, ver. 2. So also in the third year he sent both ' Levites and princes to teach through all the cities, and they went about throughout all the cities of Judah, and taught the people,' ver. 9. Well, and what was the issue of this ? ' Fear fell upon all the kingdoms about, and they made no war,' ver. 10. His garrisons of priests teaching, and princes backing it with authority, were a greater strength and fence to his kingdom than all his subjects ; and they will keep a kingdom secure from invasion, for they are the ' chariots and horsemen of Israel,' which in those days were the chief munition, as horsemen and guns are now.

And had we had that care to have fortified every village (in this plenty of able men) which our forefathers took, and wean* from popery, the souls of millions had not been left exposed to the devouring lion the devil, and the Jesuits, who are his janisaries, as they have been ; nor should we have needed to fear invasions as now we do, but should have been a terror to all round about us, as they are now to us : and had there not been auxiliary and subsidiary preachers, who have borne the heat of the day, being graciously admitted by authority, who had been swallowed ere now, and yet inquire if some have not cried them down, as they use to do mercenary soldiers, as dangerous unto the church, and that will prove fatal unto the inhabitants.

Neither is this all the cause of our people's not seeking God ; but if men preach, yet winnow their sermons, and see how much chaff you shall find among a few corns (it is Jeremiah's comparison, Jer. xxiii. 28). And when men sow chaff, what seed can be expected ? or what blessing by dew from

---

* Qu. ' won' ?—ED.

heaven to come upon it ? Or if men preach more solidly, yet still passing by the great things of the gospel, the way and signs of faith towards Christ, and repentance towards God, which yet the great doctor of the Gentiles, Paul, makes the sum of all his sermons expressly, Acts xx. 21 ; and the reason is, because often indeed in these things (even such as was Nicodemus, who was a teacher in Israel) are yet as blind hearers as they were. 'Who so blind as my messenger?' says God by Isaiah, whose name is yet a seer, chap. xlii. ver. 19 ; so blind, as they judge not of colours; *Color omnibus unus*, as he said, in the dark. And, say they, ' all the people are holy,' Num. xvi. 2, which sends men quick and alive in their own conceits to hell, and with the flattery of universal grace betrays them hoodwinked to destruction ; whereas that prophet, that is, ' God's mouth,' is to ' separate between the precious and the vile,' as God spake to Jeremiah, chap. xv. ver. 19 ; which opinion, where engendered, must needs make men regardless of seeking God, seeing they are told they are good Christians already.

Or, lastly, if they do preach those things, yet not living answerably ; ' My covenant,' says God, Mal. ii. 6, ' was with Levi whilst both the law of truth was in his mouth, and he walked with me in equity,' and he then ' turned many to righteousness ;' but they being ' departed out of the way, and causing many to stumble,' by ill and slanderous lives, ' therefore I have made you contemptible and base before all the people.' The clergy of England complain much of contempt. See here the cause of it, and all the riches and honour you can clothe and load yourselves with cannot vindicate men from it ; but that which makes our steps beautiful and persons honourable, is to preach the gospel, and to live accordingly.

And now, my brethren, to conclude this search, if the blood and spirits in which lies the life of this kingdom shall be found, upon search, thus corrupted and weak, and not having their due motion throughout the whole, we may either give it for dead, or at least fear that the death and destruction (which you see in the like case throughout the chapter he so peremptorily threatens, ver. 7, cutting off all disputes to the contrary, Hold thy peace, &c., says he, against Judah, though as then ' all his meek ones he had in the earth,' as the text shews, were found therein) is not far off our nation. For besides his general rule given, Jer. v. 9, ' Shall not my soul be avenged on such a nation?' God hath, and can have when he will, a people that shall bring forth more fruit than we have done ; who are also, at the best, but ' branches of the wild olive grafted in,' Rom. xi. 17, in the stead of this nation, the example of which I lay afore you, who were the natural ; ' and if God spared not the natural branches, take heed lest he spare not thee,' ver. 20. But yet God's ' judgments are unsearchable, and his ways past finding out,' ver. 33, past tracing ; for he keeps not always in regard of time and manner the same track of punishment, to shew the depth of his wisdom, as he there speaks.

I have done with the nation, collectively taken.

Let me now turn my speech to every particular person that hears me this day, in the fear of a decreed destruction, as it follows in the seventh verse of the first chapter of our prophet Zephaniah : God having in all likelihood bidden his guests (as he there speaks), who are making themselves ready, and in hopes have devoured us already. Let us, I say, in the fear of this, every particular man come home to himself : ' Search yourselves, O nation ;' that is, every man apart.

For indeed this duty of searching is the foundation and corner-stone of true repentance. Thus Lam. iii. 40, ' Let us search and try our ways, and turn unto the Lord.' He that is in the wrong way turns never out of it till by inquiry he finds he is in the wrong, and therefore travellers inquire often of the way, and so should we.

Only then, in the second place, it is and must be a searching of ourselves the prophet calls you to, not to search into the common faults of kingdoms and of the state, to the end to complain of them as many do, and overlook their own. No ; it is the prophet's complaint, Jer. viii. 6, ' No man repented, saying, What have I done ?' but the prodigal, when he repented, ' came home to himself.'

Yea, thirdly, and this is most seasonable and requisite in time of common danger, and when public fastings are enjoined, and when men are called thus to gather together, then to search ; therefore both are joined here and in 1 Kings viii. 38, ' If a famine be in the land, or enemy besiegeth, what prayer shall be made by any man' (that is, by any man singly and apart, for you are to pray privately as well as publicly on such an occasion), ',which shall know every man the plague of his own heart' (mark it): ' Then, Lord, hear, O God, and forgive, and do,' &c.

For, first, God hears not the prayers made till then, for the priest prayed and offered sacrifice for his own sins as for the people, Heb. v. 3.

Secondly, God forgives not till then, for God in pardoning he must have the glory of his justice which hath been provoked, and the expense of the riches of his mercy that he lays out in pardoning known and acknowledged sins. He must have a particular reckoning with every man, first, that they may know what their debt is, and what is forgiven ; that although God lose the debt, he may not lose his kindness in forgiving it.

Thirdly, Because (as there) God ' gives and doth to every man according to his ways, whose heart he knows ;' that is, God, he searcheth your hearts, and accordingly deals with particular men in time of common judgments according to their particular ways ; for judgments which you call common yet light upon particular persons. And as in common for national sins, so on this and that particular person according to his particular ways ; for a ' consumption decreed overflows with righteousness,' Isa. x. 22 ; and therefore as, to remove it in common, national sins are to be searched into, so because it lights with righteousness on particulars, every man is to search his own personal sins, and by sweeping every man his own door the street is cleansed, and so the judgment removed. The Ninevites (of whom Christ says they repented at the preaching of Jonah), upon occasion of that public fast proclaimed by their prince, did not only keep a general fast and cried mightily unto God, but that edict it is specially urged, ' Yea, let them turn every one from his evil way,' Jonah iii. 8 ; and the event was, ' God saw that they turned from their evil way, and God repented of the evil,' ver. 10.

If now you ask what you are to search in yourselves, I answer, into your sins and estates before God ; ' Search, O nation not to be desired.' Now it is sin alone that takes God's heart off from us, and that causeth him to have no pleasure in us.

Let every man therefore go home and commune with his own heart, unlock it, and search into all the written evidences and records of his own conscience, which happily have not been looked into since the first writing of them ; and to help you to order those confused reckonings, give out to every particular commandment its several bills.

Thou that hast been a swearer, think what a fearful bill the third commandment will bring in against thee, of whom God hath said that he will not hold guiltless for taking his name in vain.

Thou that hast been a Sabbath-breaker, think what a reckoning the fourth will bring in, concerning which God hath given thee a particular *memento*, 'Remember thou keep holy the Sabbath day,' in thoughts, words, actions, which it may be thy conscience puts thee in remembrance also of, and yet thou 'shuttest thine eyes,' as they are said to do, 'from the Sabbath,' Ezek. xxii. 26. Take heed lest God swear against thee, 'thou shalt never enter into his rest,' Heb. iv. 3, which, Heb. iv. 9, is called 'the sabbath of the people of God,' σαϐϐατίσμον.

Think what innumerable sins of others, pupils or people entrusted to thee, souls murdered by thy ill example or negligence to instruct them, the sixth commandment will bring in with this foot of the account: 'Their blood' (their souls' blood) 'will I require at thy hands,' Ezek. iii. 18–20.

Think how many stand on the file of the seventh, how many millions of thoughts sacrificed to speculative adultery, if not the fact itself, or man's sin committed, which latter the apostle Paul calls, Rom. i. 24, 'defiling their bodies,' ἐν ἑαυτοῖς, 'in or by themselves;' and Oh think how often with this sentence at the end: 'The Lord knows how to reserve the unjust to the day of judgment to be punished, especially them that walk after the lust of uncleanness,' 2 Peter ii. 10.

Turn over the vast heap of thy actions, sift them, see how few faithful prayers thou canst find amongst them, how few gracious speeches among as many sins as sands.

Yea, unravel all thy life and untwist each action, and see how many sins in regard of many aggravations are woven but in one.

Go down into the treasury of thy thoughts (as the Scripture calls them, Matt. xii. 35, for the abundance of them and worth in them); think with thyself if they should be melted and tried, as one day God will do every work by fire, 1 Cor. iii. 13; that when all the dross of covetous, proud, adulterous, envious, blasphemous, foolish, thoughts, as Christ musters them and calls them, Mark vii. 21, are abstracted and taken out, how little gold there remains or thoughts of any worth; so Solomon says, 'a fool's heart is little worth,' Prov. x. 20. So feel the pulse of thy desires and affections, of all thy desires, joys, &c., see how quickly and strongly it beats to what is evil, how dully, faintly, yea, not at all to what is good.

Bolt and sift out the meaning and end in every affection, thought, and action, and see how self-love, pleasure, credit, ease, is the *finis architec-tonicus* that sets all a-work, takes all, and pays all.

Observe what the motives and bribes to gratify self within thee are, which thy heart takes ere it stirs to anything is good.

Trace and scent out all the windings, shifts, and turnings of thy thoughts and inward discoursing to colour over evil.

Lastly, Cast up what thy receipts have been, what wit, learning, good example of other men, light of conscience, motions of the Spirit, tastings of the heavenly gifts, blessed ordinances and opportunities thou hast been made partaker of; and reckon thy expenses for God, and thy trading by these, and what thou gainedst for him by them.

And after you have done this, let the next inquiry be, in what estate you are before God? whether in an estate of favour, which is the thing the prophet puts to their consideration, and search whether to be desired or no; that is, in such an estate wherein God's desire or acceptance is towards thee, and so he speaks of the impenitent in the nation as opposed to the meek, in three verses, who are in estate of desire and gracious acceptance with God : Cant. vii. 10, 'I am my beloved's and he is mine, and his desire is towards me ;' and Eph. i. 6, 'He hath made us graciously accepted ;' so as though they have sins that make them in themselves not to be desired, yet God's desire is to them ; now that of all other is great controversy, which yet is to be feared, whether thou art in this state of favour with God ; few scholars beat their heads about fearing to live in that estate they are afraid to die in.

Now for the decision of the controversy, rest not only in searching the church book, and there finding you are baptized ; in Mark xvi. 16, 'He that believes and is baptized,' says Christ, 'he shall be saved ; but he that believes not shall be damned.' Suppose he be baptized, whether think you will Christ's words prove true or no ? As in Simon Magus they did, God putting no more difference between a Turk and unregenerate man, though baptized, than of old he did between a Jew and a heathen, Jer. ix. 26 ; the one is uncircumcised in the flesh, the other, the Jew, in the heart ; for as not circumcision, so nor by the same reason baptism, doth avail aught, 'but a new creature in Christ,' Gal. vi. 15.

But search you this sacred register of heaven, which is the great inquest of life and death, where all the evidences and indictments to acquit the godly, or condemn the wicked, lie.

And there you shall find that he that hath suffered in the flesh hath ceased from sin, 1 Pet. iv. 1 ; therefore he that lies in any known sin cannot be saved.

There you shall find if you make credit, or preferment, or anything but God's glory, your end, you cannot believe : John v. 44, 'How can you believe whilst you seek honour one of another, and not the glory which comes of God only ?'

There you shall find that flatterers and time-servers are not the servants of Christ : Gal. i. 10, 'If I yet pleased men, I should not be the servan of Christ.'

There you shall find that he who loves not the Lord Jesus, 'he is accursed,' 1 Cor. xvi. 22. And, 'Peter, lovest thou me ? Feed my sheep ;' you know who said so, he that must judge you also.

There you shall find that he that hates his brother, especially when he makes conscience of sin and duty, that he hates God whom he hath not seen, who gave that law he makes conscience of, 1 John iv. 20.

There you shall find that he that slights and despiseth any of God's commandments and ways appointed him to walk, shall die, Prov. xix. 16.

That he who neglects calling upon God, is a worker of iniquity, Ps. liii. 4, for sinning will either make him leave praying, or praying leave sinning.

Yea, and to make conscience of this not publicly only, but privately, for when a spirit of supplication is poured out, it makes men and women pray apart, as Zech. xii. from 10th verse to end compared.

Yea, and if men continue not to do so constantly, and delight not in God, they are no better than hypocrites, Job xxvii. 8, with 10th verse compared. If a man should take the keys of your heart, and ransack your cupboards, and see what sweet bits you delight in, he should find them full of uncleanness, ease, pleasures, &c., rather than God, and communion with him in his ordinances.

And if upon this search thy estate be found by thee to be unsound indeed, and not to be desired or rested in, be not shy or afraid to judge so of it, and to pass sentence upon thyself accordingly. For he tells them, God who is greater than your hearts doth so judge of them ; that is, think of yourselves as God doth, tune your judgments to his. Which is so far from putting you off from God, as it is a necessary preparation to coming into favour with him ; for as he that is a fool must think himself one ere he can be wise, 1 Cor. iii. 18, so he that will be justified must first apprehend himself condemned : Rom. iv. 5, 'He that believes in him that justifies the ungodly, his faith is imputed to him for righteousness.' A man in law cannot have a sentence of pardon until he be first judged, and cast, and sentence passed upon him as guilty.

And therefore it is the greatest kindness can be done you by others, and the greatest wrong you can do yourselves, for others to tell you your estate is good and blessed when it is not, or you not to be apprehensive of the truth herein. For, Ps. vii. 11, it is said, 'God is angry with the wicked every day ; if we turn not, [he] hath prepared his instruments of death.'

The next thing in the text is, to ' seek the Lord,' for there is no continuing in that estate thou yet standest in. And thou hast no way to escape but by seeking of him and turning to him.

As that wise king in the parable, Luke xiv. 32, when by consultation he had found that the king coming against him would be too strong, he sends out an embassage and desires conditions of peace ; and so must thou from God. Send up prayers day and night as messengers for peace to the court of heaven, and to obtain of Christ, that those great preparations made against thee be stopped ; and know that God will be sought too of all those shall have peace at his hands, for he doth not cast pardons away, which cost him the blood of his Son to purchase them, he will have them prized to the utmost. Now that we esteem little worth which is not worth the seeking for, when it is to be had for seeking.

Yea, and so unalterably God stands upon it and looks for this, as that though he hath engaged himself by never so faithful a promise to shew mercy unto his church, yet as Ezek. xxxvi. 36, 37, he says, ' I will ; nevertheless, I will be inquired for by the house of Israel for this,' &c.

And he looks not for this only from us, when yet his word is first passed to do it, but he looks for it from his Son Christ on our behalf, to be sought by him, who according to his Godhead is equal to his Father ; yea, and of him, who for the performance of those things also purchased all God means to do for us ; yet he must ask, yea, in the 17th of John he asks for his own glory he had before the world was. In Ps. ii. 8, ' Ask of me the heathen,' &c., which yet were his own by purchase. Much more therefore he requires this of one that is at that distance from him, who is to him but as the chaff, and wax before the fire, and dust of the balance ; as we are creatures, and who besides are enemies to him, until he be reconciled to us, and we to him.

Yea, and he resolves to be sought in earnest unto, not with a faint and a lazy seeking. Luke xiii. 24, ' Strive to enter in, for many shall seek and not be able.' If you get peace of him, you must wrestle for it ; $\zeta\eta\tau\epsilon\tilde{\iota}\nu$, to *seek*, is too low an expression ; wrestle as Jacob did all night, and with all your might too, put to all your strength, yea, use violence, Mat. xi. 12, besiege heaven with volleys of prayers and tears. Jer. xxix. 13, ' They shall seek and find me, when they seek with all their hearts.'

And faith on his graciousness and readiness to pardon, as a foundation of the seeking of him, is absolutely necessary ; and such a God thou, upon such seeking of him, shalt find him to be. Do not, therefore, now conceive him to be of so harsh and furious a disposition, as that there is no dealing with him, no coming near him ; for though he be thus great a God, yet he professeth, Isa. xxvii. 5, ' Fury is not in me' towards one who desires to be at ' peace with me.' And though he be thus strong, yet ' take hold of his strength,' as there, by faith ; and then out of faith pray to him, by prayer seek to him and wrestle with him, and thou shalt have power over him, as Jacob had. ' Then he is gracious ; and he shall pray to him, and God will be favourable, and he shall see his face with joy,' Job xxxiii. 24, 26.

If you ask, What disposition of heart, together with believing, will con-duce most to overcome him ? I answer, in the third place, ' Seek to him in meekness,' that is, lowliness and submission. As, first, acknowledging thy deservedness to be destroyed, as they, Ezek. xxxvi. 31, and thy con-tentedness to be so, if it may more glorify him, which, Lev. xxvi. 41, is called ' accepting' of a man's due punishment, putting a man's self into his hands, and referring himself to him : as David, 2 Sam. xv. 26, ' If he says of me,' says he, ' I have no delight in thee : behold, here am I ; let him do with me as seemeth good to him.' And to be content to wait and attend patiently, ' if at any time,' as saith the apostle, ' God will be gracious to thee ;' and put thy mouth in the dust. And thus God will be sought to humbly, and as a traitor guilty afore God, and obnoxious to him, Rom. iii. 19, that so his absolute free grace may appear and be acknowledged. Ezek. xxxvi. 31, they ' loathe themselves,' or as others read it, ' judge them-selves worthy to be destroyed.' And why ? For ' be it known to you, that not for your sakes I do this,' that is, to pardon you ; ' but for his name's sake,' as ver. 22 of the same chapter.

And this is the greatest violence you can use ; it is a laying hold of his strength. Indeed, it overcomes an ingenuous man ; much more God, the ' God of all grace' and mercy. It overcame David, and it was Shimei's policy, as the only way to deal with him, 2 Sam. xix. 20, who, when he saw David would be too hard for him, he cunningly comes and puts himself into his hand. And so Benhadad's servants, knowing ' the kings of Israel to be merciful kings,' advised him their master, when they saw he and they must fall into his hand, to go with ropes about their necks, testifying thereby their acknowledgment that if he would hang them up he might, 1 Kings xx. 31 ; and they came by his chariot side beseeching, and observ-ing his words that fell from him, and waited diligently to see if he would incline to mercy ; and this overcame hard-hearted Ahab.

And thus now go thou to God. Fall down upon thy knees afore him, and with a heart broken to water, acknowledge, as Shimei, thy treason and rebellions against him who never did thee hurt ; and acknowledge, with a rope ready fitted to thy neck by thy own hands, as they Benhadad's ser-vants wore ; that is, confessing that if he will hang thee up, he may. He shall need no other judge to condemn thee than thyself, no other indictment but thine own confession ; and to shew that he needed not to send for thee and hale thee to execution, thou presentest thyself to him. Tell him that he may shew his justice on thee, if he will ; and present thy naked breast, thy hateful soul, as a butt and mark for him, if he please, to shoot his arrows into, and sheathe his sword in. Only desire him to remember that he sheathed his sword first in the bowels of his Son, Zech. xiii. 7, when he made his soul an offering for sin.

Take words unto thyself, as Hosea bids, chap. xiv. 2 (he loves to be entreated). That if his end be, that his justice should be satisfied on thee, say, that his Son hath done it, and that more fully than thou ever shalt, if thou go presently to hell. He may cast thee into prison; but say, thou art not able ever to pay the debt: so as he may, if he please, lose nothing by thee if he saves thee. Nay, he shall advance the glory of his grace in one that will be ever thankful, and is already sorry for offending him.

Plead for thyself, it is for thy life, that what shall he do in damning of thee, but break a leaf that is broken already, as Job pleads: Job xiii. 25, 'Pursue dry stubble,' as there; 'chaff,' as here in the text. Say, thou art not a fit match for him to shew his power in.

Urge him, that there are few in the world that do seek him, and if he turn away those that do, he shall have fewer. Who would fear him, if there were not mercy with him. 'Soft words pacify wrath,' Prov. xv. 1, 'and soft tongues break the bones;' and so a meekened spirit, a heart of rocks; much more his who hath bowels of compassion in him.

Oh, for God to hear a poor broken soul thus truly bemoaning itself, how doth it stir him, make his bowels work within him! See what himself says: Jer. xxxi. 18–20, 'When I heard Ephraim bemoaning himself, I remember him still, my bowels are troubled for him.' Every groan went to the heart of him; if he should have damned him, it would have troubled him all his days.

But withal, you must be sure (which is the fourth) to seek righteousness: both of justification, 'God's righteousness,' as David often calls it; Christ's righteousness, 'the Lord our righteousness,' as the prophet. A righteousness out of thyself, and laid hold upon by faith, as Rom. 3d, 4th, and 5th chapters, you have urged as being witnessed unto both by the law and the prophets. And truly, that is 'God's strength,' whereby his heart is strengthened to forgive and receive sinners. So in Isa. liii. 1, 'To whom is the arm of the Lord revealed?' that is, Christ, of whom he speaks throughout that chapter. This righteousness, when revealed by an interpreter, Job xxxiii. 23, to a poor soul, and sought by him, and pleaded by him, then God is gracious to him, and says, 'Deliver him, for I have found a ransom,' which this soul seeks me in; for he will 'render unto man his righteousness' which belongs to him, and was wrought for him to justify him.

Secondly, Of sanctification: For, I say, 'the work of righteousness is peace.' For, so long as thy sins remain, how can there be peace? And Isa. lv. 6, 'Seek ye the Lord,' &c., but let the wicked man 'forsake his way'; that is, change his outward converse and course; 'and the unrighteous man forsake his thoughts,' that is, get his heart changed also to have new desires, purposes, ends, and affections, and 'he will have mercy upon him.' And get a righteousness contrary unto thy former ways and thoughts; which if you ask, what that true righteousness is? I answer, 1, that true and new *righteousness in thy heart* thou must seek, is a new bent, bias, and temper of heart, rightly disposing, swaying all the faculties and powers of it, to hate whatsoever is known or suspected to be a sin; and, on the contrary, inclining them to love and delight in those contrary ways of holiness and righteousness God hath chalked out in his word, and all this for God's cause; hating the sin, because he hates it; loving the righteousness, because he loves it. This is that which in your hearts is required; and therefore to seek it. Secondly, *in life*, is to endeavour to the utmost of a man's strength to yield a constant obedience to all God's commands, and avoid the contrary. To seek after and delight in nothing more than when thou canst avoid sin, and do what is acceptable and pleasing in God's sight; and to approve thy heart to him, and grieving for nothing more than failing and falling short in what thou aimest at, and purposest, still having it in thy eye, resting in no pitch or measure of obedience.

And without this, with what face canst thou seek pardon at his hand? For what honesty or equity is there that thou shouldst seek the pardon of thy sin, and yet live in it, or not part with it in thy full resolutions? And then how canst thou open thy mouth to ask at God's hands; or, how to desire the benefit of that all-sufficient righteousness of Jesus Christ to cover thee, and not conform to thy utmost endeavour to be 'righteous, as he is righteous,' as John speaks, 1 John iii. 7, 'purging thyself, as he is pure,' ver. 7, that is, with all thy might and endeavours after it. In Luke viii. 15, the good ground is said to have and to bring forth fruit out of ' an honest heart;' and so must thou have.

Or, secondly, if thou hadst the face to seek him, neglecting this, dost think that God would ever pardon thee? Would a king pardon a traitor, though he sued never so humbly, if he saw he would be a traitor still? Thou wouldst not pardon no man in like case thyself.

If you plead, God hath more mercy in him than is in a man, for ' his thoughts are not our thoughts,' &c., Isa. lv. 8. I answer, Yet still where he expresseth himself most merciful, as in Exod. xxxiv. 6, 7, he adds at last, ' yet by no means clearing a guilty'-hearted person, that hath a false and disloyal heart towards him, and will not be subject to him in all things, and be content to have every thought brought to obedience.

And the reason is, because, first, ' there is mercy only with him that he may be feared,' Ps. cxxx. 4. Now if he should suffer pardon to go out of his hand, and no change in men's hearts to fear and obey him, there were mercy with him to be contemned.

And, secondly, you must know that God's mercy is joined with wisdom also; for one attribute destroys not another; but to pity a rogue that continues so, it is foolish pity. God forbids it in us, and therefore will not practise it himself.

Now, till thou turnest from sin, and choosest the things that please him, he will not delight in thee: Isa. lvi. 5, 'For thus saith the Lord unto the eunuchs that keep my sabbath, and choose the things that please me, and take hold of my covenant: even unto them will I give in mine house and within my walls a place and a name better than of sons and daughters,' &c. He instanceth in Sabbath, because that day, if sanctified as it ought, in thought, speeches, and actions, is the darling and delight of the Lord, Isa. lviii. 14. Now if thou makest it thy darling day too, and such a day as this of fasting and prayer, or of those ordinances which in his word he manifests his heart is for, if thine be for them also, prayer, holy conference, &c., then he comes to delight in thee, as there, and otherwise not; for ' can two walk together as friends (says the prophet), and not agree?' hating what he discovers he hates, &c.

Therefore, resolve either to leave every known sin, and submit to every known duty; or else never look to find favour and mercy from God.

Now the last clause and condition the prophet puts in, is to do ' before the decree come forth.' There is a space, as Solomon observes, Eccles. viii. 11, between sentence or decree, and the execution of it; and that time is space to repent: Rev. ii. 21, ' I gave her space to repent.' Now what and when God will decree against thee, and serve an execution upon thee, thou knowest not; and thou dost not know what decree is bringing forth, as they know not what is in the womb till it be born: Prov. xxvii. 1, ' Thou knowest not what a day may bring forth,' so as thou neither knowest what nor when an execution may be served upon thee; he may serve an execution of death ere to-morrow; as upon him, 'thou fool, this night;' death's serjeants may arrest thee, and bring thee before the judge; and therefore take our Saviour's counsel, given in the like case: Mat. v. 25, 'Agree with thine adversary whilst thou are in the way, lest at any time he deliver thee to the judge, and the judge to the officer, and he cast thee into prison.' And how near this serjeant from God is thou knowest not. James tells thee, James v. 9, 'Behold the judge is at the door,' and then his officer death is not far off.

But if God should spare thee yet, and let thee live, yet in the mean time an execution of hardness of heart and blindness of mind may be served on thee, as on the Pharisees: John xii. 40, 'He hath blinded their eyes, and hardened their heart, that they should not see with their eyes, nor understand with their heart, and be converted.' If not so, yet, which is all one, a decree [may] pass against thee, that thou shalt never have a pardon granted, though thou shouldst sue for it; as against Esau, who, Heb. xii., 'neglecting his birthright,' though he sought to revoke it 'with tears,' he could not; and against the Israelites in the wilderness, against whom 'God swore they should never enter into his rest,' though they lived many years after.

But the most fearful execution of all the rest, which all these tend to, is yet behind; you have it in the text, 'the anger and wrath of the almighty God;' that is, the child which in his decree is conceiving, and is already quickened. Ps. vii. 11, 'God is angry with the wicked every day.' This child strives in his heart every moment, so as he is ready every day to fall in travail, only because this child must have a time fully to be come to its growth, therefore he forbears; yet so as in the mean while he is 'a-preparing his instruments of death' (as there) for the execution of his anger, when his anger shall be brought forth.

And to that end there is a day appointed, 'the day of the Lord's anger,' in the text, which though thou knowest not, yet Ps. xxxvii. 13, God 'sees this day a-coming.' A birth when God's decrees bring forth anger, and thy 'sin brings forth death,' James i. 15, and that then when thou least dreamest of it, 'For when they shall say, Peace and safety, then sudden destruction cometh upon them, as travail upon a woman with child, and they shall not escape,' 1 Thes. v. 3. Yea, and it shall be the 'fierce anger of the Lord' also, the longer the child goes in the womb, the bigger. *Fierce*, because 'without mercy,' James ii. 13. 'Judgment without mercy,' called also 'pure wrath' without mixture, because not a drop of mercy to moderate the fierceness of it.

And what art thou this fierce wrath shall cease on? Thou art but 'chaff,' Nahum i. 3. His anger is a whirlwind; a small ordinary blast scatters chaff away, much more a whirlwind. There is no resistance, and if thou couldst resist the whirlwind, yet there it is said to be 'poured out as fire,' which therefore must needs consume thee; and if it rend the rocks, melt the hills, burn the earth, ver. 5, 6, how much more chaff? 'Who can can stand before his indignation, who can abide the fierceness of his wrath?'

I should now, in the last place, speak to those that are already truly turned to God, 'the meek of the earth.' And herein the prophet seems to act as one out of hope to prevail with the impenitent; yet seek you, says he, as when that great sin was committed, Ezra ix., though others were regardless of the danger would follow, yet every one that feared the Lord assembled to him, to pray and seek God, ver. 4.

Thus here doth the prophet speak to the godly amongst them, ' seek *you;*' as if he had said, Though others do (according to their kind) go on in hardness of heart, to treasure up wrath against the day of wrath (formerly spoken of by him), yet *you*, who are, and profess yourselves, ' the meek of the earth' (which is the general title given the saints in the Old Testament style, and imports all the whole of religion), upon whose hearts the word useth to take impression, do *you* according to your kind, take and receive this word of exhortation with meekness.   Which is,

First, To seek your God, for so in dangerous times he expects you should, and wonders if you do not ; so Isa. lix. 16, he ' wondered there was no intercessor' (it was in evil times, as appears by the former verses).   God wonders not that wicked men should be so bad, but that his people should be so negligent.   What ! (says he) have I no children on the earth, that upon such occasions, and such threatenings, use to intercede with me for the nation they live in !   Where are my Noahs and Daniels ?   We wonder at things their not doing according to their kind, as when we see the sun stand still, or fire not to burn, &c.

And, *secondly*, you are to seek righteousness and meekness, as thereby to condemn and be witnesses against the wicked for God, when judgments come and condemn the rest (as Noah did by fearing God aforehand, Heb. xi. 7), as also to save your own souls ; for as nothing but an ark saved Noah, so nothing but righteousness can save you, Ezek. xiv. 14 ; if Noah, &c., be saved, it is by their own righteousness.

If you say you have done it already, that answer will not be taken, for God, though he acknowledgeth they had wrought his judgment, yet exhorts them the more unto it against such a time as this, when to be saved when the judgment should come would be so great a mercy, to have their lives for a prey in such dear years of life ; though God forgat not what they had done, ' ye that have,' &c., says he, forget what was past, and seek after righteousness afresh, as if you had never yet sought any.

And to quicken them to it, he tells them, ' ye shall be filled,'[*] that is, when God comes to burn up the chaff ; yet then he will save his wheat, for he will preserve seed-corn to sow the world withal after harvest.

And if it should be asked how it is possible that they should be hid whilst the judgment is in general, consider he hath many chambers of his providence, as Isa. xxvi. 20, ' Come, my people, enter into thy chambers, and hide yourselves till my wrath overflows the earth ;' then, when others shall have nowhere to hide their heads, but shall wish the rocks to cover them, ye shall be hid.

Yea, but you will say, this is but half a promise here, and ' it may be.' But now, I had rather have God's *it may be*, than that *and it shall be*, from all the kings of the earth.   God loves to speak with the least, and do with the most, to be better than his word, who is abundant in kindness and truth.   Now it is not put to shew any uncertainty (see Junius on this place), it is put in a case of a certain promise, and yet withal to shew some difficulty in the performance of it, as when Peter says, ' the righteous shall scarcely be saved.'

And last of all, lest any of his saints should through discouragement or otherwise be slack, as either to think that for their weakness their prayers would do no good, nor prevail with God to remember them in the evil day, or that many particular persons should deem that there are enough besides

---

* Qu. ' hid' ?—ED.

them to seek God, and they need do the less, he therefore bids them all:
' Seek the Lord *all* ye meek.'

And God hath chambers enough to hide you all in, and it must be your
own righteousness must prevail for you, Ezra xiv. 14; and besides, he hath
need of all your voices; as in elections or great canvasses a voice casts a
matter this way or that, so in the great business of the church; therefore,
Isa. xxxvii., when ' the children are come to the birth, and there was no
strength to bring forth,' Hezekiah goes a visiting for another voice, sends
to Isaiah the prophet, as to a man-midwife, to come and help. But you
will say he was a prophet, a great saint; know that God often stands upon
a number, ten in Sodom, reckoning and counting small and great. The
number would have cast it, if of persons righteous. How many ten thousand
in England by proportion to this number for Sodom are there we know
not.; now Europe is a-bringing forth, and so the parliament, and yet they
have no strength, therefore come all to help; it was never known that when
all the lower house on earth did all petition to God, but they prevailed.
' If two agree on earth,' says Christ, then much more when all. I will
conclude all with that in the 3d chapter of this prophecy, ver. 9. God
being determined to pour his anger on all the earth, as now it may be he
hath begun to do, yet he meaning to spare his own in those general calamities, he says, that he ' will turn to them in peace, and they shall all call
on him and serve him with one shoulder;' so say I, lift up prayers with
pure hands and lips, and do it all of you, and all with one consent, and
God will visit you in mercies when he is in the way of his judgments.
And so let us do again this day.

CHAPTER 2

*Gather yourselves together, yea, gather together, O nation not desired; before
the decree bring forth, before the day pass as the chaff, before the fierce
anger of the Lord come upon you, before the day of the Lord's anger come
upon you. Seek ye the Lord, all the meek of the earth, which have wrought
his judgment; seek righteousness, seek meekness: it may be ye shall be hid in
the day of the Lord's anger.*—ZEPH. II. 1–3.

The doctrine is, that in times when public and common calamities are
threatened and feared, God's people should then especially practise these
duties mentioned here: ' Seek the Lord,' &c.

This I will demonstrate, *first*, in the general, by Scripture and reason;
then, *secondly*, enforce the particular duties, upon particular grounds also.

First, In the general, they are before public judgments to practise holy
duties. Because the promise of hiding being made only to the practice of
them, as here, and a godly man being only a wise man, for the fear of the
Lord being the beginning of wisdom, and the knowledge of the holy understanding, Prov. ix. 10, this is one main privilege and benefit which he
doth and may get by this his wisdom, to ' foresee the evil, and to hide
himself:' Prov. xxii. 3, ' The wise man foresees the evil, and hides himself; whenas the simple,' that is, unregenerate person, ' passeth on, and
is punished.' For indeed wherein doth wisdom excel folly, and what privilege hath it above it? But in forecasting things to come, by insight
into their causes, and so accordingly using means to prevent them if evil,

to attain to them if good. Eccles. viii. 5, 'Whoso keepeth the command-ment shall feel no evil.' And why? For a wise man's heart discerneth 'time and judgment,' the hints, nicks, and opportunities, the want of which is the great misery of all other men, ver. 6. This want of wisdom in others God complains of, Jer. viii. 6, that they are as a horse that goes on fearing no colours as foreseeing no danger, and so 'rusheth,' as it is said there, 'into the battle;' whereas the stork, and crane, and swallow have an instinct of wisdom to know the times of their removing before winter and cold weather, take their times to build their habitations; but, says God, you 'know not the judgments of the Lord,' that is, foresee not judgments in the causes in like manner to hide yourselves.

Answerably in the 25th of Matthew, at the beginning, though they slept and were secure in the time when the bridegroom was far off, yet when the cry and noise came that he was come, they trimmed their lamps that were wise virgins, and began to set fire to them again. In the 26th Isaiah, verse 9, 'When thy judgments are in the earth, the inhabitants of the world will learn righteousness.' Now, who are the inhabitants of the world but the meek here in the text? for, Mat. v., they are the meek to whom the promise of inhabiting the earth is made (for wicked men their own place is hell, Acts i. 25); and if any learn righteousness it is they, and if at any time then especially when judgments are abroad in the earth. But to name no more places, to enforce this by reason.

First, Consider the chief end which God hath in threatening and send-ing public calamities on the world is to purify and make his own better and fitter for heaven, to put them upon seeking him and seeking righteous-ness. As the winter and cold winds are sent for the good of the corn and herbs as well as the sunshine days in summer and spring, so the winters of calamity which the world hath successively after days of peace and prosperity, are for the bettering of his own people; for 'the world is theirs, things present and to come,' 1 Cor. iii. 22. Winter chokes the weeds, mellows the heart of the earth, and so furthers the rooting and growth of the corn. The winds purify and fan the air, and cause the flowers to cast forth a pleasing smell. So in measure doth God deal with his, Isa. xxvii. 8, when first the seed begins to bud forth; and though he stays the roughness of the winds and storms that might blast, and kill, and destroy grace in them, in the same verse, yet debate with them he doth in measure. And his end is to purify them: 'By this shall the iniquity of Jacob be purged;' yea, and this is all his end, this is all the fruit, to take away the sin. And so in Dan. xi. 35 those heavy storms which there befalls the world are but to purify and make white the wise: God's laundresses, to wash away their filth, and whiten them as men hung out and wetted to be whited by it. And as he sends not the rain of his word in vain, Isa. lv., it returns not empty, but accomplisheth the ends for which he sent it, so nor shall these storms, but he will have his end in this blessed effect of learning his people righteousness ere he hath done; they bring forth the quiet fruit of righteousness in the end in and to them that are exercised thereby, Heb. xii. 11. Now, if this then be God's end, which he will bring about ere he hath done, our duty is to prevent him in it, and take out this lesson, and then therefore especially to seek him and his righteousness, and make it our especial aim and busi-ness. For otherwise we despise God in his judgments threatened, because they lead to this end, and are appointed to it; even as they do that despise his mercy, Rom. ii. 4, 'which leads to repentance.' And so instead of treasuring up mercy against that evil day, whereby we might be spared, we shall treasure up wrath.

Secondly, Besides that it is God's direct end and most principal, when he brings them thus, to learn them righteousness. So to avenge their quarrel as well as his own, and the wicked's misusing of them, yea, and for their sakes he forbears a long while, and puts up many wrongs wherein he could have righted himself immediately. And this must needs be a further engagement to his own to learn and seek more righteousness in and against such times: 'Destroy it not for their sakes,' Isa. lxv. 8. He forbears the principal long for them, loseth much glory he might presently recover, therefore they had need pay use in the mean time to keep off the suit; to bring in the more righteousness daily, and then seek and gather up more to pay him when the bond is like to be presently sued; a decree coming out with an execution. And as that he thus forbears is an engagement, so that his coming to judge at such a time is to avenge their cause, is much more. Now, that he doth so is evident, Deut. xxxii. 35, 36, compared, where to be revenged on his enemies is to judge his people, which as in the next words is interpreted is to judge for them, and for their sakes; 'he shall repent for his servants;' and so it is called also pleading their cause, and taking vengeance for them, Jer. li. 36. Have they not reason then to take part with him, when he comes purposely to take part with them; to walk in righteousness more especially then with him, when he comes to judge with righteousness for them; to fight his battles when he fights theirs; to remember him in their ways, when he cometh to make inquisition for their blood and wrongs, remembering them? Ps. ix. 12.

Thirdly, If it were God's end only to avenge his own cause, yet then they are to be called forth as his witnesses, and so to join with him in condemning the world in time of public visitations; therefore, Rev. xi. 1, 2, they are called witnesses that, ver. 6, do join with God in smiting the earth with plagues; and as at the latter day, the day of the great visitation, they by their works are to glorify God, and witness that the wicked's condemnation is just, 1 Peter ii. 12, and so judge the world, so in days of lesser and more particular visitations also. And so Noah, by fearing and believing God, and preparing an ark beforehand, condemned the world, Heb. xi. 7. God must have some to justify his proceedings; now, he hath none but you: Isa. xliii. 12, 'Ye are my witnesses;' now, if ye should be as unjust and unrighteous as they, as guilty, and negligent, and secure as they, and had as little sought God as they, and his righteousness, ye were disabled to be witnesses then. With what face could you do it? They might except against you justly. And how could God take your testimony if so obnoxious as they? *Testimonium qui dat, habeat*, says the law.

Nay, fourthly, he must otherwise be forced to cut you off else with the wicked, for he cannot spare you of all others, you having known his name, Amos iii. 2; for he, though a Father, yet judgeth 'without respect of persons,' 1 Peter i. 17; and if there were not a great, broad, and evident difference between you and others, he would seem to be a partial and indulgent Father, which he forbidding and punishing in others, as old Eli, will not be guilty of himself; yea, and therefore judgment takes hold on his own house, nay, it begins there; therefore he is fain to teach his own by chastising them beforehand, Ps. xciv. 12–14, that when he comes as the judge of all the world to execute vengeance (ver. 1, 2 of that psalm), he may then spare his own, and they rest in the day of trouble, ver. 13;

that, as the words are, 'God may give him rest in the day of trouble:'
that is, with justice and equity may do it. And the reason given in the
14th verse is, because God hath a mind to spare them and not cast them
off, therefore in wisdom and mercy he corrects them and teacheth them out
of the law, until the pit be digged for the wicked; as also 1 Cor. xi. 32,
therefore 'we are chastised, that we should not be condemned with the
world,' but hid and preserved when others are destroyed.

Fifthly, If he should spare you; yet otherwise, you should not be fit
men to intercede for them, which yet is your duty and honour, for you
are his remembrancers and watchmen, Isa. lxii. 6, intercessors, Isa.
lix. 16, such as God seeks out and would fain find ere he destroys, Ezek.
xxii. 30. Now it is righteousness extraordinarily sought that only can
ingratiate you so far with him as to give you the lives of others, as he did
theirs to Paul who were in the ship with him; not ordinary courtiers, but
especial favourites they must be who prevail so far, men greatly beloved,
as Daniel was; if you deliver the island, it must be by the pureness of
your hands, Job xxii. 30.

First, To seek the Lord; and seeking having reference and relation to
finding, Isa. lv. 6, thereby must be understood the practice of such acts of
the soul as whereby God's favour is won and obtained against the evil day,
and because that it is made a distinct thing from seeking righteousness, &c.,
whereby also God's favour is to be obtained; therefore seeking the Lord
I interpret to be meant those inward immediate acts and dispositions which
are more immediately terminated upon him, and whereby we do ingratiate
ourselves with him; and then to seek righteousness is to practise the duties
of repentance and new obedience, whereof meekness is a particular branch,
more especially needful to times of judgment.

Now those acts of the mind which have God for their immediate object
requisite at such times, are,

First, To take him for your portion and refuge; and so all saints have
done upon such occasions in a more especial manner; so did David still
when he was in any distress.

And so the church, when under the greatest pressures that ever; in the
third of Lamentations, from the beginning to ver. 17, 'Yet still the Lord
is my portion, saith my soul; therefore I will hope in him. The Lord is
good to them that wait for him, to the soul that seeks him,' ver. 24, 25.

And so the church, when she was beset about with briers, and every man
was as 'a thorn in her side,' Micah vii. 4, therefore, ver. 7, she resolves,
'I will look to the Lord;' seeing I can have comfort in none of my friends,
I will look to him.

And so Jonah in the whale's belly, when the weeds were wrapped about
his head, and the waters came about him, so that he thought he should
have died no other death: 'When my soul fainted within me,' Jonah ii. 7,
'then I remembered the Lord;' and 'they that observe lying vanities,'
ver. 8, and seek to other shifts, at such times they 'forsake their own
mercy;' they leave, as those with Paul would have done, the ship in a
storm, and commit themselves to a cock-boat, that every wave overturns.

God is worth something at such a time as this; for be thou in what place
thou wilt, or in what distress soever, he is a very present help in trouble:
Ps. xlvi. 1, and 'if I be in the ends of the earth, I will cry to thee when
my heart is overwhelmed,' Ps. lxi. 1. And though 'my heart hath often
failed me,' says David, yet 'God never failed me,' Ps. lxxiii. 26, nor never
will. And 'he is a Rock that is higher than I,' says Ps. lxi. 1; and if I

could but get up on him, though the waters would soon drown me that am but weak and low, I am soon overborne, or at least soon overwhelmed; yet he is a Rock, and an high Rock; so high as that when the overflowing flood and waves of great waters come, 'they shall not come nigh thee,' Ps. xxxii. 6; when mountains and great men of the earth are covered with waves, carried into the sea, covered and overborne, Ps. xlvi. 2, 'thou shalt be safe.'

On the contrary, if thou beest in a parched land, where no water is, as David elsewhere speaks, Ps. lxiii. 1, yet there, 'he that trusts in God, and whose hope is in the Lord,' as Jer. xvii. 7, 'he shall be as a tree planted by water, and spreads out her roots by a river, and shall not see when heat comes; but its leaf shall be green, it shall not be careful in the year of drought, nor cease to bring forth fruit.' All other trees, whose roots are shot into dry earth only, they must have rain from without to keep them green, else in a year of drought they wither and die; and so that man that makes flesh or a creature his arm, ver. 5, whose souls and the affections of them are shot only into riches and honours, &c., as the soil they live in, if there be a drought without, a want of earthly comforts, they are like the heath in the wilderness, ver. 6, for they want moisture; and so all the joy and frolicness, which is their leaves and fruits, withers and dies, and falls off. But now a tree that is rooted by a river that never dries up, and thence the root secretly doth draw sap and juice, regards not drought above ground. So now a godly man, whose soul and all the faculties of it are shot and rooted in Christ, the spring of all comforts, and God of all consolations, sees not or feels not when heat cometh, viz., persecution from without, that dries up all others' moisture. Such soul is not careful in years of drought, though there be a decay of outward comforts; for there is a secret river runs by its root continually, 'a river which makes glad the city of God,' Ps. xlvi. 4; and though Euphrates may be dried up, as it was when Babylon was taken, Jer. li. 36, yet this river can never, because it springs up to eternal life, and no enemy can ever sever these streams from that spring; yea, and though the hogs of the earth may root up other trees, the Spaniards may root you out of your pleasures and riches and houses, yet what God hath planted in his Son shall never be rooted up, as the opposition shews, Mat. xv. 13. 'But my vineyard and the trees therein, I the Lord do keep it; I will water it every moment, lest any hurt it, I will keep it day and night,' Isa. xxvii. 3.

Therefore choose God, and take him for thy portion aforehand, for when the evil day comes else, thou wilt be sent to the things you delighted in, as they: Jer. ii. 28, ver. 27, 'In time of their trouble they will come to me,' says God, 'but where are the gods that thou hast made thee? let them arise, if they can save thee in the time of thy trouble,' ver. 28. 'Wherefore plead you with me? whom you have transgressed against all your days,' ver. 29.

Secondly, Trust perfectly in him; that you shall find in all the places quoted the consequent of making him their portion. Wait for mercy from him, cast thyself on him for relief; live by faith, trust perfectly on the promises made, and the experiments of his former dealings with his people at such times as these; it is the only way to quiet your minds. See the counsel given the church, and what the church did in such times as these: Isaiah xxvi. 4, 'Trust in the Lord for ever, for in the Lord Jehovah is everlasting strength;' not strength only for the present, but which never decays. Other things may strengthen the heart a while, but he for ever.

He is a rock, and a rock of ages; and, ver. 5, this motive is added, ' Thou wilt keep in perfect peace the mind stayed on thee :' so as a soul that rests itself in Jehovah, and hath cast anchor there, shall be at peace, and at perfect peace, when all the world is at war about thy ears. ' According to thy faith be it to thee.' If thou wouldst have perfect peace, then trust perfectly, as Peter says; for if thou beest strongly settled upon him as thy basis, they must shake him ere they can shake thee. Ill tidings, that make the hearts of hypocrites appalled, as Isaiah xxxiii. 14, yet shall never move him; ' he shall not be afraid of evil tidings,' Ps. cxii. 7; for why, ' his heart is fixed' (it is pitched upon all good it looks for; hath got a standing), ' trusting in the Lord.'

Now, in the same 26th of Isaiah, at the 8th verse, what doth the church answer to this? Why, ' In the way of thy judgments have we waited for thee.' Though God be never so angry, and come out as a judge, yet one that trusts in God dares stand in the way of judgments, looks for mercy from him then. In Isaiah lxiv. 1, when God did terrible things, ver. 3, and was wroth, ver. 5, yet then he that rejoiceth in him, and works righteousness, meets him, and remembers him, and so trusts in him in his ways; for ' all his ways are mercy to them that keep his covenant,' Ps. xxv. 10. He is never out of the road of mercy unto them. So as the church says, Isaiah viii. 17, I say, and his disciples, ver. 16, say, ' I will wait upon the Lord, that hides his face from the house of Jacob, and I will look for him;' that is, when he looks in wrath upon all else, yet then I will look he should be merciful unto me, as he promiseth, ver. 14, that he would be a sanctuary to them, when a snare to all else.

Therefore trust him, and trust him perfectly. Go, study all the promises, this in the text among the rest; distil the juice and comfort of them all, drink them down. All that ever he promised to his people, or hath done for them, were written for our comfort. There is not a promise but it is a tried truth; and still in all ages, upon all occasions, God's people have found the faithfulness, and purity, and soundness of them, that there is no flaw or dross in them; which is David's meaning, when he says as often in the Psalms, ' The words of the Lord are pure,' and ' tried;' still he speaks so of the promises of deliverance from danger; as in Ps. xii. 6, which was penned in shewing the oppression of godly men in Saul's time, who persecuted the godly, killed the priests, and exalted the vilest men: ver. 8, ' Now I will arise, says the Lord, I will set him in safety,' ver. 5; and what is David's gloss on this promise? Ver. 6, you may trust him, says he, for ' the words of the Lord are pure words, as silver tried in a furnace of earth purified seven times;' that is, still in all straits and difficulties, even in the fire, God hath made good his word.

They have been tried again and again. Abraham tried them; ' in the mount the Lord will be seen.' Jacob, he tried them, when he was in a strait, Gen. xxxii. 9, and he found them true. So David fell often, seven times; yea, seventy times seven times. There are so many *probatum ests* to them, that thou mayest build upon every one of them.

' A friend,' says Solomon, ' loves at all times,' Prov. xvii. 17, ' and a brother is born for adversity.' Now God hath been a friend to thee from everlasting, and all those *sæcula* have not worn it out; and is nearer than a brother, as tender as a mother, Isaiah xlix. 15, and thou ' art graven on the palms of his hands, and thy welfare is continually before him,' ver. 16, and ' remembered with everlasting kindness,' Isaiah liv. 8. He never had his mind off thee, and dost thou think he will forget thee for a little adversity? No; he should not be a friend then. Now is all the trial of him; he will not fail thee in thy greatest need. Therefore, says David, 'Trust him at all times,' Ps. lxii. 8, for 'God is a refuge,' and that especially in the evil day: Jer. xvi. 19, 'O Lord, my strength, &c., and my refuge in the evil day.' The chiefest use of him lies then, and if it were not for that, we were in worse case than others, for all our hopes are in him, as Jer. xvii. 17, 'Be not a terror to me,' says Jeremiah to God, 'for thou art my hope in the evil day;' all the hope he had. He were undone if he should find him look aloof off from him then. No; then is the blessedness of a godly man seen: Ps. ii., 'If he be angry, then blessed is he that trusts in him;' then especially.

And if he seem never so angry, yet trust him, for he means thee no hurt: Jer. xxix. 11, when they were carried into captivity, they thought he meant to destroy them; nay, says God, be not jealous of me, 'I know the thoughts that I think towards you; thoughts of peace, and not of evil, to give you an expected end;' as good an end as you can look for, if you but let him alone, and do his do.

And this is the strongest motive to move him to be merciful to thee, for thereby thou becomest his guardian,* his pupil, and he is engaged to take the tuition of thee. It is against the law of nations to betray those that fly for succour to us. In the captivity of Babylon, says God to Ebed-melech, Jer. xxxix. 18, 'I will surely deliver thee, and thy life shall be given thee for a prey; because thou hast put thy trust in me, saith the Lord.' That is all the reason; and so Isaiah xxvi. 3, 'Because he trusts in thee.'

Only, in the third place, carry thyself fearful of offending him; which is another way to win his favour, as indeed the best of you have cause to do: in time of judgments, Rev. xv. 4, 'who shall not fear thee?' For he is a Father, who without respect of persons judgeth every man 'according to his works,' 1 Pet. i. 17; therefore fear.

When Uzzah was stricken for that small and but rash act, as the Holy Ghost himself acknowledgeth it, 2 Sam. vi. 7, it is said of David, that he was afraid of the Lord that day, and thought with himself, how shall the ark of the Lord come to me, that am as sinful as Uzzah, and committed many a worse error, not rashly, but presumptuously. So when thou shalt see God come out of his place with fury, to punish the inhabitants of the earth, because there is wrath; as they say to Job, 'Beware lest he take thee away with his stroke,' Job xxxvi. 18; that is, whilst thou lookest at thyself and thy obnoxiousness. It is good to fear; it is a sign of stubbornness if thou dost not. If children see their father beat but the servants, if they fear not, it is a sign they are stubborn children.

And to fear is a means to prevent thy being stricken in thy particular. If shaking the rod works awfulness, God loves not to strike; and therefore in Hab. iii. 16, when he saw pestilence and sword a-coming as God's harbingers; says he, 'I trembled, that I might rest in the day of trouble.'

Only this, 'Fear not their fear,' as God says, Isa. viii. 11, that is, not punishment only, but fear to offend, fear sin. 'Sanctify God in your hearts, and let him be your dread; fear him in all your ways.' To fear punishment only is not to sanctify him. My brethren, take heed of walking rashly now in these times, that is, hand over head, as not caring what you do, as Levit. xxvi. 40, which is translated 'walking contrary,' and is read by others, 'walking rashly,' not much minding what he doth. It be-

* Qu. 'ward'?—ED.

hoves you to look about you, always walking circumspectly, lest for want of taking heed you grievously offend God ere you are aware ; take heed, for God will walk rashly to such, strike a rash stroke as it were, and cut off even one otherwise dear to him, as it were unawares ; because there is wrath, take heed lest he take thee away by his stroke.

Fourthly, Make him now the end of all thy actions, more than ever : Rev. xv. 4, ' Who will not glorify thee' when thy judgments are made manifest, ' for thou only art holy ;' and this holiness of his God manifests in his judgments, as much as in any other works ; and his end when he comes, is to glorify himself of those that would not do it aforehand, to recover his glory of men that regarded it not. Ezek. xxviii. 22, ' Behold, I am against thee, and I will be glorified in the midst of thee : when I shall have executed judgments.' And therefore you had as good give glory to him beforehand, as Jeremiah says, chap. xiii. 16, ' before he cause darkness ;' for God will be glorified either on you or by you, for he made all things for himself. All things are by him, therefore for him ; and if therefore he get nothing by you, nor you pay your rent, look to be turned out. Are you such vines that bring forth fruit to itself, as Hosea x. 1, so as God gets nothing done for him, eats not of the tree he planted, he stubs it up, why cumbers it the ground ? Especially look to yourselves when God's axe is lifted up and laid to the root of the tree ; now down with all unprofitable ones, not only those that do not bring forth fruit, but that do not bring forth fruit to God, Rom. vii. 4, that bring not forth fruit ' meet for him that dresseth them, and rains on them ;' as Heb. vi. 7, he that doth not is ' nigh to cursing,' and so to burning.

But now, a soul that is a fruitful soul, and desires in all things to glorify him, and to bring forth much fruit, and that to him, it were not for his profit to do it ; nay, God should be a loser if he should cut him off, as Deut. xx. 19. What, cut down a tree that is full of fruit, and that not ripe yet ? No, he will not. God will not ' sell his people for nought, and not increase his wealth by their price,' as they plead, Ps. xliv. 12. He may get more by them, and let them stand. Nay, see what God says, Ps. xci., when ' thousands fall besides thee,' &c., why, says God, ver. 14, ' because he hath set his love upon me, therefore will I deliver him.'

Yet, fifthly, pray to him, and call upon him, and keep communion with him, which indeed is more especially and particularly put for to ' seek him ;' and is the next condition required in that Ps. xci. 15, ' He shall call upon me, and I will answer him,' which hath three parts, first, ' I will be with him in trouble,' secondly, ' deliver,' and thirdly, ' honour him.' He will answer thee, first, by being with thee in thy trouble, manifesting his presence ; and what if thou beest in the fiery furnace with the three children, if God and Christ walk with thee. Now thou hast his promise as well as they, I will be with thee in the fire, Isa. xliii. 2, and in waters ; be with thee as a friend, bemoaning thee, and bearing the burthen with thee, which is a great ease to a man. Isa. lxiii. 9, be with thee, and tender thee, and visit thee, if sick, or in prison, &c., to bring thee cordials and refreshments, as Ps. xli. 3, to ' make thy bed in thy sickness, and strengthen thee when languishing.'

And as he will be with thee, so he will plot to deliver thee, and not rest till he hath done it ; and not only so, but bring thee out, as Joseph, out of prison into greater honour, or as Daniel, out of the lions' den.

And this he would do, if men would seek him, and preserve communion, and be much with him, as the church did, Isa. xxvi. 8, 9, ' in the night

sought him, and sought him early, when his judgments are in the earth.'
'When I awake,' says David, 'I am still with thee,' Ps. cxxxix. 18, yea,
and all the day long he kept communion with him : Ps. lxxiii. 23, 'I am
continually with thee,' and do walk as in thy presence, and dare not suffer
my heart to go far from thee ; for I am not able to subsist unless thou
holdest me by thy right hand, especially not then when waves of trouble
come ; then, unless he hold thee, how wilt thou do ? as Peter, if Christ
had not put forth his hand. Therefore keep nigh him, still have him by the
hand ; for the Lord says, verse 27, 'Those that are far from thee shall
perish,' else, when troubles come, I am in a miserable case. Ps. xxii. 11,
' Oh be not far from me, for trouble is near,' for there is none to help, none
else ; and therefore if thou wouldst not have him far off thee, then walk
not aloof of him now. Oh, ' it is good,' says David, verse 28 of the same
73d Psalm, ' to draw nigh to God,' that is my best and only way for safety,
and therefore seek him and follow him hard, as David : Ps. lxiii. 8, ' My
soul followeth hard after thee,' as one not willing to lose sight of him ;
follow him up and down, give him no rest night nor day. It is not enough
to trust him and fear him, but pour out your hearts before him, Ps. lxii. 8,
' for he is a refuge for us.' And to strengthen their faith and quicken
their prayers, I have heard it spoken again and again, that power belongs
to him, and mercy belongs to him ; that he is able, and merciful, and therefore willing to do abundantly above all we can ask or think ; and therefore
it is not in vain to seek him, and to trust him.

And this God expects ere he delivers you. In Jer. xxix., he had promised to keep them safe in the captivity, yet he bids them pray to the
Lord for it, verse 7, and that after seventy years he would return them,
verse 10 ; yet says he, ' You shall go and call upon me, and pray to me,
and I will hearken : yea, ye shall seek me, and find me, when ye shall
seek for me with all your heart,' verses 12, 13.

And so much for seeking the Lord.

The second general head commended to the godly, is, ' seeking righteousness,' which is meant of righteousness of justification, which is called ' the
righteousness of God,' that is, of Christ. It is most necessary to get assurance of that, and to get your conscience sprinkled with his blood, as the
doors of the people of Israel were with the blood of the Lamb, and so God
passed them by when he destroyed others ; for that pacifies the wrath of
God only. Isa. xxxii. 1, ' Behold, a king shall reign in righteousness, &c.
And a man,' namely, Jesus Christ, ' shall be as an hiding-place from the
wind, a covert from the tempest ; as rivers of waters in a dry place ; as the
shadow of a great rock in a weary land,' to shelter thee, and cool thee, and
cover thee from God's wrath, when he rains down snares. ' Kiss the Son,'
as well as the Father, ' lest ye perish,' Ps. ii.

Or, secondly, if meant of the righteousness of sanctification, it is also
needful to practise the duties of repentance and new obedience more than
ever ; for ' overflowing, it shall overflow with righteousness,' as he said,
Isa. x. 22, Ezek. xiv. 14.

As, first, to turn from sin, put a stop to that, for this is that which makes
God angry, Isa. xlii. 25. Why is Jacob given up to spoil, and God's fury
burn as fire ? Is it not because they have sinned ? Sin is the fuel of this
fire, and makes a man tinder to a judgment, that the least spark take
presently.

And, secondly, the end why God afflicts us is, to take away the sin. Isa.
xxvii. 7–9, ' By this it shall be purged ;' therefore, make use of lesser

afflictions aforehand, as purges to work it out, that God may not be provoked to give a stronger, both to take away the humours and purge also. You see that is all his end to take away sin ; this is all the fruit. Do it aforehand, and you prevent him.

And if you will not take your sins away, know God will take you away, for cleanse a land at one time or other he will, Ezek. xxiii. 48. At the 47th verse, they should be stoned, &c., and ' thus will I cause lewdness to cease out of the land.' If you will not cause it to cease by severing it and your persons, God will take the persons themselves away, so to purge the sin away. And so, Isa. xiv. 23, if they would not sweep their hearts themselves, but let heaps of filthy thoughts, speeches, desires lie, I will come with my besom, and cleanse all for you ; but it shall be ' the besom of destruction.'

Let every man, therefore, put a stop to sin ; as they reasoned, 2 Chron. xxviii. 13, have we not sin enough already ? Especially preserve thyself from the sin thou art most addicted to, whether by custom or inclination, be it a disposition of pride, worldly lusts, uncleanness, idleness. As David in the 18th Psalm, which he makes in the day that he was delivered from all his enemies, as appears by the title ; and vers. 17, 19, ' He delivered me from my strong enemy,' &c. ; and why ? because he kept close to God, did not wickedly depart from him ; if he did, it was weakness rather than wickedness ; ver. 21, I have put away none of his statutes, and ' I have kept myself from my iniquity.'

And so the king of Nineveh, Jonah iii. 8, bade the people turn every one from his evil way ; and because oppression was the chiefest sin, he mentions that : violence in their land. And God delivered them you know.

Worldliness and unjust dealing, and seeking riches, and honours, and great things, is, of all other, the most vain at such times as these ; whenas thou knowest not how soon it may be all one with the buyer and the seller, as Isa. xxiv. 2, that is, both have a like bargain, for the enemy comes and takes away both. And ' dost thou seek great things for thyself ?' says Jeremiah to Baruch, Jer. xlv. 5, projecting great matters, when I am a-rooting up all things in the land. ' Is this a time,' as he said to Gehazi, 2 Kings v. 26, ' to receive vineyards ?' &c.

Take heed, also, of being drowned in sensual lusts and pleasures, surfeiting and drunkenness, Luke xxi. 34, Mat. xxiv. 38 : ' They ate and they drank, and the flood swept them away ;' for they make a man secure, presumptuous, more unfit and unwieldy to suffer.

Keep yourselves also free from the sins of the times ; if you mean to be free then, ' partake not of their sins, lest of their plagues.' This was the lesson that God taught Isaiah : chap. viii. 11, ' God instructed me that I should not walk in the way of this people.' It was when God threatened the Assyrian to come in'; and having care of his people, he bids them seal that, ver. 16, among them, not to be carried with the stream of times, and then ' I will be a sanctuary' unto them.

What corrupt practices in state, what corrupt opinions do men raise up, free yourselves of them. If they say a confederacy, an unlawful league or peace, say not thou so ; but go to God, and there give your voice at least against it. Indeed, in an evil time a prudent man is fain to be silent, as Amos v. 8, to man namely ; but go to God, and complain to God, and mourn for them, and so thou shalt wash thy hands of them, 2 Cor. vii. 11.

How did Lot wash his hands of the sins of Sodom ? He was vexed at them, 2 Pet. ii. 7, and God delivered him. How did the people of Israel clear the land of murder, when it was not known who did it? Deut. xxi. 6, 7. The priests should slay a heifer, and wash their hands of it : We have not shed this blood, &c., and so put it away.

Not only mourn for, but intend your zeal against, the sins of the times and places you live in, so far as your callings do extend. For because that Jeremiah (and his remnant) was a man of contention against the sins of those times, &c., they 'cursed him,' Jer. xv. 10 ; therefore the Lord said, ver. 11, ' Verily it shall be well with thy remnant ; and I will cause the enemy to entreat thee well in the time of evil and affliction.' Even so it seemeth just and good to our good and wise God, that when he recompenseth ' tribulation to them that trouble you,' then to give ' rest to you that are troubled,' 2 Thes. i. 6, 7, as the apostle there speaks in another case ; and because we contend for God with the enemies of his glory, therefore the enemies of our peace shall deal well with us.

And indeed, if ever godly men's zeal and valour for the truth was to be quickened and stirred up, it is most at such times as these. For now, God himself begins to be zealous, and his displeasure against sin to wax hot. In Isa. lix. 13–15, when God saw nothing but ' oppression and departing from God,' and ' judgment turned backward,' that ' truth was fallen in the streets,' and that ' equity could not enter,' ' the Lord saw it, and it displeased him,' vers. 15 and 17 ; he ' clad himself with zeal as with a cloak,' coming forth to repay them according to their deeds, ver. 18. When, therefore, we see like times, and that God begins to take up his cloak, to come abroad into the world amongst us in fury and displeasure, we should sympathise with him, and be affected as he is, as courtiers are with their kings.

So Moses, Num. xi. 1, 10, when the people murmured, and it displeased God, ver. 1, and his anger was kindled greatly, the text adds, ' and Moses also was displeased.' For this is a general rule given, 1 John iv. 17, that as God is in this world, so should we be, to behave ourselves in the exercise of the same moral virtues that he doth exercise, as to shew forth kindness and longsuffering to the persons of the evil and unthankful, as he doth, so to be zealous against their sins, according to our calling, as he shews himself to be ; and then most especially when he clothes himself with it.

See what God says of Phinehas, Num. xxv. 11, because he was ' zealous with my jealousy ;' so out of the original interpreters read it, though we translate it, ' for my sake,' that is, he was affected as God was at the unclean act ; yea, and this is the speediest way to abate his zeal. When he shall see us take his part here below, and begin to be hot and valiant for his truth, he thinks then that he may be quiet, and so his wrath slacks, as it did there. Though men grow the more furious in such a case, when they see others back them and second them, yet God doth not. And if we in our places, and our rulers in theirs, would strike through the loins of sinners : we with reproofs nailing their souls to hell, and they with the execution of laws ; and do it with God's zeal, as Phinehas did, that is, with grief and indignation that God is so dishonoured, for of those two affections is zeal a compound, Mark iii. 5, as appears by Christ there. God, he should not need to be furious. ' Phinehas,' saith he, ' hath turned away my wrath, whilst he was zealous with my zeal amongst them,' Num. xxv. 11. However, if you be so, yet with you God will make a covenant, as with Phinehas there, that he and his posterity should continue, as they did in all the evils and troubles that befell the nation of the Jews till Christ's time, and rubbed through the Babylonish captivity and all. Ezra was of his race, Ezra vii. 1, 5, and fared and scaped as well then as any other.

And though we have not such public callings and spirits as he then, yet so far as our commission reacheth, let us exercise and shew the like to the full : thrust javelins through men's hearts by reproofs, reform our families, and those we have authority over, and contend with all the world by keeping the law, as Solomon speaks, Prov. xxviii. 4 ; putting iniquity far from our tabernacle, as they exhort, Job xxii. 23, with this promise, ver. 29, ' When others are cast down, thou shalt say there is lifting up.' God will remember thee, as good Nehemiah prays in his last chapter, for thy zeal for God.

But above all, my brethren, be now ' zealous of good works,' as the apostle speaks, Titus ii. 14. Greedy devourers of all the duties of new obedience, abounding more in all the fruits and works of righteousness, you that have ' wrought his judgments,' says the prophet here, ' seek righteousness ;' that is, still and more than ever. Whatever part of righteousness you before were conscionable in, set upon it afresh, as if you had done nothing yet. Mend your pace, they are not hours to stand still in. After John in the Revelation had declared what terrible things were to come on the world, the use he makes in the conclusion is, that the ' righteous be more righteous.'

To instance in some particulars, still enforcing them upon the same ground.

You that have searched your hearts heretofore, search and search again ; it is the exhortation in the text, enforced with this motive, ver. 12 of the first chapter ; for God comes to ' search Jerusalem with candles, when he comes to punish.' Prevent God's searching. If a man can dress and search a wound himself, it is less pain to him than to have the gentlest chirurgeon.

You that have watched over your corrupt hearts and dispositions afore, do it now more than ever. It is Christ's motive against such times as these : Luke xxi. 34, 36, ' Take heed lest your hearts be overcharged' and overrun with any sorts of lusts ; but ' watch therefore and pray always, that you may be accounted worthy to escape all those things that shall come to pass,' ver. 36. In Rev. xvi., when the sixth vial is poured out, and that great and last battle is fought wherein antichrist is to be destroyed, before that great overthrow under the seventh, there is a *caveat* given which personally may and doth, for aught I know, concern men living in this age (and it is put in by way of parenthesis) : ' Blessed is he that watcheth, and keeps his garments,' that watcheth over corruptions, suffers not them, as the tares, to grow whilst he sleeps ; that watcheth and suffers not graces and the flame of them to die, as the virgins did whilst they slept.

You that have been fruitful in good speeches and heavenly thoughts, out of the abundance of which the mouth speaks, be more fruitful, Mal. iii. 16–18 verses, and beginning of the 4th chapter compared. Who were they that were spared in the day when the wrath of God ' burnt as an oven,' others as stubble, as in the beginning of the 4th chapter, but they that spake of it one to another in evil times before, and that ' thought upon his name' ? ver. 16. ' Then,' &c. You may see what times they were in the verses before : ' Them' (says God) ' I will spare, as a man spares his son.' You that have thought much of him before, he will then think of you, and then you shall ' discern between the righteous and the wicked ;' a great and a broad difference God will then put.

You that have sanctified the Sabbath strictly, and sought God upon your fast-days diligently, and made conscience of humbling yourselves thoroughly, do so still; for see what comfortable promises you lay up for yourselves and your posterity against the evil day, Isa. lviii., where he exhorts to a thorough observation of both: at ver. 11, 'God shall guide thee continually,' and in evil times a man had need of God's guidance, to lead and dispose of him into ways and places, and conditions of safety and deliverance, which all the wit of the world cannot do; and 'he shall satisfy thy soul in drought,' when all comforts without fail, as you know not how soon they will; 'and thou shalt be like a watered garden, and a spring of water whose waters fail not.' And at ver. 12, 'Thy posterity shall build the old waste places,' that is, the desolations of the church; which suppose it be not done in thy days, yet thy children happily shall be great master builders of it for time to come, and thy prayers put up at such times shall lay a foundation for a settled condition of the church for many generations, as our martyrs did of ours by their prayers and sufferings.

And all this promise is made to strict sanctifying of fasts and of the Sabbath day, which are called Sabbaths, because to be kept holy as Sabbaths are; so in the verses before and after, ver. 13. And if fasts are to be kept so strictly, then Sabbath as strictly, for that is the *regula* and *primum in isto genere*, as appears by the fourth commandment, 'Keep holy the seventh day,' that is, *primum*, and therefore *regula reliquorum*, and so is to be kept as strictly as fasts are. Though indeed thanksgiving is more to abound in the one, humiliation in the other, yet not to speak our own words, or take our own pleasure, &c., in both. For equal it was, that if they kept not the Sabbath, the land should not keep her inhabitants, Lev. xxvi. 34, 35, and they instead of resting should then find trouble; whereas, Jer. xvii. 24, 25, if they would not profane it, God says, the 'city should stand for ever.'

Be exceeding conversant with the word of God, in reading, meditating, and applying it to your hearts; get as much of the engrafted word into your hearts, turned and digested into pure grace and strength, and likeness thereunto; pray it as much into your hearts aforehand as ever you can, there may come a dear year of it all the world over, you know not how soon; therefore as the angel said to Elijah, Eat again and again, for you may have a long while for to go in the strength of what you get now beforehand. 'Let the word dwell richly in you,' as Col. iii. 16; furnish yourselves with as much of that precious treasure as you can, for a little money will not carry you through a long journey, but will soon be spent. Only trust it not in the purses of your memories or brains, but lay it up in your hearts, and believe it, brethren, you cannot be robbed of it.

Acquaint yourselves much with it, and be familiarly conversant in it now, as God commands in Deut. vi. 7, 'And thou shalt teach them diligently unto thy brethren, and shalt talk of them when thou sittest in thine house,' &c.; and answerably it will be a constant and familiar companion with thee, and be familiar to thee in all the evils that thou shalt meet withal. Prov. vi. 22, 'When thou goest it shall lead thee,' and guide thee into the ways of peace and safety; 'when thou sleepest,' and art in any danger, 'it shall keep' and preserve thee; and 'when thou awakest, it shall talk with thee, be familiar to thee, yea, and in all distresses comfort thee. Ps. cxix. 92, David vows he had perished long ere this, if God's law had not been his delight. And all outward evils will but make it the sweeter: 1 Thes. i. 6, 'They received the word in much affliction, with joy of the of the Holy Ghost.'

Yea, and this will be an argument and motive to God to spare thee, when he cuts off others; and so Jeremiah useth it, chap. xv. verses 15, 16, among other motives why God should not take him away, but remember him, ver. 15, as in the 11th verse he promiseth to do: 'Thy words,' saith he, 'were found, and I did eat them, and thy word was unto me the joy and rejoicing of my heart.' And so in Job xxii. 22 and 29 compared, 'Receive, I pray thee, the law from his mouth, and lay up his words in thine heart;' and among other promises in the 25th verse, &c., this is one at the 29th, 'When men are cast down thou shalt say, There is lifting up,' namely, for thee. Because Josiah had a melting heart at the reading the law, therefore God brought it not in his days, 2 Kings xxii. 11, 19.

Do as much as thou canst to others, and use all the abilities and opportunities God hath put into thy hand to the utmost advantage to do good to men's souls. Heb. x. 25, 'Exhorting one another, and so much the more as you see the day approaching.' Those especially that are near to thee, by getting them into Christ before the evil day comes and cuts them off in their sins, warning them to 'save themselves from this froward generation,' in Acts ii., that is the common destruction and general desolation that will befall this generation if we turn not; especially your children, kindred, friends: Gen. xix. 12, 14, when Sodom was to be destroyed, said the angel to Lot, 'Hast thou here any besides, sons-in-law, &c.? And Lot went up and spake to his sons in law,' &c., but he seemed as if he had mocked; though it took no effect, yet therein he discharged his duty.

If thou canst but get thy friends or any of thy children into Christ, then thou needst be no more solicitous for them, for God is bound to take care for them, and will do; come what times will come, they are well enough then.

Do good also with thy estate, to the bodies of men, especially the saints, and for the propagation of the gospel and good of the church. It is a thing I find enforced by Solomon upon this very ground also: Eccles. xi. 1, 2, 'Cast thy bread upon the waters, give a portion to seven and also to eight, for thou knowest not what evil shall be upon the earth;' he exhorts to this, you see, in evil times, and the motive is rational and strong, if we take in that also in the former verse, that in 'many days he shall find it;' and that he that doth good with his substance 'lends to the Lord,' Prov. xix. 17.

For, first, then he disposeth it himself, whereas otherwise the enemy that comes and takes all away may be his executor, for aught he knows.

Secondly, He gives it to the Lord, that gave him it at first, and he had better, and shall have more comfort that *he* hath his goods than *they*.

But, thirdly, he doth not give it or cast it away, as yet in the first words Solomon speaks to shew what freeness should be in the donor, but he lends it to the Lord, who after many days will return it again; and that when evil times come, when thou shalt have most need of it, and thou hast not men's bonds for it, but God's also, who is their surety.

To conclude, therefore, this part of the exhortation, to abound in all these and the like practices of righteousness of what kind soever. With these general considerations to quicken you thereto,—

Work as hard as you can whilst you may. For,

First, Believe it, there is nothing here in this world desirable but to have ability, opportunity, and a heart to do God service. Eccles. iii. 12, 'There is no good in them,' speaking of all things here below, 'but for a man to rejoice and to do good in his life.'

Secondly, Consider that every one of you have some work to do. You

are some way to be profitable to God and men, in the duties of your calling and talents committed to you, and duties of religion; and all this
work is to be done whilst it is day: John ix. 4, 'I must work the work
God sent me to do whilst it is day.' God appointed his own Son work,
and this made him abundant in it, because he could work only whilst it
was day. God had bespoke a great deal of work, and but a little time
allotted for it; therefore our Saviour hastened the more to get it done
before candle-light; he that made the first day, and was Lord of time, must
yet take this opportunity. Now there was an 'hour of darkness a-coming,
as he tells the Pharisees, Luke xxii. 53, when they attacked him first;
'this is your hour and the power of darkness,' when they were to do their
works; and so Christ must cease to do his. Now that which was Christ's
case is ours also; 'for when the night comes,' says he in the next words,
'no man can work:' as Ps. civ. 23, 'Man goeth forth unto his work, and
to his labour, *until the evening;*' for then the beasts go forth to raven, as
there.

Now, thirdly, besides that, death seizeth upon all. Years of darkness,
'and those many,' as Solomon says, Eccles. xi. 8; there are hours of
darkness to the church of God, when the enemies thereof, as the Pharisees
of old, have the power in their hands; so as then no man can work, or if
he doth but a little, as in the days of popery, when no man might buy or
sell that would not receive the mark of the beast, Rev. xiii. 17; and it is
to be feared, that there is yet an hour of temptation, and the power of
darkness a-coming over the world, as some interpret that place, Rev. iii. 10,
when the witnesses shall be slain, Rev. xi. Popery may have a reviving,
as heathenism had after Constantine's reformation, in Julian's time, sixty
years after, and then it will prove a time of suffering rather than doing;
your shop-windows will then be shut, the night may come when none can
work, or if they do, do only work within doors; for your hearts may pray,
let the enemies do what they will or can. Therefore let us now bestir ourselves, and do good whilst we have time (as the apostle's exhortation is,
Gal. vi. 10), and indeed opportunity. The devil, the shorter time he thinks
he hath, indeed rageth the more, Rev. xii. 12. *Fas est et ab hoste doceri,*
learn this of your enemy: 1 Cor. vii. 29, speaking of times of persecution,
as appears by the 26th verse, 'Brethren,' says he, 'the time is short,
therefore use the world as if you used it not,' for you know not how long
time you have to enjoy it. Like travellers, if they fear night draws on,
they put spurs to their horse and ride away the faster, so do you.

But, fourthly, consider that you may be cut off among others; the best
may. Now 'in the grave there is no work,' says Solomon, Eccles. ix. 10,
and therefore do what thou dost with all thy might; and as speedily rid
as much work as thou canst. It will grieve you to die and to have brought
no more glory to God, to have sowed no more seed to the Spirit, which
you may reap in heaven; to be hewn down with so many leaves and little
fruit, and that not ripe, many buds of good purposes of being more zealous
scarce brought into act.

Therefore fall to work and bestir yourselves; if you die, how can you die
better than so doing? 'Blessed is he whom his Master finds so doing.'
This will make you ripe and loaden with ears against the sickle comes;
and when you have done your work, you may say with Paul, 'I have
finished my course;' no matter if you be cut off, you then will glorify God
in your deaths, and be vessels prepared for glory, as saints are, Rom.
ix. 23. As, therefore, good housewives scour and make bright their ves-

sels against some great day, so do you against the day of the Lord. That you may be ' meet,' as the phrase is, Col. i. 12, ' to partake of the inheritance of the saints in light,' as therefore Peter exhorts, 2 Pet. i. from 5 to 12th, add grace to grace, and abound too, ' so shall you make your election sure ;' and when you come to die, ' abundant entrance will be made into the kingdom of Jesus Christ ;' you shall not scarcely be saved, creep through a narrow hole, have much ado, but a large way, an abundant entrance, shall be opened unto you.

The last thing is to seek meekness, which is a contentedness to be disposed of by God, either in doing or suffering his will, without murmuring or repining ; such as was seen in old Eli, in 1 Sam. iii. 18, and in the church when under the greatest and sorest pressures, Lament. iii. 26–31, and expressed there by quiet waiting, bearing the yoke, sitting alone ; a meek person is silent, hath his mouth stopped, nothing to complain of, because ' he hath laid it' (as others read it) ' upon him ;' going alone to meditate of and mourn for his sins, put his mouth in the dust, and gives his cheek to him that reproacheth him, takes it patiently, and as it is Levit. xxvi. 41, ' accept his punishment,' which is also joined with a constant cleaving to God, notwithstanding all he has laid on him, as the church : Ps. xliv. 17 to the 20th, ' All this is come upon us ; yet have we not forgotten thee, neither have we dealt falsely in thy covenant. Our heart is not turned back, neither have our steps declined from thy way ; though thou hast sore broken us in the place of dragons, and covered us with the shadow of death. If we have forgotten the name of our God, or stretched out our hands to a strange God.' They forsook him not, nor did deal falsely in his covenant, ' though thou hast sore broken us,' &c.

And this disposition ariseth out of two things.

First, A thorough conviction of a man's sins, and the offence to God in them, and obnoxiousness and deservedness to be destroyed for them. So the church, Micah vii. 9, ' I will bear the indignation of the Lord, because 1 have sinned against him ; ' and the church in Lam. iii. 39, ' Wherefore,' says she, ' should a man complain or murmur for the punishment of his sins ? ' as being a most absurd and uncomely thing, that a man that is so obnoxious should think much to be corrected ; as if a thief that deserved hanging should complain of being burned in the hand. Especially when one considers, as Ezra ix. 13, that ' God punisheth less than a man deserves.'

Secondly, So far as this is joined also with hope of mercy, for otherwise a man's soul flies in God's face, as did Cain, and thinks out of self-love (if not subdued by the love of God in the heart) the punishment too great, and more than he can bear ; therefore in the fore-named places, Lam. iii. 26, hope is still joined with quiet waiting ; yea, and in the 29th, made a condition pre-requisite, he ' puts his mouth in the dust, if so be there may be hope,' otherwise not. This makes him quiet, and for a while content, that (as it is ver. 31) ' God will not cast off for ever ; but though he cause grief, yet he will have mercy according to the multitude of them.'

And this disposition of contentedness to suffer thus arising, is it which God requires especially of all graces to abound in us at times of judgment ; and therefore, speaking to his people here, his compellation is, ' Ye meek of the earth,' and his exhortation, ' Seek meekness,' this appellation, suiting so well with the matter he had in hand, threatening a day of anger. As therefore, when we speak to God, we usually call upon him as the God of that grace we sue for. If we ask wisdom of him, we look and call upon him by the name of ' Father of lights ; ' if consolation, ' the God of all comfort.' So when God speaks to us, he gives us that especial appellation, and denominates us by that grace (as here of meek ones) which best becomes us in receiving the message he is delivering.

And when God speaks of a 'day of anger,' and of his 'fierce anger' a-coming, it becomes us, who are obnoxious as well as others, to be meek, and silent, and still. Then, 'seek meekness;' not to entertain a murmuring thought to the contrary; for it is the most absurd and unseemly thing to see one that deserves to be in hell, and have the lowest place there, to complain of lesser punishments; and therefore, Lam. iii. 39, Jeremiah brings it in as a most unreasonable thing to be wondered at, ' Why doth an evil man complain, a man for the punishment of his sins?' He wonders that a man obnoxious to God in so great a guilt; what! that he should complain of punishment, of punishment of his sins? betwixt which there is no proportion. A rogue that deserves hanging, drawing, and quartering, complain if he be sentenced but to whipping or burning in the hand! Down on thy knees, wretch, and thank the Judge for his mercy that thou art 'not consumed' (as they, ver. 22 of the same chapter), as infinite mercy by which thou escapest. Be content to welcome that punishment which is less than thou hast deserved. If any had cause to complain, Christ had, who was innocent; and innocency makes men speak when guilt would stop their mouths; but ' as a lamb led to the slaughter, he opened not his mouth;' prayed indeed the cup might pass, but yet 'if possible,' else not; 'Not my will, Father, but thine;' and 'he was heard in what he feared.' So do thou. The promise of hiding is made to it; if there be any hiding-place to be found on earth, a meek man may challenge it: Ps. xxxvii. 8, 'The meek shall inherit the earth;' and therefore they are here called the 'meek of the earth, and the 'inhabitants of the earth,' Isa. xxvi. 9.

And the reason why God so especially regards this disposition, and makes a promise against ill times to it, and spares them, is,

First, Because God desires but to overcome when he comes to judge, Rom. iii. 4; to have the victory over men. Now, a spirit that confessing it hath sinned willingly submits to and accepts its punishment: over that spirit God is acknowledged a victor already. And it is not a fit match for him to shew his power on; but a Pharaoh that will not stoop, he will shew his power on him to choose and break him in pieces. You whip your children but till they kiss the rod, and then you fling it away.

Secondly, A meek soul will still be thankful to him, and give him all the glory, let him deal with it how he will, and he doth desire no more, apprehending itself worthy to be destroyed. It magnifies the least mercies in the midst of judgments, and still thinks judgments small, confessing God just and merciful in them, if its being be but preserved: 'It is of thy mercy we are not consumed,' Lam. iii. 22; and ' Great is thy faithfulness.' So Ezra ix. 13, he there aggravates his sin: ' All this is come upon us for our great trespass;' but extenuates and thinks nothing of the punishment: 'Thou hast punished us less than our iniquities;' but he magnifies the least mercy: ' hast given us such a deliverance as this,' sets an emphasis on that.

Thirdly, A meek soul will not forsake God, but serve and obey him still, let God do what he will with it: Ps. xliv. 17, 18, 'All this is come upon us; yet we have not forgotten thee, neither have we dealt falsely in thy covenant. Our heart is not turned back, neither have our steps declined from thy way; though thou hast sore broken us.' For a meek heart still knows that obedience is due, that imprisonment satisfies not for the debt. Now, such a soul therefore God cannot find in his heart long to punish, and therefore the promise is made to them.

Now, to exhort to this, consider but this one motive, that besides that a man is obnoxious, God also hath an unlimited prerogative to bring on thee what he will. And if he will bring a judgment on thee, all the world cannot hinder it nor take it off. So as there is no dealing with him, but submitting; for he keeps prosperity and adversity under lock and key, and shuts and none can open; men must lie close prisoners till he will let them out, Job xii. 14. It is Job's expression in this very case: 'Behold, he breaketh down, and none can build up; he shuts up a man, and there can be no opening,' and so on to the end of that chapter. And upon this ground see what counsel Elihu gives, Job xxxiv. 29–31, he having the prerogative to 'give quietness,' so as then 'none can give trouble;' and when he 'hides his face, who can behold him?' whether it be done against a man; and not only so, but a whole nation. They cannot all keep an affliction off, nor all the world cannot hurt them, if he will give quietness. If he will set an hypocrite over them to ensnare them, they cannot all get him down till he will, ver. 30. And what then? 'Surely it is meet to be said, I have borne chastisement, and I will not offend any more.' No way but to kiss the rod and say, 'I will do so no more.' And if a man sees not cause why God should thus chastise him, and so be apt to repine, yet let him think there is a cause; therefore in verse 32, 'That which I see not, teach thou me; if I have done iniquity, I will do so no more.'

And to say as Jeremiah upon the like occasion, or the church in his person, Jer. x. 22–24, when there was the noise of the bruit of an invasion from the north, to make the cities desolate, what say they? Ver. 23, 'O Lord, I know that the way of man is not in himself: it is not in man that walketh to direct his steps,' whether he shall have fair way or foul to walk; neither do I know whither to run for safety; my life and all is in thy hands; therefore 'O Lord, correct me, but with judgment.' The church is willing in such a case to be whipped, only desires God to deal gently with her; and so must we.

www.ingramcontent.com/pod-product-compliance
Lightning Source LLC
Chambersburg PA
CBHW060742100426

42813CB00027B/3026